ON THE TRAIL OF THE PONY EXPRESS

Jerry Ellis

With a new afterword by the author

UNIVERSITY OF NEBRASKA PRESS

LINCOLN AND LONDON

First paperback printing: 2002

Library of Congress Cataloging-in-Publication Data
Ellis, Jerry
[Bareback!]
On the trail of the Pony Express / Jerry Ellis; with a new afterword by the author.
p.   cm.
Originally published under title: Bareback! New York: Delacorte Press, c1993.
Includes bibliographical references (p.   ).
ISBN 0-8032-6746-0 (pbk.: alk. paper)
1. West (U.S.)—Description and travel.   2. Pony Express National Historic Trail.
3. Ellis, Jerry—Journeys—Pony Express National Historic Trail.   I. Title.
F595.3.E45   2002
917.804'34—dc21
2002020313

DEDICATED TO THE PONY EXPRESS RIDERS

and

THE SPIRIT OF ADVENTURE IN ALL OF US

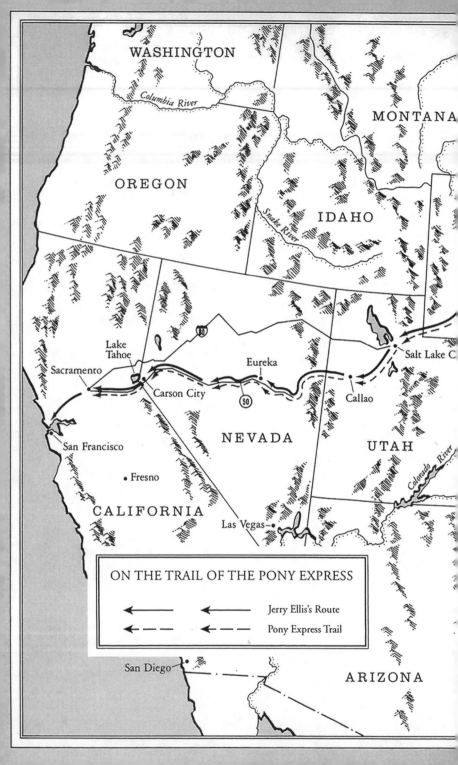

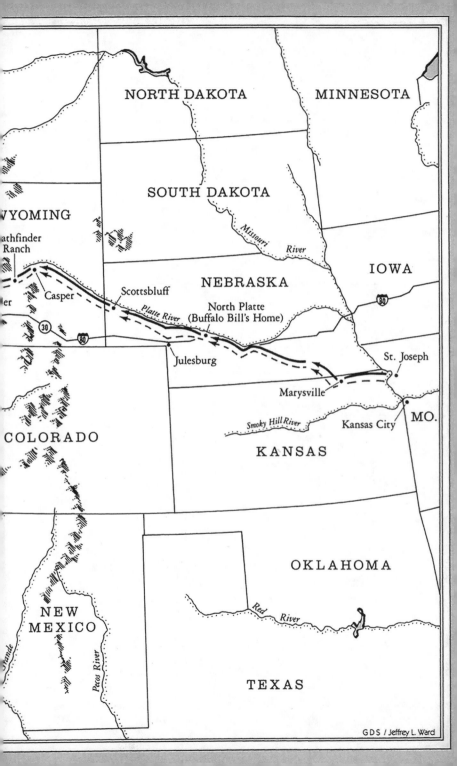

ACKNOWLEDGMENTS

I sometimes have a great need to feel close to people, even to the extent that we have joined forces in some wondrous conspiracy to make life richer and more exciting. I feel that with my editor, Emily Reichert, who has to be the best editor in all of New York. She worked with me on this book with such dedication and enthusiasm that I'm still thrilled and honored by it. How lucky I am to have her in my life. Thank you, Emily. Another prized conspirator is my tough, honest, beautiful, and brilliant agent, Susan Ginsburg. Without her, my footing wouldn't be as solid. The members of my family? Don't get me started on thanking them for all their support or I'll never shut up. Morris Pearsall, thank you for the many fine conversations we had about the Old West and Buffalo Bill. You, dear reader, and especially those who wrote to me after reading *Walking the Trail*, I thank you from the warmest place in my heart. You helped keep me reassured, giving me courage. Debi, I love you.

AUTHOR'S NOTE

This book is based on my true-life experiences traveling along the Pony Express Trail by foot, horseback, covered wagon, canoe, and hitchhiking, although the names and other details of certain individuals have been changed.

CHAPTER ONE

I'm packing a bag for what I hope will be the greatest adventure of my life. I'm at my home in the mountains of North Alabama, but tomorrow I leave for St. Jo, Missouri, where I plan to start my journey along the Pony Express Trail. I'll be traveling across Kansas, Nebraska, Colorado, Wyoming, Utah, and Nevada to San Francisco, California. The Trail is twenty-one hundred miles long and meanders across plains, deserts, and mountains. I plan to make the journey by horseback, covered wagon, foot, thumb, and canoe. The trek will take three or four months. At times I will follow country and state roads; other times I will follow the original Trail.

I'm forty-three now, but ever since I was a child I have been fascinated by the Old West and the Pony Express daredevil riders. I used to imagine myself as one of these brave young men when I was a kid. Buffalo Bill, the most famous of the Pony riders, was my childhood hero.

I wish I had been living in 1860 to see the first ad for Pony Express riders when it appeared in a San Francisco paper. It read:

WANTED—young, skinny, wiry fellows, not over 18. Must be expert riders, willing to risk death daily. Orphans preferred. Wages $25 a week. . . .

Before 1860 mail made its way from East to West on boat via South America and took as long as two months to reach its destination. The Pony Express promised to deliver the letters in *only ten days*. This was great news to more than four hundred thousand people who had poured into California after gold was discovered at Sutter's Mill on the American River near Placerville in 1849. With hopes of striking it rich, men abandoned freight ships in San Francisco and tore down the masts to make tents to live in throughout the gold fields. They were joined by thousands from the East who left their families with promises of returning or sending for them once they had their pockets full. Not many became rich, and most became starved for letters from home.

I remember reading about the Gold Rush in books when I was a boy, and learning how this Great American Dream to connect East and West in only ten days was put into operation by Alexander Majors, William B. Waddell, and William H. Russell. These three innovators hired eighty riders to carry the mail, with forty galloping East and forty racing West day and night.

A rider usually rode fifty to a hundred miles along the Trail and changed horses every twelve to fifteen. He prided himself on the speed at which he could drop from one horse and leap atop the next. He carried his letters in a *mochila*, Spanish for purse, which fit over the saddle, with only his body weight fastening it down beneath his seat. Each of the four corners of the *mochila* housed a leather box to carry the precious letters. Three of the boxes were locked, and the only keys waited at the end of the Trail, in St. Jo and San Francisco. The fourth box was unlocked to allow the addition of mail along the way. A rider averaged carrying about sixty pieces of mail, including telegrams, each trip.

There's a wonderful description by Mark Twain, who rode a stagecoach West in 1860, and who immortalized the Pony Express rider in his book *Roughing It:*

We had a consuming desire, from the beginning, to see a pony-rider, but somehow or other all that passed us and all that met us managed to streak by us in the night, and so we heard only the whiz and a hail, and the swift phantom of the desert was gone before we could get our heads out of the windows. But now we were expecting one along every moment, and we would see him in broad daylight. Presently the driver exclaims: "Here he comes!"

Every neck is stretched further, and every eye strained wider. Away across the endless dead level of the prairie a black speck appears against the sky, and it is plain that it moves. Well, I should think so! In a second or two it becomes a horse and rider, rising nearer—growing more and more defined—nearer and nearer, and the flutter of the hoofs comes faintly to the ear—another instant a whoop and a hurrah from our own deck, a wave of the rider's hand, but no reply, and man and horse burst past our excited faces, and go winging away like a belated fragment of a storm!

So sudden is it all, and so like a flash of unreal fancy, that but for the flake of white foam left quivering and perishing on a mail-sack after the vision had flashed by and disappeared, we might have doubted whether we had seen any actual horse and man at all, maybe.

It was a hazardous journey for the "swift phantom of the desert." The Pony rider was threatened by tornadoes, lightning, floods, rattlesnakes, bears, mountain lions, murdering outlaws, and warpath Indians. In the winter there were snowstorms and golf ball–size hailstones; in summer the desert sun scorched the rider and there was always the danger of his horse stepping into a prairie dog hole to make him tumble or collapse on top of the rider.

I'm intrigued by a boy who would brave these dangers and wonder what compelled him to risk his life along the Trail. I identify with his spirit of adventure and his solitude. The rider always traveled alone. Like him, I'm a loner. Even when I was a teenager, the age of most of the riders, I traveled apart from others. I took risks that others wouldn't. When I was seventeen, I ran away from my little mountain town of Fort Payne, Alabama, and hitchhiked to New York to visit my sister. It was such an exciting experience that I began to thumb all over America. By the age of twenty-six I had thumbed enough miles in six countries to circle the globe five times.

I also see myself in the Pony Express rider because he was such a tough, strong figure. When I was a kid, I was small and not very strong. Sometimes this made me afraid of boys bigger than myself, and this haunted me. I began to lift weights and soon found my body growing muscular and more powerful. This new strength gave me a lot of confidence; I no longer feared anyone. It also fueled my desire to be one of the toughest and most daring teenagers around.

Sometimes I'd stand in front of a mirror and practice showing no emotion in my eyes or face. I thought that would make me appear strong. And I'd do things to act tough. On Friday nights, my two buddies and I would race in our cars to the Lookout Mountain bootlegger and buy beer or moonshine. We'd get high and roar back into Fort Payne to arm-wrestle on the hoods of cars at Jack's, the local hangout. By that time I'd been lifting weights for three years and I prided myself on my strength and muscles. Yes, sir, my buddies and I thought we were about as macho as they came. Other kids thought so as well, for none of them dared to mess with us. My Cherokee cousin, Rodney, won respect for being in two car wrecks in less than twenty-four hours. I was riding with him for the first wreck. We turned over a souped-up '56 Chevy three times down the side of Lookout Mountain. The second time, Rodney was alone in his '57 Chevy when he totaled it racing another car up Sand Mountain. It was during that summer that I began to feel ashamed of some of the things I was doing and trapped in this macho image I'd found so appealing. That's what drove me to thumb my way to New York that first time and open my mind to different kinds of people with different thoughts and beliefs than many had in the Deep South. I'm not saying all this just to drift back into personal memories. I wonder if many of the young Pony Express riders were also bored and frustrated living in one-horse towns, and if they craved finding a new image of themselves as well as adventure.

I'm happy to say that I've changed a great deal since I was a teenager, but I'm still curious about this whole issue of growing up and what it means to be a man. I'd like to see what I might discover about that in myself as well as in others as I travel the Pony Express Trail.

Being a fan of the Pony Express riders, I'd like to claim that I'm daredevil on horseback, but I'm not. I haven't even done a great deal of riding. I've been cautious around horses ever since I was kicked in the head by one when I was five years old. But I like to challenge myself, and this trek seems like an ideal time to get into the spirit of riding horses.

It's now the first of May, and I hadn't planned to leave on this journey till the middle of the month. But I heard about a wagon train leaving in two days down the Oregon Trail, which follows the same route as the Pony Express Trail for almost a thousand miles. The wagon train flyer promises:

FUN and FELLOWSHIP
MAKE NEW FRIENDS
CAMPFIRES and MUSIC EVERY NIGHT

The idea of fun and new friends convinced me that I should change my plans and leave early with the wagon train. I broke up with my girlfriend two months ago and I feel a bit lonely. Maybe starting out on my travels with a group of people will ease some of that.

I fold the wagon train flyer and place it in the journal inside my backpack. The pack is now loaded with two changes of clothes, a camera, film, boots, tent, sleeping bag, plastic inflatable mat and pillow, cooking utensils, canteen, maps, and a diary by Sir Richard F. Burton titled *The City of the Saints and Across the Rocky Mountains to California.*

Sir Richard Burton traveled the Pony Express Trail in 1860 by stagecoach when he wrote this diary. I plan to read it as I follow the same route to compare what he found then to what I find today.

I didn't know much about Burton before I started doing some research into my upcoming trip. He was born in England in 1821. His father wanted him to become a minister and sent him to Oxford to study, but Sir Richard fell from grace with the professors in only two years when he criticized their accents in non-English languages. Obsessed with comparative religion, though he never reached an inner peace about God, he set out to explore the world and learn more about man and his spiritual nature. He spoke several languages, including Arabic and Somali, and wherever he traveled he joined the locals in food and drink, sometimes even wearing their costumes to blend in like one of their own. He wasn't above entertaining them with wild stories, horoscopes, and card tricks.

I like that Burton, a wanderer like myself, will be making this long journey with me. I push his diary a little deeper into my pack and zip-close that compartment.

I have only one other item to add to my pack, and to get it I must walk back into the woods behind my house. I leave my bedroom and go outside, where the moon has just risen over Lookout Mountain. Its light reflects from the window in the barn as I walk past it. An owl hoots from the pines, and a whippoorwill calls.

Two lightning bugs flicker yellow as I follow a moonlit path beneath the pines and oaks. It meanders up a hill for a half mile to my cabin. I go inside and strike a match to light five candles, for there's no electricity or running water in here. I built this cabin six years ago with my father. I use it as a retreat to collect my thoughts and listen to my heart. It is a kind of friend. There is a fireplace, and its light offers warm company for conversation and a bottle of wine. The walls and shelves store my folk art. I'm part Cherokee and I make gourd masks in the shape of birds and animals similar to the ones my ancestors made. I also carve soapstone for pipes and make spears, bows, and arrows. Indian artifacts I have found over the past thirty years lie here and there on the mantel, in a glass case. Just out the window, some thirty feet away from my cabin, is a special grave no bigger than a man's hand. Buried there are items people gave me when I walked the Trail of Tears in 1989. The items are meant to honor the four thousand Cherokee who died on the Trail of Tears when they were forced to march from their homes in this area of Alabama to Oklahoma. I learned a great deal about myself and others along those nine hundred miles. It was that journey that strengthened my faith in man, myself, and the Great Spirit, and that now helps lead me to retrace the Pony Express Trail.

On the mantel by a photograph of my Cherokee great-grandmother sits a leather pouch containing the last item I need to pack in my bag. It is a whistle made from the wing bone of a dead hawk I found near my cabin. I was relieved to discover that it was not one of the pair that has circled high over my cabin for the past three summers.

I blow out the candles and leave the cabin. I walk down the hill to the garden behind my parents' house. Ever since I walked the Trail of Tears it has become a ritual for me to dig my hand into this soil before I go on a long journey. My father and I plant the garden in this soil and my mother prepares meals for us from the vegetables that grow there. It connects us to each other and to the earth. It helps me feel whole.

Every time I go on a long journey I'm faced with the possibility that one or both of my parents could die while I am away. I am always torn by my need to set off on my own and my fear of losing one of them, for while I do not cling to them they are, by far, my best and dearest friends.

I go into the house. My parents are asleep. I pause to hear them breathing.

I go to my bedroom at the other end of the house. It is time for me to go to bed. I need a lot of rest to begin the long journey tomorrow. But first, I open the leather pouch. I remove the hawk-wing bone whistle and gently blow into it. It creates the faint whistle of a hawk, sounding like the two that circle over my cabin. This is no attempt to call those birds; I just want to hear the familiar sound that reminds me of home and will be a comfort on my journey. I gently blow again, asking the Great Spirit to protect my parents while I am away. I am not above accepting a Helping Hand myself.

CHAPTER
TWO

I awake early the next morning with the Alabama sun shining down from Lookout Mountain. My bedroom window is open and I hear a crow calling from the oaks. As I get out of bed and get dressed I look out the window to see a blue jay squawking from a grape vine growing out in the pasture.

After a moment the blue jay flies from the grape vine and I leave my bedroom to have breakfast with my parents. I know their eyes and voices so well that I see and hear a mixture of excitement, anxiety, and sadness about my leaving on this long, uncertain journey.

Don't worry about me, I say at the breakfast table. I'll be just fine.

Do you have to take a canoe down that river by yourself? my mother asks.

I'll wear a life jacket, I say.

Don't get stranded out in the desert without water, says my father.

I won't, I say.

Sometimes those deserts get flash floods, says my father. They can wash you away.

I'll have plenty of water then, I say.

I hope you travel with those wagon train people most of the way, says my mother. There's safety in numbers.

I understand why that 1860 San Francisco newspaper ad

for Pony Express riders stated *orphans preferred*. All those years I spent thumbing alone around America put my mother through many worried and sleepless nights. I feel a trace of guilt about leaving on this new trek because I'm concerned that she will lie awake again many nights till I reach the end of the Trail.

I'm excited, I tell them. I've never been on a wagon train before. I hope it's as much fun as the ad promised.

After breakfast I place my backpack in the trunk of my parents' car for them to drive me a hundred miles south to Birmingham Airport. I will catch a plane to Kansas City, which is only thirty miles from St. Jo, where the Trail begins.

I close the trunk and search the yard for our cat, Rosco. I want to pick him up and rub his neck and head before I leave. I go to the barn, but he isn't inside. Sometimes he sleeps at the foot of my bed and I'm disappointed that I can't find him there either.

My parents and I get into their car and head south. It takes two hours to drive to Birmingham Airport.

We'll wait till your plane leaves, says my mother.

No, I say, taking my pack from the trunk of the car. Y'all go on. It'll make saying good-bye easier.

When I was eighteen, my parents drove me to the south end of my hometown so I could thumb to California. I was fed up with Alabama and thought I wanted to live in Los Angeles. When I parted with my parents on the side of the road, my mother had tears in her eyes.

Could you at least shake my hand? she asked.

I shook her hand. I thought it was unmanly to show more emotion than that.

Today, standing outside Birmingham Airport, I open my arms and pull her to my chest, my heart. It feels right to hold her.

Now don't worry, I say. I'll phone.

My father is about to cry and this warms me. I like to see his face get soft. His body stays stiff as I put my arms around him. His shoulders stick out like aged guards. I understand his defenses.

Take care of the garden till I get home, I tell him.

We'll still have corn and tomatoes when you get back, he says, if it doesn't get too hot and dry over the summer.

I carry my pack aboard the plane. Before I place it in the overhead compartment I unzip its small pocket and remove a strip of leather two and a half feet long.

I take my red-handled knife from my pocket and sit by a window. I cut the leather strip in two, then remove my hat from my head and make a tiny hole on either side. I feed one end of the leather into each hole and make a knot to prevent it from sliding through. I feed the loose ends dangling to my neck into a hole in a piece of basswood an inch long and an inch in diameter. I can now push the basswood toward my neck to tighten under my chin. This will keep the hat from blowing off my head when I encounter the strong prairie winds. The basswood, according to my Cherokee ancestors, will protect me from being struck by lightning. In the side of the hat is a tail feather from the same hawk where I got the wing bone for my whistle. Sticking from the band at the back of the hat is a rattler from a snake. I wore this hat when I walked the Trail of Tears and I feel like it is part of me.

I have on an old faded pair of jeans and a pair of hiking shoes I bought just a few days ago at Sears. I have a second-hand pair of cowboy boots in my pack for when I ride horses. My belt buckle is real silver and was handmade by a Navajo in Arizona. In its center is a small sun.

It takes only two hours for the plane to fly from Birmingham to Kansas City. As we prepare to land I gawk at the Kansas and Missouri rivers snaking across the prairie. The land seems to stretch forever, and adrenaline shoots through me as I wonder who I'll meet and what will happen as I retrace the Trail, meandering over the very earth I now behold.

The plane lands and I swing my pack over my shoulder to make my way through the airport terminal to look for transportation to St. Jo.

We have a van that goes to St. Jo, says the clerk at the counter. But it'll be another two hours before it leaves.

I don't want to wait that long. I find a cardboard box at the newsstand and use my knife to cut a flap from it. With a black Magic Marker, I write:

ST JO

OREGON TRAIL WAGON TRAIN

As I walk a mile from the airport to the highway the straps on my pack begin to rub my shoulders raw. It will take a while for that skin, as well as my feet, to toughen. It's May, but today is cold, windy, and cloudy. I hold out my sign to the approaching cars and trucks.

It begins to rain and I push the collar of my leather jacket up around my neck. Those new leather straps on my hat are paying off because the wind from the big trucks tries to blow it from my head. Some of the water flies into my eyes. Many of the motorists stare as if my sign doesn't say WAGON TRAIN at all, but HOMELESS, WILL WORK FOR FOOD, and they don't stop.

I'm standing here for almost an hour and begin to wonder if I'll ever get a ride, when a van pulls over in front of me. I lift my pack from the ground and run to it.

I open the door to the van. A smiling man in his early twenties greets me.

Going to St. Jo? I ask.

Yes, sir, he says. That's where I live. Be happy to give you a lift out of this rain.

I hop in and close the door, holding the pack in my lap. It's warm and dry inside and we take off down the road, his windshield wipers leading the way.

You going on that wagon train? he asks.

Sure am, I smile.

I envy you getting to go through Wyoming, he says. When my parents divorced a few years back, it tore me apart. Wyoming is where I went to begin getting over it. I climbed up on this boulder. Got up there and just sat, looked out over the land. Best medicine in the world.

When we arrive in St. Jo, the rain has lightened. Miles to the west the clouds are parting and sunlight shines down. Rolling green hills fade into the prairie.

Want me to drop you off anywhere special in town? the driver wonders.

I'm a little hungry, I say. Maybe a café.

I know just the spot.

He stops on a cobbled stone street in front of a Victorian building. A sign over the door says Johnnie Frye Bar and Grill. I open the van door to exit.

Thanks for the lift, I say.

Have a good summer, he says. I wish I were going with you.

CHAPTER
THREE

The van disappears down St. Jo's cobbled street. I lift my pack and enter the Johnnie Frye Bar and Grill.

As I sit at a table near the back of the enormous single room I feel as though I have stepped back in time to the Old West. The ceiling is fourteen feet high and a handcarved wooden Victorian bar stretches twenty feet along the south wall. A bullet hole peeks from the top of the bar near the man-size mirror, as if someone tried to shoot his own reflection and missed.

A waitress comes my way and hands me a menu. She eyes my pack on the floor.

Just get to town? she says, her voice warm and tender.

Yes, I'm here to join the wagon train headed down the Oregon Trail.

I saw some of those people this morning on my way to work, she says. They're gathered just a few blocks from here down by the river. A horse had gotten loose and they were trying to catch it. You know what you want to eat yet?

In a few minutes she brings me a cheese sandwich and a cup of coffee. As I enjoy the food I'm happy to see the rain stop. The clouds part just enough for blue to peek through and the greening trees promise spring. Just beyond the café window, water drips from the roof to the cobbled street. Between bites of sandwich and sips of coffee I make notes in my journal about when, from the plane, I spotted the Missouri and Kansas rivers snaking across the prairie. I'm still awed by the land's vastness. It makes me feel so small, but hungry to see who and what awaits me out there on the Trail. But am I truly ready to face any dangers that come my way? Am I tough enough to make it all the way to California? As I write in my journal, a great mounted elk head on the wall casts shadows from his horns onto my pages. I wonder if he once grazed along the very Trail where I will soon journey. That he is no longer alive to run and leap across the great prairie makes me just a bit sad. His glass eyes seem to ponder me.

My heart lightens when the waitress appears with her warm, friendly face. I return a smile.

How's the coffee? the waitress asks as she pours more.

It's fine. Thanks for brewing a fresh pot.

Sure, she says, I wanted a cup myself.

On the wall near the elk head hangs a painting of Johnnie Frye. While some locals like to think he was the first Pony Express rider out of this town, the *St. Joseph Weekly West* of April 7, 1860, names Johnson Richardson as the first man. But I don't care. Johnnie Frye is more fascinating to me because he is still a folk hero a hundred years after he died. Back in 1860, so the story goes, some of the women around St. Jo liked to give the good-looker cookies they had made, but he rode so fast through town that it was difficult for him to take them. One creative woman is said to have invented the doughnut so Johnnie could capture it as he rode by, his finger in the hole. Another determined woman chased him till she tore free a piece of his shirttail for a quilt she was making.

I finish the sandwich and coffee and place my journal back in my pack. I ask the waitress for the check.

More coffee? she asks.

No, I say, I've got to walk across town to see a man about renting a horse.

* * *

Two hours later, after an unsuccessful talk with the horse trader, I walk down a cobbled street toward the Missouri River, where the waitress said the wagon train is camped. The sky has darkened with clouds again and the wind is cold. I hope the wagon train has a big campfire like the ad promised so I can warm myself before it. The flyer pictured a giant black pot hanging from a tripod while people lined up to fill their plates. Some thirty covered wagons encircled them, just like I have seen in movies and old photographs.

But when I get to the end of the street near the river, I see only four wagons. They aren't at all like the ones I had in mind. They're no bigger than compact cars, and the wheels don't have wooden spokes and steel rims, like those that dared the Oregon Trail in the 1840s and 50s. The little wagons rest on rubber car tires. There's no big black pot to eat from and the only fire I see is on the end of a match as a man in a cowboy hat lights a cigarette. I wonder if these little wagons are mascots for the real wagon train that hasn't arrived yet.

There is, however, very real excitement in the air. A man leads a horse from a trailer, and a TV cameraman films him. Eight or ten pickup trucks with campers are parked among some fifteen horses and mules. Men, women, and children walk about with cameras to snap pictures as if a circus or carnival just hit town and the main tent were about to be raised. Two cars ease down the road toward me and the passengers gawk and point. Everyone is grinning so much that it makes me wonder if something big and miraculous is about to happen. If it is, I want to be part of it.

The animals, however, seem more nervous than excited. Horses and mules, tied to ropes, pull hay from bales with their giant teeth while their tails swish through the air like brooms of witches as they leap from the earth. Then one of the mules bites another on the neck and he kicks, making the first one jerk backward to pull the rope tied to a wagon. A man with a long black beard is squatted by the wagon as he straightens a two-inch metal rod by pounding it with a hammer against an anvil, an iron block. He then inserts the rod into a leather harness on the ground, but drops it when one of the mules kicks again. He leaps to his feet and raises his hammer toward the massive animals.

You settle down now, he shouts. Stop that biting and kicking before I work on your head.

The mules seem to understand, for they return to eating the hay. The man with the beard squats back at his anvil and begins to pound the rod again.

I walk down to the river, where a man in his fifties fills two buckets with water. He wears a cowboy hat with a red lace garter around it. A long turkey feather sticks from the band. He pulls the buckets from the river and one of them splashes onto his boots.

Can I give you a hand? I ask.

Looks like I need one, he says, handing me a bucket. You here to join us? I just got to town yesterday myself. I was afraid I wouldn't make it. I retired last week after twenty-six years carrying the mail and went to the doctor for a pain in my leg. He discovered I had a clogged artery, but he did that balloon surgery and took care of it. I'm sure glad, too. I've wanted to ride the Oregon Trail ever since I was a kid. How far you going with us?

I don't know, I say. I just went to see a man on the other side of town about renting a horse to ride for the first hundred miles. He wanted five hundred dollars cash and said I'd get half of that back when he picked up his horse in one piece. I liked the horse, but I didn't get a good feeling about the man. I told him I'd let him know before dark.

Five hundred dollars? says the man. That's highway robbery. You can almost *buy* a horse for that. I tell you what. I bet we can find you a wagon to ride in for free. Then later on somebody's bound to join the wagon train with a spare horse you can ride.

That sounds good, I say, offering my hand. My name is Jerry Ellis. I'm from Alabama.

I'm Josh Wilson, he says, returning a firm handshake. I'm from Arkansas. Let's find you a ride.

We carry the buckets of water to his horse, tied to a rope that is linked to the bumper of a truck. Josh then leads me past the TV cameraman to a man in a cowboy hat who smokes a cigarette and brushes a mule.

This man needs a ride in a wagon, Josh explains. I told him we'd help him out. Is the reporter and photographer from that London newspaper still leaving with you in the morning?

No, says the man. They faxed their story back to England yesterday and their boss told 'em to fly back home. I'll have room in my wagon.

That's great, I say, offering my hand. My name's Jerry.

I'm Peter Jacobs, says the man, knocking ashes from his cigarette. Sure, you can ride with me and I'll feed you for twenty-five dollars a day.

I turn to Josh and he lowers his eyes. I want to be part of this wagon train and the FUN and FELLOWSHIP that the ad promised. I don't want to be viewed as a customer.

I don't have that kind of money, I say. Thanks anyway, but I'll just walk.

Let's check with the wagonmaster, Josh suggests. He might have room in his wagon.

I follow Josh to the wagon where the man with the beard is still squatted by an anvil. He uses his hammer to pound the rod into the harness. Josh introduces us and explains the situation. The man's name is Charlie Green; he's from near Knoxville, Tennessee.

You'll be welcome in my wagon, says Charlie. There's just me and my wife.

I can help you feed and water your mules, I say, or do anything else I can to help out.

That won't be necessary, says Charlie. But have you signed up yet and paid your dues? You need to see Sally Tyler over there in that camper. If you don't, she may blow a fuse.

I'll do that now, I say.

Be here by eight in the morning, Charlie warns. We won't wait on you.

I walk to the camper Charlie indicated. Inside I find a woman with red hair and a puffy white face seated at a table. In her sixties, she wears a tight red sweater, and gold earrings dangle over flakes of dandruff on her shoulders.

Are you Sally? I ask.

That's right, she snaps. Who are *you*?

I'm Jerry Ellis. I just talked to Charlie. I'll be riding with him and his wife. He said I should pay my dues here.

It's twenty-five dollars for each month you stay with us, she says. How much is Charlie charging you to ride in his wagon?

Nothing, I say, giving her twenty-five bucks.

Nothing, huh? she says, giving me a tin badge with a picture of a wagon train like the one in the ad. You want to buy a T-shirt?

On the table next to her box of badges is a stack of T-shirts. They picture the wagon train from the ad—the one I have yet to see in real life. I pick one up and eye it.

They're nice, I say, hoping she can't see that I really don't like them. But I guess I'll pass on one right now.

Did you read the rules? she asks.

I wonder if one of the rules is that I have to buy a T-shirt to ride on a wagon. I shake my head.

That badge you got in your hand, she says. You got to wear it at all times. Put it on your hat so everybody can see it.

She is so crusty that I'm almost amused. She reminds me of a drill sergeant. I take my hat from my head and fasten the badge to it. I place the hat back on my head.

See you in the morning, I say, hoping that she has simply had an off day and will be in better spirits after a good night's rest.

Yeah, she mumbles as I leave the camper.

The sun has set and I walk down the dirt road among the horses and mules. At the end of the road, all by itself, is an old wagon painted green. It is parked under a towering cottonwood, its leaves quivering in the cold wind. Two small mules, eating hay, are tied to ropes linked to the wagon. On the side of the wagon, painted in red as if by a child, are the words DAVID STEIN. A man of about eighty years old is standing by the wagon, lather on his wizened face. He uses a straight razor to shave before a cracked mirror hanging on the side of the wagon. A tiny light glows over the mirror.

Hello, I say.

He turns and the razor shakes in his wrinkled hand. His eyes are cautious, his voice gentle.

Oh, hello, he says.

I didn't mean to startle you, I say. I was just looking around. There aren't as many wagons on this train as I thought there would be. I like yours. Did you build it?

No, I traded a mule for it eight or nine years ago. My wife helped me paint it last week. She had planned to come along with me, but she got to feeling weak a couple of days ago. I didn't want to leave her, but she made me come anyway. I phoned her a little bit ago. She said she was feeling a lot better. But I'm not sure she was. She doesn't like for me to worry about her. We're both getting up in the years. If I can just go on the ride for a week or two, I'll be happy. Helen is an understanding person. She knows what this trip means to me. Are you married?

No, I say. I just broke up with my girlfriend a few weeks ago. I was married once, but it didn't work out.

My first wife died, he says. She was helping me feed the cattle when her heart gave out. I lifted her into the truck and drove to the doctor. But he was twenty miles away and it was too late. I don't let my second wife feed the cows.

He turns to the mirror. He touches his cheek with two fingers.

Your soap is getting dry, I say. I'll leave so you can finish shaving. I'm riding with the wagonmaster and his wife. I'll see you in the morning.

That's good, he says, easing the razor to his face.

His hand is shaking as he pulls the razor and I walk on. Twilight is falling on the wagon train when I stop and look back. I'm intrigued that the old man parked his wagon away from the others. I wonder if he's lonely. He reminds me a bit of my grandfather, whom I loved a great deal. When I was a boy, he owned a mule and buggy. He was the last person where I grew up still to go to town and back by that means of transportation. I once rode with him in the buggy as he returned from town to his farm on Sand Mountain. The dirt road we followed snaked along a cliff and it was a cold and windy November afternoon. He placed a quilt over our legs to keep us warm and I felt so safe and happy that I wanted that day to last forever.

I stand watching the tiny light by the cracked mirror as David Stein continues to shave. It glows like a candle in the night. Then I turn around and head for town.

CHAPTER
FOUR

As I walk up St. Jo's cobbled street the tiny light on old David's wagon fades into the night. In the distance, lightning flashes yellow. Thunder rumbles. The wind becomes stronger and colder. I put my hands in my pockets.

I walk pass the Johnnie Frye Bar and Grill and see the mounted elk head on the wall near where I sat this afternoon. I spot my waitress carrying two mugs of beer to a table. I'm tempted to go inside, but I've already met so many people today that I want to be alone to savor a walk through this little town before I leave tomorrow.

I stroll another four blocks down the darkened streets, when I spot a metal statue at the corner. It's a horse positioned in an eternal gallop while a bigger-than-life Pony Express rider sits atop his *mochila* stuffed with letters as they race toward the Missouri River. They appear so real and powerful that I can almost hear hooves pounding against the cobbled streets. The rider's spurs jingle and jangle as his six-shooter hangs from his leather belt. My adventurous side wants to mount this horse and feel the wind in my hair, the thrill in my heart. This is not the first time I have wondered if life itself were not like some wild and beautiful stallion to ride bareback as hard and fast as possible before I die.

As I marvel at the statue, hailstones the size of marbles

begin to fall. They bounce from the metal horse and rider. The ground starts to become white.

With my pack tossed over my shoulder, I run down the street. My hat protects my head, but a couple of the hailstones sting my neck.

I've made plans to stay at the Pattee House tonight and run that way. By the time I spot it, looking just like it did in old photographs I've seen, I'm out of breath. I hurry up on the porch to get out of the howling storm.

The Pattee House stands four stories tall and in 1860 it was the finest hotel in St. Jo. It offered good meals, beautiful rooms, and excellent service. Anyone about to take the stagecoach to California stayed here to savor a bit of luxury before daring to cross the Great American Desert. Mark Twain was one of those. So was Sir Richard Burton.

Along with housing some of the most famous figures of the time, the Pattee House also served as the headquarters for the Pony Express. When newspaper ads appeared for riders, this is where the hopeful teenagers of the area flocked from little farms and ranches to be interviewed. Records are thin, but they were probably interviewed by Alexander Majors himself. When he and his partners, William B. Waddell and William H. Russell, founded the Pony Express and the Central Overland California and Pike's Peak Express Company, Majors had the most experience with horses and the rugged men who earned livings by sweat and backbreaking work on the frontier. For several years he had contracted to haul military supplies by wagon for the U.S. Government down the Santa Fe Trail. He wasn't afraid to dirty his hands on the Trail as he worked side by side with his men. He demanded that they treat their horses, mules, and each other with respect.

When Sir Richard Burton stayed in the Pattee House, he was introduced to Alexander Majors. He wrote about that meeting in his diary:

> He forbade his drivers and employees to drink, gamble, curse, and travel on Sunday; he desired them to peruse Bibles distributed to them gratis; and though he refrained from lengthy proclamation commanding his lieges to be good boys and girls, he did not the less expect it of them. Results: I scarcely ever saw a sober driver. . . .

Mail delivery by horseback was not invented by Mr. Majors and his courageous partners. Relay horses and riders carrying mail date back as far as the thirteenth century, in China. Kublai Khan had organized such a system for his great empire.

In 1856 the U.S. Government tried to create its own relay mail system across the Great American Desert. It bought seventy-five camels in Arabia for thirty thousand dollars. But the hard desert in America was unlike the soft sand in the Middle East. The animals' hooves couldn't take it. They also scared the hell out of mules and horses. So the plan was scrapped. Some of the camels were bought by circuses. Others were released to roam the wilderness.

It was the Pony Express, however, with its headquarters in the Pattee House here in St. Jo, that created perhaps the greatest and most heroic story of the Old West. A couple of weeks before that first historic ride, several of the young Pony riders were housed in the luxurious hotel. They got to eat fine meals and dance with pretty women. They wore their spurs as they swaggered about the admiring onlookers and well-wishers. Then, a week or so before the Pony Express began on April 3, 1860, all the riders—except the one out of St. Jo—were sent to desolate and lonely way stations along the Trail to fulfill their promises to risk their lives daily to make sure the mail got through.

* * *

Over a hundred years later the Pattee House is a museum. Shivering and alone on the porch, I take my pack from my back. When lightning flashes to reflect from the many windows and cast eerie shadows onto the street, it looks a bit like a haunted house.

The hail stops, but is followed by pouring rain. The wind blows sheets of water onto the porch and I crowd the doorway with hopes of staying dry. But the back of my jeans becomes wet and my face cold.

I'm relieved when a car arrives and a man I've been expecting, Gary Chilcote, overseer of the Pattee House, gets out to greet me. He is in his fifties, small and thin, with a spark in his eyes. He writes for the local newspaper and saved the Pattee House from rotting to the ground several years ago when no one else came to its rescue. He is also president of the St. Jo Pony Express Association. Each summer, all along the Trail, members of this Association, and others like it, ride horses at breakneck speeds to celebrate and honor the Pony Express riders.

What a night, says Gary as he runs from the rain and howling wind onto the porch.

I appreciate you letting me stay here tonight, I say.

It's no trouble, he smiles, unlocking the museum door. Just watch out for the Pattee House ghost.

I lift my pack and we go inside. The house smells musty and old.

Ghost? I ask as we walk through a pitch-black hallway.

If you believe in that kind of thing, he says. Back in 1857 a woman jumped from a window upstairs to her death. They say her spirit is still here. Sometimes people hear her footsteps. Across the street there on that hill in the trees is where Jesse James was killed. He was playing poker in his house when a friend shot him in the back of the head. We moved his house behind the museum. It has a lot of the things in it that belonged to him and his brother, Frank. When Jesse was killed, his wife and kids lived here in the hotel for a while. I don't want to be rude, but I got to hurry back home. My wife and I have friends over tonight. I'll leave the light on back here for you by the bathroom and turn on the heater. You did understand when we talked on the phone that I've got to set the alarm?

Yes, I say. I don't mind.

He goes to his office, sets the alarm, and returns. He eyes some thirty or forty giant pictures of famous outlaws on the walls. Their rugged, leathery faces seem to snarl.

Don't let these guys get to you, he says.

I'll do my best, I tell him. See you in the morning around six-thirty?

He nods and hurries out the door to beat the alarm. I peek out the window to watch his car disappear into the rain, kind of glad that he left as soon as he did. I've been looking forward to being alone here, as if it were my own private Old West museum. It's just a bit spooky, though, as a tree limb brushes against the window and the wind continues to howl. A dog barks up the street.

I only have access to the ground floor of the Pattee House, and most of it's dark. I dig into my pack and pull out a small flashlight. Shining it around the room, I see a glass case the size of a writing desk. It looks like a casket holding a carved wooden cane. I step closer to it and discover a little sign saying that the cane belonged to St. Jo's fur-trading founder, Joseph Robidoux. I can almost hear the old man tapping his way down a dark, cobbled alley.

I shine the light about the room, and spurs, saddles, and pistols are ghostly in the twilight. A female mannequin, dressed in lacy Victorian clothes, holds a fringed parasol as she stands at the foot of a high post wooden bed. Lightning flashes, and her face seems to come alive for a split second with something warm, inviting, and risqué.

On the other side of the room a shelf holds an old whiskey

bottle, which makes me wonder what happened when the liquor was consumed. Did the drinker down the whole bottle in one evening to gather up his courage or forget his pain, or did he sip it with others to savor excitement about their journey by stagecoach to California? Below the bottle is an oak desk with a telegraph machine atop it. I walk to it and click out dots and dashes as if I knew what I were spelling. Still, I'm amused at the machine's metallic little song. I've seen so many Westerns that a part of me feels compelled to jot down an urgent telegram I've just received and race it over to the sheriff.

I walk back to the rear door and shine my light through its window. I see the little house where Jesse James was killed. In the howling wind and rain, it looks shabby and lonely— and just a bit haunting. I wish I could disconnect the alarm and go outside to enter the famous outlaw's home.

When I was five years old, I loved to go to the Saturday cinema with my older sister, Sandra, and watch cowboy movies. Roy Rogers, Gene Autry, and Hopalong Cassidy were my heroes. They could outride, outshoot, outlasso, and outfight all those mean outlaws dressed in black. Roy and Gene could sing, too, and they were always kind and happy. They treated old people, kids, women, and animals with respect. I thought they were real. I wanted to be like them. If my sister ever wanted me to do anything, she would refer to them. A real cowboy would eat his eggs, she might say. A real cowboy would let me put lotion on his face. A real cowboy would never hurt anybody again: That's what she said after I shot her with my BB gun. I was sorry. I had gotten a little confused between real bullets and movie bullets. It hurt to see her cry after I shot her. She was as much my heroine as Roy and Gene were my heroes. She said something about a *good cowboy* having a clear conscience. I didn't understand the big word. But I promised her that I would never shoot or hit her or anybody else again.

* * *

Something shakes the door, and my heart begins to pound. I use the flashlight to find my way back to the front of the museum. The door, only eight or ten feet away, rattles again and louder than before. I tell myself that it's just the wind, but adrenaline shoots through my system and my heart races faster. Lightning flashes and I see someone on the porch. When I pull back the curtains to peek outside, though, no one is there.

Then I hear footsteps on the second floor. Or do I? Yes, there they are again. No, maybe it's just a rat running over timber so old and dry in the ceiling that it magnifies the sound. But I don't buy my own logic, for the creaking now becomes so loud that it seems to rattle the very walls themselves.

I shine the flashlight all around the room till I stop on a photograph of Jesse James. He is dead in the picture and his eyes are closed. The floor over me creaks again and my face flushes as hot air drifts against my cheeks and lips. Then outside the window I see someone on the porch. I'm sure this time. Staring in through the old panes of glass in the window, he turns a flashlight on me while overhead the footsteps on the floor are racing back and forth, and I swear I can feel someone's hot breath blowing into my face. Then it sinks in that the man on the porch is my reflection in the window. The footsteps are giant metal gears in the heater, its fan circulating hot air. Some night watchman I'd make.

It's been a long day and I'm beat. I take my sleeping pad from my pack and blow air into it, then unroll my sleeping bag. I take off my clothes and crawl into it. My flashlight is at my side.

Rain continues to fall and I can hear it pouring down on the porch outside. The wind howls and tree limbs brush against the windows. A train whistle blows in the great distance, like a soothing song in a storm. The heater clicks on and sends footsteps across the second floor, but I'm getting used to that now. I snuggle deep into my sleeping bag with my head on my leather jacket. When lightning flashes, I see the tiny sun in the center of my silver belt buckle. It was a Christmas gift from my girlfriend I broke up with a couple of months ago, and thinking of her here, alone in the dark on such a rainy night, makes me just a bit lonely. I suspect that this will not be the last time I lie alone in the dark on the Trail and long to hold a woman in my arms who I love and trust.

CHAPTER
FIVE

 The next morning I'm awakened from my night on the floor of the Pattee Hotel by the rattling of the front door. It opens and Gary Chilcote steps inside.

Good morning, he says, hurrying toward his office. I've got to turn off the alarm.

My body is stiff and my lower back hurts as I crawl from the sleeping bag and get dressed. I wish I had a cup of coffee. I stuff my flashlight into my pack as Gary returns.

See any ghosts last night? he asks.

Just the one who lives in the heater, I say. Thanks again for putting me up.

I step out from the Pattee House to find the street empty except for more cold wind and rain. When Pony Express rider Johnson Richardson stepped through the same doorway for that first historic ride, he was greeted by hundreds of well-wishers who threw a party in the street for him. They had hoped that he would've left hours earlier, but he had to await his mail from the East. It finally arrived aboard a special locomotive—the *Missouri*—and one car, which roared out of Hannibal: With smoke puffing from its stack and sparks flying from its great iron wheels, it set a speed record that lasted for fifty years.

It was all the young rider could do to make his way through this wild crowd to his horse. When he finally leapt atop his bay mare and settled onto the saddle with the *mochila* beneath him, he waved his hat at the crowd in celebration that he was off! As he pushed his way through the mob, frantic well-wishers, hungry for souvenirs, plucked hair from the horse's mane and tail to make rings and necklaces.

The horse and rider then charged down the cobbled street while a band played and a cannon boomed. The wild crowd cheered and seconds later young Richardson was out of sight. The rider raced toward the Missouri River to board a ferry to carry him and his horse to the other side of the river, where he could continue his ride toward Troy, Kansas.

No such party crowd waits for me, just cold wind and black clouds as I hurry down that same cobbled street past the Pony Express stables, still standing and now a museum, and toward the Missouri River to join the wagon train. I've walked only two blocks when the wind sucks the hawk feather from the band in my hat. I try to catch it, but it drifts about like a darting butterfly and lifts high over my head into the blowing mist. A gust now catches my hat, but its leather straps make quick and certain hands to hold it on my head.

I spot the wagon train. It's still far from being the one pictured in the ad or on my badge, but a fifth little covered wagon has joined it and eight or ten horses are saddled with riders. For three or four blocks leading from the wagon train to the bridge that crosses the Missouri River into Kansas, some hundred or more onlookers have gathered to watch us leave town. I'm a bit surprised to feel a sudden swelling of pride.

A police car with its red light flashing sits at the head of the wagon train. A TV crew with a camera and a microphone moves about the crowd. Josh, who helped me get a spot on the wagon train, sits atop his horse, which wears a tiny brass bell, dangling from the massive belly held tight by the leather straps of the saddle. As the horse trots, the bell rings.

Can your horse play a tune? I say.

Oh, no, grins Josh, that bell just keeps me awake.

As he smiles I spot two front teeth capped with gold. One of the removable gold caps has had a star design cut in it to reveal the tooth's white enamel. A turkey feather sticks from his cowboy hat, which is also decorated with a red lacy garter. I find his appearance so colorful that I can't help but stare.

At the end of the wagon train sits the little green wagon owned by David Stein. He sits in the seat with leather reins in his hands; they lead to his two mules. I wave and David waves back, a big, warm smile revealing his perfectly white false teeth.

I feel a bit uneasy when I spot Sally on a horse. Red hair, sticking from her cowboy hat, blows in the misty wind. Her puffy face looks even paler than it did last evening when I paid her my dues. I'm glad I'm wearing the badge.

How you doing today? I ask.

It's cold, she says. I don't like it when it's cold.

It'll warm up.

Yeah, she mumbles, I guess.

I move up to the head of the wagon train, where I find the wagonmaster, Charlie. His wagon is hooked to the three mules he scolded yesterday when they bit and kicked each other over hay. Instead of a cowboy hat he wears a baseball cap. The plastic cover over his wagon shakes in the cold wind gusting off the river.

Want a chew? he asks, sticking a piece of tobacco into his mouth.

No, thanks.

It's some I grew and cured myself, he says. It ain't none of this store-bought stuff. Go ahead and put your pack in the back of the wagon. Make yourself at home. My wife will be back in a few minutes and I think we'll be ready to roll.

It feels good to take the heavy pack from my back and place it in the back of the wagon where I'll be riding. When I return to the mules, I find that Charlie is gone. In his place stands another man, huge and in his late fifties, holding something that looks a bit like a tripod some old folks use as a walking cane.

Hi, I say, eyeing the odd metal device in his hand.

You seen Charlie? he demands in a voice that is so loud that I wonder if he is hard of hearing or thinks I am.

He was here just a second ago, I say. You on the wagon train?

That's right, he says, his voice growing even louder. I'm Ted Simpson. I'm the *trail boss.*

His handsome, leathery face becomes hardened as the corner of his eyes wrinkle. So does the skin on his forehead. He does, however, offer a smile. I'm curious about the mixed messages he's sending me. He stands as though his body is a bit stiff. His shoulders stick out like my father's did when we parted at Birmingham Airport yesterday.

You a rancher? I ask him, still curious about the metal device in his hand.

A retired truck driver. What do you do?

I'm a writer. I write books.

I don't do a lot of reading. I'd rather be doing something outdoors.

I agree, I say. I spend a lot of time in the woods. What's that in your hand?

A rattlesnake catcher, he says, lifting it a few inches and sticking out his chest a bit with pride. I wanted to show Charlie.

You hunt for snakes often?

Every spring in Texas. We roast them over a mesquite fire. Tastes a lot like chicken.

I've eaten part of one, I say. I had a high school buddy in Alabama who bit a live one in two. He did it on a dare to win a six-pack of beer. You do some crazy stuff when you're a kid.

He continues to eye me as if he isn't sure what to make of me. I don't like feeling uncomfortable like this.

Catching rattlers is some hobby, I say, trying to win his confidence. Could I see your catcher?

I reach out to take the metal device, but he doesn't offer it. When I start to lower my hand, however, he eases it my way. I'm careful not to pull it from his huge hand too quickly.

This is some device, I say, squeezing and releasing the handle, which opens and closes the metal fingers at the end of the four-foot-long snake catcher. I like snakes myself.

When I return the device to him, his long fingers wrap around it quickly, as if it might vanish if they don't.

I'm Jerry Ellis, I say, offering my hand. I'm riding with Charlie and his wife. Glad to meet you.

He offers that beautiful smile again and I like the way he shakes hands. Maybe he's simply under a lot of pressure from all the responsibility of heading this wagon train. I'm a bit relieved when Charlie, his big black beard blowing in the wind, steps from a camper.

You about ready to go, trail boss? says Charlie, his voice playful but a bit strained and I wonder what's bothering him.

I been waiting on you, Mr. Wagonmaster, says Ted, his voice once again rising as if he or others have trouble hearing.

I been waiting on *you, trail boss,* says Charlie, his voice now less playful and harder.

Ted hands the snake catcher to Charlie, and he works its handle to make it open and close like I had done. I continue to study Ted's eyes. He seems disappointed when Charlie returns the device to him.

It squeaks a little, says Charlie, spitting tobacco juice to the ground. You need to oil it.

A cop sticks his head from his car parked in front of Charlie's wagon. The mist is becoming rain.

We got the road cleared, shouts the cop. You folks ready to go?

Ted climbs onto his horse as Charlie and I get into his wagon. There in the front seat now is a small woman in her fifties. She wears no makeup, but her skin has its own beauty. Her eyes offer a warm gleam.

Good morning, she says with an accent I recognize from back in the hills of Tennessee. I'm Charlie's wife, Lily.

My pleasure, I say. I'll try not to be in your way.

Plenty of room, she says, brushing hair from her eyes as wind gusts and rain falls.

Ted, on his horse and ahead of the wagon train, is joined by Josh, who carries a red flag to warn traffic of our presence. Next to them is a blond woman in her late forties who rides a palomino. Fringe dangles from her buckskin jacket.

With its red light flashing, the police car eases forward along the street. Ted takes his hat from his head, turns to face the wagon train, and swings the hat in the air.

Wagons hoooooo, he shouts with his thundering voice.

He returns his hat to his head, and his horse starts forward as if the whole world might follow. The hundred or so onlookers wave and snap photographs as the wagons rattle across the railroad tracks.

Leading the wagons and other riders, Josh guides his horse toward the bridge when suddenly the massive animal begins to slide on a patch of ice that formed on the road. Fear flashes across Josh's face as his horse's front legs begin to fold. It looks as though the horse will fall and bring Josh down with him before we've even gotten started. But the horse regains his balance, the tiny brass bell on his saddle straps jingling, and I breathe a sigh of relief.

We don't have time for any ice skating, shouts Charlie, guiding his three mules with the leather reins.

I know, shouts Josh. Tell my horse.

The police car leads us out of St. Jo and onto the bridge to cross the Missouri River into Kansas. We're only five little wagons and eight or ten horses with riders, and when I think about the vast prairie I saw from the plane yesterday, we seem so very small. Still, the spirit of adventure swells big within me as we roll down the Trail.

CHAPTER
SIX

After the wagon train crosses the bridge into Kansas it starts down a narrow country road. The police car turns off its red flashing light, turns around, and disappears back over the bridge into Missouri. So much for the parade.

We rattle down the road past modest farmhouses, barns, and gardens barely green with sprouting lettuce, turnips, cabbages, and onions. Fenced horses and mules along the route snort, prance, bray, and kick, as if desperate to be free.

Farmers and their families hurry from their houses to point and gawk. Some of the faces intrigue me and I wish we could stop to talk. A few children run alongside our wagons and look eager, almost envious as they watch us disappear down the road.

It continues to rain and the strong wind is so cold that I begin to shiver. I dig into my pack and find another pair of jeans and a shirt. I put them on and slip my hands back into the pockets of my leather jacket.

From end to end the wagon train stretches only some seventy-five yards long. We don't have to worry about creating any sonic booms. We're making only three to five miles an hour. I'd like to say that I'm still on fire with excitement after the first hour, but the cold, wind, and rain and the repetition of the slow wheels rocking the wagon and the constant flutter of the plastic cover dampen my spirits.

Lily? I shout above the wind. Would you like to sit back here where it's dry and a little warmer?

Yes, she says. That would give Charlie somebody new to talk to. He already knows all about me, she adds, a hint of sadness in her voice.

Lily and I exchange seats and I sit beside Charlie, who's chewing his tobacco as wind blows sheets of rain into our cold faces. I lower my head and let my faded hat act as a shield. I look up, however, when Charlie shouts at his mule —Jack—and jerks the leather reins with his fist as if trying to pull a tooth from the animal's giant mouth. Charlie holds the reins tight for several seconds, forcing the mule's head to face us. His big eyes look almost human and I feel a bit sorry for him.

You better straighten up, shouts Charlie, or I'll put a lip screw on you.

Oh, Charlie, Lily mutters from the back of the wagon as she snuggles inside a blanket.

You trying to say something back there? he asks.

You and that mule, she says, her eyes making contact with mine as if to apologize for her husband. Jack can't understand what you're saying. He's just cold and wet like the rest of us. This wagon is heavy to pull.

He better *try* to understand me, shouts Charlie, if he knows what's good for him.

Lily shakes her head and pulls the blanket close to her neck. Her hair blows in the wind. Then even her head disappears under the comforting blanket.

Say you're from up around Knoxville? I ask, hoping to get Charlie's mind off the mule because the anger in his voice when he shouts grates on my nerves.

Yeah, says Charlie, that's where I was born and raised. I got a little tobacco farm there down near the Tennessee River. You can't depend on it to make a living, though. I've worked the past thirty-five years in a glass factory making windows for cars.

Thirty-five years? That's a long time.

No, he says, spitting tobacco onto the road. That's a *helluva long time.* You work yourself to the bone and the government taxes you to death. But I had four kids to support. You married?

No, I say. I'm divorced. My first wife got involved with another man. I never wanted to be married again. There have been a few women since then. I'm used to coming and going as I like now. Sometimes I get lonely, but my freedom means a lot to me. I can't imagine working in the same place for thirty-five years. I'd go nuts.

Charlie turns to me. His eyes harden. I feel I may have offended him, but that was the last thing on my mind. I try to correct my possible mistake.

That's good you got four kids, I say. I miss having children of my own. Sometimes I like kids more than adults. I—

I retired a month early, says Charlie, his voice rising, to take this trip.

I think that's great, I say. I like to see people—

For years now, he says, I've had this picture in my mind of my wagon rolling down the Oregon Trail. I'm going to make it the whole way or die trying.

I don't like that he has interrupted me twice in less than one minute. But I do like hearing his dreams. His eyes are taking on a beautiful gleam.

I keep seeing my wagon and mules, Charlie continues, making tracks in the sand on the Oregon beach. *Gal-darn you, Jack, how many times I got to tell you?*

Charlie slams on the brakes and the mules continue to walk, dragging the wagon a foot or two before they stop. He jerks the leather reins with such force now that Jack's head is pulled sideways, his lips and eyes looking as vulnerable as a scolded child who doesn't understand what he's done wrong.

Now you walk right, shouts Charlie, hitting Jack over the back with the tip of a six-foot whip.

Something wrong? shouts Ted, the trail boss, riding back to the wagon on his horse.

No, says Charlie. Jack just ain't broke in good yet. He'll start behaving by the time he's walked across the state of Kansas, though. Now go on, Jack, and stay in line with Hank and Red.

Ted drives his spurs into his horse's stomach and the horse gallops back down the county road to join the blond woman in her leather fringed jacket, riding the palomino. Charlie's wagon rolls on as Jack, Hank, and Red walk into the wind and rain.

I turn back to see the wagons and riders on horses. David, in his old green wagon, meanders down the Trail as if he's had a drink or two, or just doesn't care if his mules don't toe the line. They wear little American flags sticking from their harnesses and they wave in the constant wind. From time to time Josh, riding at the end of the train, will shout *CAR* and wave his red flag. Ted, on seeing a *car* at the head of the caravan, will shout the same and wave his red flag. What a mirage we must be to those unsuspecting people in cars and trucks as they spot us coming around a curve.

After three hours the rain lightens up and we stop at an old abandoned farmhouse to take a break and stretch. The women have the back of the barn first. The men are next. I return to the wagon to find Lily by herself all wrapped up in the blanket. She holds the reins and her face looks a bit perplexed, as if she worries that the three mules might try to run away any second now.

Well, she says, what d'you think of this wagon train?

I'm not sure yet, I admit. It's my first time on one.

I'd rather be home myself, she says. But Charlie would be lost without this trip. Lord, I hope we make it. I saw you writing in a journal earlier. I'm trying to do that myself so I can give it to my grandchildren, but it ain't easy. I can't get past the postcard stage. I work at a school cafeteria. Kids know so much more today than I did when I was their age. Some of the kids are so sweet when they come through the food line. I'm not supposed to, but I give a few of them bigger helpings. I can't help it. One boy can't talk plain and some of the other kids mock him. I don't scold them. I just make sure he gets the biggest piece of pie. I learned that from my mother. She always said God looked out for the weak and weary, but He welcomed a helping hand. My mother's gone now. I still miss her. I never saw her mistreat a living soul. Daddy's gone, too. He had his days. He never was happy with himself. Sometimes I wondered why Mother didn't just walk off. Your mother living?

Yes, I say. My father, too. We're very close. My whole family is. I have two sisters.

That's good, says Lily. We're close, too, except for Charlie and two of the four girls. They just can't talk without fussing with their dad. They say he doesn't listen.

Charlie comes from behind the barn and she turns back to the mules as if I had vanished. I hope that this does not become a pattern. I don't want to be a sounding board for Lily only when Charlie is not around. Still, I savor that she has been so open with me.

We travel about thirty miles today and arrive on the outskirts of the tiny town of Troy, Kansas. The wagon train rolls under trees outside a barn and 4-H building where we are to camp for the night.

The rain has stopped and the sky is clearing. The wind has died down. I climb from the wagon with stiff legs and an aching lower back.

You sure I can't help feed and water the mules? I ask.

I'm sure, says Charlie, taking the bit from Jack's mouth and rubbing the floppy ears with a tenderness that surprises me after all the jerking he did on the reins today.

I'll see y'all later then, I tell him. I'm going to stretch my legs and wander into town. Lily, y'all need anything from the store?

No, she says. We got our camper stocked full. We'll go get it back in St. Jo as soon as the animals are taken care of.

Troy is only a few blocks away and it feels wonderful to be out of the confines of the wagon and away from Charlie's shouting. The walking also loosens up my legs and releases the tension from my lower back.

Downtown Troy is little more than a block long. The sun is already setting and only one small grocery store is open. I go inside and order a turkey sandwich along with a cup of coffee. I don't mind standing as I eat, for I get to watch the locals come and go with life's demands: eggs, milk, cornflakes, coffee, and cigarettes—despite the surgeon general's promise for the user to grow alien life forms in his lungs.

Anybody unusual or outstanding I should meet here in Troy? I ask the pretty store clerk, making change.

Yes, she says, dropping a penny on the floor. You got to meet Ernest Ditlamore.

Who's he? I ask.

He's a wonderful old man, she says, picking up the penny. He lives in a hole.

A hole?

Straight down in the ground, she says, like a rabbit.

Yes, I say. I would like to meet him. How do I do that?

I'll phone Larry and see if he'll take you out to the little farm where Ernest lives. Larry takes him groceries once a week.

She dials the phone and I get more excited when she finds Larry home. I'm disappointed, however, when she covers the mouthpiece and her eyes become apologetic.

Larry can't take you today, she says. How about tomorrow afternoon?

The wagon train leaves in the morning.

She speaks the same into the receiver and hands it to me. Larry tells me not to worry, that he'll come tomorrow to the wagon train camp and give me a lift back to Troy to meet the Rabbit Man of Kansas.

That's a lot of trouble, I say.

No, says Larry, almost giggling as if he guards a secret I could never guess. It's no trouble at all. Ernest loves to meet people.

We make arrangements to meet tomorrow and I hang up the receiver. I wish it were tomorrow already. I've never met a Rabbit Man before.

Thanks, I say, heading out the door.

You're welcome, says the clerk. Tell Ernest I said hello.

A trace of mischief livens her face and I wonder all the more about this man who lives in a hole as I walk back to the wagon train. When I arrive at the 4-H building, I'm disappointed to find that everyone has gone inside the campers for the night. What happened to the music and campfires that the ad promised?

I walk down a hill to the barn where the horses and mules are tied. Jack stands next to Hank and Red. They smell of sweat and hay. I start to rub Jack on the head, but Hank lifts his great leg and kicks. I back away and leave the barn.

I spot a tiny light at the top of the hill. It burns inside old David's wagon. I go to it. I find David crawling into a bed in the back of the wagon. I'm about to say hello when he turns off the light. The night air feels even colder as I stand there alone in the sudden darkness.

The stars are out and a coyote calls as I head for the 4-H building with a tin roof and a concrete floor. A gas heater is on at one end of the building. I take my sleeping bag from my pack and unroll it atop my inflatable pad.

I remove my clothes and get into the sleeping bag. It makes me a bit sad that I am alone and that my campfire is a gas heater. Its dozens of tiny flames make delicate hissing sounds like people whispering in the distant darkness, but I know there's no one here. I close my eyes, hoping to fall asleep and dream away this lonely feeling.

CHAPTER
SEVEN

I awake at dawn in the 4-H building. I've just had a dream in which a small boy was staring at me. I know I've seen him before, but I can't remember where. Then as I become fully awake I'm a bit amused and concerned to realize the boy was *me*. Yes, I'm clear now. It was me in my first-grade class picture, surrounded by the other boys and girls in school. I didn't like the first grade, seated in a row. I felt trapped in the classroom; I wanted to be outside in the fields and woods. I feel as though the dream is trying to tell me something.

I get dressed and stuff my sleeping bag and pad into my pack. I carry it outside to place it in the back of Charlie's wagon and discover that the rain and clouds have all vanished. It's a beautiful May morning, with birds singing as they hop about in the trees. It's still cold, but the clear sky and the rising sun give hope of a warm day. I spot Charlie in a plowed field down near the barn. His eyes scan the moist earth.

Looking for arrowheads? I ask. I do that sometimes.

I wouldn't pass one up, says Charlie. But I mainly collect unusual rocks. I got one I found down by the Tennessee River that's shaped like a goat. Another one looks like a pig. Lily doesn't think so, but that ain't the first thing we don't see eye to eye on.

Do I have time to run into town to get coffee before we leave? I ask.

Oh, yeah, says Charlie, his voice smooth and gentle compared to yesterday's shouting at Jack. It'll be an hour before we head out.

I walk into town and find a little café. I go inside, take off my hat, and sit at a table near the coffeepot. The waitress pours me a cup. As the caffeine gets my heart to pumping faster I find myself thinking more about the dream I had this morning. It may not mean a thing in this world, but the fact that I can't shake it bothers me a bit.

The waitress brings me two fried eggs, potatoes, and toast. As I chew I listen to the locals having breakfast.

How cold did it get last night? asks a man pouring sugar into his coffee.

I don't know what the thermometer said, says a guy spreading jam on his toast, but my wife kept her big feet next to mine. Must've gotten down into the twenties. You see that wagon train hit town yesterday?

No, says the man.

Yeah, says the guy with the toast, they're camped down at the old 4-H barn.

My God, the man pouring sugar complains, every time people come through here playing cowboys and pioneers we spend a month cleaning horse shit off the streets.

I pay my check and leave the café, heading for the little grocery store where the clerk told me about the Rabbit Man. I want to say hello to her, but the store is not open yet, so I walk on.

When I get back to the wagon train camp, I find that Charlie is having trouble with his mules. Jack won't move from the barn and begins to kick the wooden walls.

What's the matter with you? shouts Charlie. Are we going through this again today? You're just begging for that lip screw, ain't you?

Lily holds the other two mules, Red and Hank, by their halters and leads them to the wagon. She looks at me and shakes her head as Charlie struggles to get Jack out of the barn.

It stopped raining, I say.

Yeah, she says, I just wish Charlie could see some blue in the sky.

Charlie finally gets Jack to the wagon and hitches him along with Hank and Red. David hitches his two small mules and straightens the little American flags sticking out from their harnesses.

Did you stay warm outside in your wagon last night? I ask.

No, says David, his right hand trembling slightly. I chilled a little in the middle of the night. But I wanted to hear the coyotes and see the stars. I can't understand coming on this trip and not doing that. Where did you sleep?

In the building, I say. But from now on I'll sleep in Charlie's wagon. I like to hear owls hoot.

He smiles as if he has found a kindred spirit. I do the same. When he starts to get into his wagon, his foot slips and he almost falls to the ground.

Careful, I say, offering my hand.

I don't have the strength I once did, he says.

I help him into his wagon and he eyes me with a look so warm that it melts my heart.

You're welcome to ride with me sometime, he offers. Can you drive a team?

I never have, I say, wanting to do just that.

That's okay, he says. It's easy. I'll show you how. My mules are well trained. Well, most of the time. Ever now and then one will get a little wild.

I don't want to feel confined on a wagon today like I did yesterday so I've taken off my cowboy boots and put on my new Sears hiking shoes. I will walk and run today alongside the wagon train. When I leave it, days or weeks from now, I will be mostly on foot, and I want my legs and feet to be in excellent shape. The rest of my body is already strong and tough. I've continued to lift weights faithfully ever since I was a teenager who dreamed of becoming Mr. America and one of the strongest men on earth.

As Ted, the trail boss, leads the wagon train down the hill along a dirt road, I find myself thinking about my teenage years and how the Pony riders were, like myself, loners and risk-takers. Nothing thrilled me more than to thumb to New York or Mexico and not know who I would ride with next or what would happen. I was rarely ever scared because I felt—probably like most young American males—*indestructible.* Didn't I have the muscles to prove it? I could outlift anybody in my weight category in the state of Alabama. I had trophies to prove it. And hadn't I thumbed rides with Hell's Angels and other thugs and not gotten a scratch? When one driver pulled a knife on me, didn't I call his bluff and tell him I would make him eat the blade if he didn't put it away in five seconds? Still, I cannot deny the other side of that macho coin either: One Halloween night my two buddies and I went to the bootlegger on Lookout Mountain and bought some whiskey. We got high and joined three other kids in a '56 Chevy. The driver had had more to drink than I realized. He missed a turn at the top of the mountain and crashed into a truck parked outside a grocery store. He panicked, threw his car into reverse and then into first gear. His hot rod was the fastest in town. The wheels burned rubber as we flew from the scene of the accident.

We better not run, said one of the boys in the backseat.

Don't listen to him, said my cousin.

Yeah, said my other buddy. He's just chickenshit.

The driver started down the mountain. It was filled with curves. His tires squealed.

I want out, said the boy in the backseat.

Yeah, said another kid. You're going too fast. You won't

make that curve at the bottom. Tell him, Wild Man. He'll listen to you.

My nickname was Wild Man. Me and the whiskey I had drunk wanted that name to earn its honor. I was seated next to the driver.

Give it hell, I said. See how fast it'll go.

The driver stomped the gas pedal and it was all he could do to stir it, the tires squealing louder with each new curve. My shoulders knocked against those of the driver and then against those of my cousin as we swerved from side to side. When we met a car coming up the mountain, it shot into a ditch to avoid a crash.

We ain't going to make that last curve, shouted the boy in the backseat. We'll wreck. Stop it, damn it.

Give it hell, I said, thinking it sounded tough.

I felt indestructible and was sure that we would round that last curve with a thrill that would last a lifetime. But as we entered the curve the hot-rod Chevy flew from the road and rolled over three times down the side of the mountain. Glass shattered and bodies bounced about the car. When the car came to a dead stop against some oaks, it was turned upside down. It seemed like a miracle that four of us made it without a scratch. The driver, however, had broken both his arms. I felt horrible about his injury. The next day my two buddies and I went to see him in the hospital, but he didn't have much to say to us that day or any day that followed in the years to come. His arms are stilled wired together with iron pins. Sometimes even today at the age of forty-three when I'm at the gym doing barbell curls for my arms, I'll think of him. I wonder if I called him and told him that I was sorry about what had happened if he would think I was foolish after all these years have passed.

As I continue to run down the dirt road alongside the wagons where the Pony riders once raced I can't help but think about what happens to the human body as a man ages.

When I was the age of the Pony riders, I felt nothing could hurt me. Muscle and bone were stronger than steel. The Pony riders must've felt the same way to take the risks they took. But now, with my youth gone, as I see old David, fragile and weathered driving his mules I know I, too, will one day become that vulnerable, as surely as all the Pony riders are now dead and turned to dust. These thoughts don't depress me. They make me realize once again just how short and precious life is. At least in this heightened moment I don't even mind that my lungs begin to burn from running. I feel lucky to be in the race against time.

CHAPTER
EIGHT

Green hills roll before the wagons as far as the eye can see. Thick green grass eight to ten inches tall wavers in the constant wind. I like that the road has many curves, because I never know what might be around the next bend. Some of the earthbanks on the sides of the road are ten feet tall and the massive roots of oaks twist and turn to look like giant snakes coiled on a warm day. A creek winds to my right and a mockingbird sings atop a small cedar, gently rocking back and forth as if to give the bird a ride for his song.

After jogging for a mile or so my feet begin to hurt. I slow down to walk, but it's difficult to keep up with the wagons. I have to run again to catch them every couple of minutes, and it bothers me just a bit that I'm chained to the wagon train's pace as long as I'm with it.

I feel a bit apart from the folks on this wagon train and not only because I'm having trouble staying apace with them. I don't feel like I know any of the travelers yet. I have to say that I'm disappointed that there are no children with us. They can be so easy and open and I like their company. And the only single women are Sally, the crabby drill sergeant, and the blonde in the fringed leather jacket who usually rides alongside Ted at the head of the train; women are usually good to talk to. Funny, I once believed that saying very little made me more masculine and now I'm hungry for conversation. Still, this is only my second day on the journey and I need to give myself and the others time to warm up. When I jog alongside the wagon driven by Peter, who wanted to charge me to ride in his wagon, I decide it's time to try to break the ice.

You got two good-looking mules, I say.

They'll do, he says, puffing on a cigarette. You look a little out of breath.

A little, I admit, my lungs and feet burning like hell.

Want to ride up here for a while? he asks.

You charge by the mile or by the minute? I grin.

No charge, he laughs. Climb on up.

With his wagon rolling down a hill, I hop aboard and sit beside him. I'm surprised to see a woman seated in the back of the wagon. Her very long nails are painted a bright red and she thumbs through a copy of *Cosmopolitan*. Life is rough on the old Oregon Trail.

I'm Kathy, she says. Peter's wife.

She is a beautiful woman with a sensual smile and eyes filled with what I take as healthy and intellectual curiosity. It makes me feel good just to look at her. But when Peter turns to see us smiling at each other, she loses her smile and starts thumbing through the magazine again.

I appreciate the ride, I say. My feet were really starting to hurt.

Josh, carrying his red flag, rides toward us on his horse. Its little brass bell, dangling from his stomach, jingles. The horse jerks his head sideways and raises his big ears before a mailbox made from an iron plow.

He see a spook? laughs Peter.

I reckon, says Josh, pulling on the reins and trying to get the horse moving down the dirt road again. Yesterday he almost bucked me when he saw a tractor tire leaning against a barn.

Josh finally gets the horse convinced that the mailbox isn't a monster and they ride on up to join Ted and the blonde on the palomino.

What makes horses and mules do that? I wonder aloud.

Who knows? says Peter. I've traded horses my whole life and still haven't figured it out. Sometimes they'll even spook at a fence post. My daddy and me had one old mule who'd spook every time he saw a woman in a bonnet. My great-aunt always wore one and he'd go crazy when he saw her. We finally traded him to a man in Georgia.

You trade horses for a living? I say.

Horses and mules, says Peter. I'm in business with my father. What do you do?

I write books and plays, I say.

Really? says Kathy, lowering the magazine and coming to the front of the wagon. That sounds interesting. I read a lot. I was in plays in high school.

Peter eyes her and spits to the side of the road. She eases her fingers into his hair, kisses his cheek, and goes back to her seat, disappearing behind the *Cosmopolitan* again. Her long red nails appear on the edge of the pages as if at least that much of her will stay in the conversation. I feel in the way, but I'm determined not to let that stop me from getting to know these people. I pride myself on helping folks drop their walls. I know a little about walls because I spent so many years hiding behind them. I certainly don't mean any harm to Peter or his wife, Kathy. I'm just looking for that fun and fellowship the wagon train ad promised.

That's interesting that you and your father both trade horses and mules, I say. I guess he taught you the business?

I been trading and breaking horses back in Kentucky ever since I was in the sixth grade, says Peter, his face beaming and his chest sticking out just a bit as he lights another cigarette.

I raised pigeons when I was in the sixth grade, I say. I've always liked birds. I got two hawks that circle my cabin each summer. Did you have a horse of your own in the sixth grade, or did you just train them to sell?

I had a pony, says Peter, his voice softening for the first time. Me and the other kids played tag and I'd ride him to the middle of the pond. Nobody else's pony would come out there. I got wet, but I always won. When I got home one day from school, I couldn't find that pony. Daddy had sold him. I never let myself get that attached to another one. No, I didn't even have a real childhood. I was breaking horses while the other kids were out playing. I'll say this much, though, I was the only kid in grammar school to carry a hundred-dollar bill in his pocket.

He has a faraway look in his eyes, as if he can still see that pony. For all I know he is a kid again racing to the middle of the pond, where he always won. Then that look vanishes. He puffs on the cigarette and spits to the dirt road as if to get a bad taste from his mouth.

What's the problem, Charlie? shouts Peter.

Charlie and Lily are in the wagon in front of us. Charlie has stopped the wagon and is jerking on the long leather reins.

Jack thinks he can do whatever he wants, shouts Charlie. I'll get him straightened out, though.

Charlie cracks a whip over Jack's back and the wagon rattles on. Lily turns my way just long enough for me to see a pained look in her face.

Charlie has a time with Jack, I say.

I'll tell you something about Charlie, says Peter, his voice taking on a defensive tone. We had just met on another wagon train a few years ago, and I had some money problems. He pulled me aside and gave me a check for five hundred dollars. Said pay him back when I could. Now, that's a friend.

This makes me think more highly of Charlie. I also envy the bond between him and Peter. Both my hometown buddies are dead now, and I miss them.

What Trail were you on, I ask, when you and Charlie met?

The Trail of Tears. You heard of it?

This seems like a wonderful opportunity to get closer to Peter and Charlie. We have a lot in common I didn't know about.

Yes, I say. Both my grandparents were Cherokee. I walked the Trail of Tears in 1989.

You *walked* it? snaps Peter.

Yes, I had read in a newspaper where a wagon train re-traced it. I had no idea y'all were part of it. My walk was the greatest experience of my life.

You walked nine hundred miles? asks Peter.

Yes, I say, feeling and savoring all the warmth and kind-ness of people I met along the Trail.

How many people did it with you? says Peter, as if doubt-ing my story.

I did it alone. I had more freedom that way.

Hmmm. He spits onto the dirt road.

The look on his face makes me feel as though I have said something wrong. I don't know what it was. How could two men have followed the same Trail and not feel a closeness? Then it slowly dawns upon me that maybe we only traveled the same exterior Trail. The Trail that is inside a man may cross different streams and mountains as he seeks the heart's home.

CHAPTER
NINE

The wagon train rattles down a dirt road across Kansas as I continue to sit in the front seat of the wagon with Peter. There is so little conversation that I turn to the constant wind blowing over the rolling hills of grass and imagine that it has a voice—discreet and muffled—and speaks to me as if I were a loyal listener. Still, sitting next to Peter, I cannot help wondering what became of the boy who once rode that pony to the middle of the pond. If he is still inside Peter, I wish I knew how to bring him out from behind the guarded walls of manhood. When I glance to the back of the wagon, my eyes meet those of Kathy. She's looking at me over the magazine. For a fleeting second, I wonder if she, too, is thinking about a different Peter.

At noon the wagon train follows the curving dirt road toward the Iowa/Sac/Fox Indian Mission, which has been converted into a museum. Two yellow school buses are parked before the old mission, and some two hundred schoolchildren stand gawking, pointing, and shouting just outside the building as we approach. They wave, as if their hands in the air can somehow magically touch the horses, mules, and wagons, though we are still some fifty yards from them.

The children are held back by four or five adults, who I presume are teachers, as the wagons rattle to the top of a grassy field overlooking the mission. Between us and the children is a line of small oaks and the old original Oregon Trail, with ruts three feet deep and stretching some thirty or forty yards. When the wagon train finally stops, I hop down from Peter's wagon. I'm surprised to see Josh having trouble with his horse again. It is spooking, trying to get away from a stump sticking two feet from the ground.

Settle down, shouts Josh, fighting the horse with the reins. The horse's hind leg kicks into the air and his mighty neck jerks and twists as if he wants to throw Josh as far as his giant eyes can see. Josh no sooner has the horse calmed down when Jack kicks Hank, the mule lined up next to him. Red, the third mule, now swishes his mighty tail high into the air. This sense of uneasiness in the animals makes me feel a bit edgy, too. The day has warmed up and foam drips from their mouths. Their massive, sweaty bodies seem so huge compared to the children only thirty yards away, begging the teachers to let them come closer.

I want to ride in a wagon, shouts a boy.

Me, too, says a boy next to him.

Yeah, shouts the first boy. We want to drive it.

I want to ride a horse, screams a little girl. I know how. I have one at home. Can I, *please*?

We'll take a closer look in just a minute, says a woman standing before them.

But the first boy pushes the second one beyond an imaginary line the teacher seems to have drawn between the horses and children, and he runs toward the animals. Two other boys follow.

Get back here, shouts the teacher.

But it's too late. All two hundred children break through the imaginary barrier to become an excited mass of small legs, arms and heads. As they run laughing and screaming toward the wagons, the animals try to back away but are bound to reins and harnesses.

I don't like this, says an onlooker standing beside me. All these kids around these animals scares me.

Me, too, I say.

I scan the crowd with hopes of seeing Charlie, wagonmaster, or Ted, trail boss, moving toward the children to take control and make them move back to the mission. But Charlie is talking to his wife, Lily, and Ted is laughing along with Josh and Peter about something.

All you kids, shouts the man beside me, get back away from these horses and mules.

A few of the kids listen and back away. But there is so much talking and laughing as the kids stick their noses into the wagons and pet the horses and mules that most don't pay any attention to the warning. The children seem to think that the wagon train in the greatest show that ever hit Kansas.

Put me on your horse, mister? says a little girl. Please?

It's a mule, says David, struggling to lift the girl from the ground and onto his animal.

Atop the mule, she smiles as if this were the biggest thrill in her life. She holds on to the little American flag sticking from the animal's harness and waves at her schoolmates.

Then, in the blink of an eye, everything changes. One of the mules kicks. The other one bucks, and the little girl screams as she falls from the mule to the ground. Dozens of kids now scream and begin to run. A couple of the children fall to the ground, and several others trip over them.

The mules break free from their spot and begin to run down the hill. Now all the kids are screaming and running as the wagon wheels and thundering hooves aim right at them, unable to distinguish clods of earth from children's heads, arms, and legs. It is a human stampede parting for two terrified mules, their tiny American flags waving in the prairie wind.

The muscles in my legs, arms, and back tighten as I stand watching all the confusion. I'm torn between running after the mules to try to stop them and pulling children from the ground and to safety. But it all is happening so fast that I, like other adults around me, stand frozen with panic.

David, who has been holding tight to the long leather reins of both mules ever since he stood by the mule he placed the girl on, hits the muddy ground. He is dragged down the hill, his old, frail body twisting and turning as his head bounces over the earth; the mules' hooves sling mud onto his face as they thunder on.

The children's screams grow louder as David finally lets go of the reins, and he rolls to a stop. The mules and wagon shoot ever faster down the hill toward a ditch. When they collide with the earthbank, the wagon crashes and turns over on its side. Two of the wheels spin in midair as the mules come to a dead halt, their eyes wild with terror.

David lies on the muddy ground halfway down the hill between his wrecked wagon and a second wagon atop the hill. I fear that he is seriously hurt, but I'm relieved to see him rise to his knees. I start toward him to help him to his feet, when I hear a scream behind me. I turn to see what's wrong.

At the top of the hill, the two horses pulling the wagon that was parked next to David's wagon have become spooked. They are charging toward a group of children who run for safety, only to stumble into the ancient ruts of the Oregon Trail. One of the kids, a thin blond girl of ten or eleven, avoids the ruts by running another way. But the two runaway horses, pulling the wagon, race in her direction and she runs into an oak. The horses crash against the tree as well and she screams as she is pinned against the trunk. I fear that her insides are so crushed that she might not survive.

Two men run to her. They pull the horses and wagon from the trunk. It's discovered that there's been a stroke of luck, that the wagon's iron tongue—to which the horses are fastened—caught its end against the tree and spared the girl the full impact of the crash.

You're not hurt, says a teacher as she pulls the girl into her arms. You're not hurt, she says again, as if trying to convince herself more than the girl.

Tears roll down the girl's face. She is so limp that she can barely walk, and she looks pale enough to be in shock.

I . . . the girl mumbles. I . . .

She breaks out crying again and the teacher leads her back to the mission, where eight or ten picnic tables are loaded with food. The other children hurry that way, too. Many look back to the hillside where the nightmare erupted, their faces still frozen with fear and disbelief.

David limps just a bit as we turn his wagon back upright. While there's quite a bit of crying and anxious activity all around me, I'm a bit perplexed that I don't hear any conversation about how the accident could've been prevented if Charlie or Ted had taken control and made sure the kids were held back.

David's mules are unfastened from the wagon and led from the ditch. A sledgehammer is used to pound the wagon's bent iron tongue back as straight as an arrow.

You okay, David? I ask as he limps around, trying out his shaky legs.

I think so, he says, his clothes, hands, and face muddy, his right hand trembling slightly. I think I'll phone my wife.

The people who run the Indian mission museum begin to serve lunch at the picnic tables. They're working hard to make the kids feel safe and sound again, but their young voices are still filled with fright. I don't know about the other grown-ups, but I'm not hungry.

CHAPTER
TEN

After lunch, the wagon train rolls down a dirt road, leaving behind the old Indian mission and the children waving good-bye. They fade into the distance, but I'm haunted by their screams when the stampede occurred. David has cleaned the mud from his clothes and face, but his aged eyes still look uneasy from the day's tumble down the hill.

That evening, when we arrive at the night's campsite in a lot next to a football field, I find a young man with a chubby face coming my way.

Are you Jerry? he grins.

Yes, I say, shaking his hand.

I'm Larry. We spoke on the phone last night. I've come to take you to meet Ernest.

The gleam in his eyes makes me feel like there's a real treat in store for me in this mysterious Rabbit Man of Kansas. We crawl into Larry's truck and start for Troy, which is some thirty miles back to the southeast.

Have you known Ernest for long? I ask.

Oh, yes, my whole life.

He really lives in a hole?

Yes. Larry giggles like he did last night when we talked on the phone.

You take care of him?

Oh, no, says Larry. He takes care of himself. I just take

groceries to him. I've been doing it for years. He makes out a list each week and puts it in an envelope with a stamp and my address on it. The mailman picks it up, marks through the stamp with a pen, and drives down the dirt road to my mailbox about a mile away. It's always the same list, more or less.

That's kind of you to take him groceries.

It doesn't take long. I have a lot of spare time.

What do you do for a living? I ask.

I work at a feed mill three days a week. I did work every day, but things have dropped off the past year.

He slows his truck and we roll up another dirt road toward an old barn, hay sticking out from the loft. Chickens are running around and scratching the ground as they cackle. Larry stops the truck and we get out to face a banged-up and rusty old trailer house. I'm disappointed that Ernest may be fudging on the truth and live here some. I want a full-time Rabbit Man.

Does he live in the trailer sometimes? I ask, wary of the answer.

He wouldn't think of doing that, Larry explains. This is just where he keeps his animal feed and a deep freeze for his ice cream. The door's cracked a little, so he's probably in there now. He's expecting us.

Larry knocks on the trailer door. It swings open to one of the strangest-looking people I've ever seen.

Ernest appears to be in his seventies and he hasn't shaved in a week or two. He wears two pairs of coveralls with the knees worn from the first pair to reveal the second, red pair underneath. He's as dirty as a coal miner, but his eyes beam with warm, life-giving curiosity. He has no teeth within his big smile and he leans on two canes. One is a store-bought cane. The other was cut from the limb of a tree; his fingers rest in its Y.

Good to meet you, he says, extending his hand like any

fine and caring gentleman. I'm so happy you came to see me. Would you like an Eskimo Pie?

Not just yet, I say, still staring at this kind, homely stranger.

Five or six kittens meow and crawl over his dirty, heavy shoes. He continues to stand in the doorway, and on the wall behind him is a tempting calendar from the fifties: a pinup girl with long, smooth legs descending from short shorts, while her big breasts are peeking from inside a dangerously revealing halter top. It takes me several seconds to realize that she holds a spark plug with a tiny yellow flame blazing from it. She's either advertising car parts or she has human electricity for sale or rent.

That's some girlfriend you got there, I say.

Ernest leans on the tree limb cane with the Y as he turns to study the calendar beauty. He laughs as if I don't know the half of it.

Yep, he says. She's a sweet one.

Where's the hole you live in? I say, feeling only a moment later that I may have been too forward too fast because Ernest gives me a funny look.

We'll head that way now, Ernest offers.

The kittens run from his giant shoes and the sensual gal in the calendar disappears behind the closed door as Ernest hobbles down from the trailer. He uses two canes with ease as we wander over to an old shed where a 1930 Chevrolet is parked. It's covered with dust, and boxes, boards, wire and tin have been piled on the hood.

My daddy bought that car new, recalls the Rabbit Man. He's dead and it doesn't run anymore. This airplane in the other shed over here was built in 1946. I was flying her myself till just a few years ago. I could land her right out there in that field. Well, it's grown up some now.

I look to Larry to confirm the truth. He nods that Ernest is, indeed, a pilot, whether he has a license or not. I like this whimsical little Rabbit Man and his old plane covered in as much trash as the 1930 Chevrolet. I almost expect him to suggest that we pull it from the mess and take it for a flight, his canes sticking out the window to shake at Troy as we buzz the little police station.

I miss flying that old plane, Ernest confesses. But sometimes I have two friends who come by and I go with them to model airplane meetings. I get all cleaned up when I do that. Sometimes I put on a tie.

I try not to stare, but his face is such a wonder to behold because of all the joy in it that it's difficult not to.

Up here is what's left of the house I lived in before I moved into the hole, he says. My mother and daddy built it back in the 1880s. It burned to the ground except for this rock foundation. But I know, you want to see the hole. We're almost there. Just a little farther up the path.

Why do you live in a hole? I ask him.

I don't have to worry about tornadoes, he says with the convincing clarity of a hole salesman. It's also easy to heat. When the house burned, I just got a pick and shovel and starting digging.

I live part time in a cabin, I say, that started out as a giant tree house.

A tree house? he grins, pausing on the path and leaning on his canes. I always wanted one.

We walk past some bushes and an apple tree green with new leaves. A small shed—which looks like it might collapse if we sneeze—has a tin roof over a wooden trapdoor. Ernest lifts it to reveal his hole-home, going straight down into the sweet earth. It's as dark as the tunnel of love.

Want to come see? invites the Rabbit Man. I'll go down first.

The Rabbit Man eases down into the hole with his canes and disappears into the darkness. When I begin to do the same, Larry giggles and his big belly shakes.

Have you been down there? I ask.

No, says Larry, and I don't plan on it either.

No, comes the voice of Ernest from the earth, Larry never comes into my home.

When I ease down into the hole, the Rabbit Man lowers the trapdoor. We're in total darkness except for a few rays from the setting sun coming through a dirty skylight. My eyes begin to adjust and I see that the room is barely big enough for us and a potbellied stove where he burns wood for heat and cooking. I like the smell of the damp earth as I strike a match. The flame shows the Rabbit Man's proud smile.

Where's your bed? I wonder aloud.

You're standing on it, says Ernest without judgment.

I discover that I'm standing on a pile of flattened cardboard boxes. Then the match goes out.

Sorry about standing on your bed.

No harm done, he says. I walk on the boxes all the time. I sleep just fine. It's cozy and warm down here when it snows a foot deep *up there.*

Ernest reminds me of Jimmy Stewart in the movie *Harvey,* which is about a six-foot rabbit most people can't see. Both Ernest and Jimmy Stewart's character seem to accept life as it comes while others get in a hurry and bent out of shape.

I like your hole, I say, trying to eye his impish face in the dark. It makes me feel good.

I'm glad you like it, says the Rabbit Man. I couldn't live any other way now.

I wish I had brought my backpack, I say. I'd pitch my tent here on your farm, if that was okay. I'd like to get to know you.

That's a good idea. Can't you go get your pack and come back?

I'm with a wagon train. It leaves in the morning.

Oh, that's too bad.

You want to leave the hole first? I say.

No, insists the Rabbit Man. After you.

I crawl out of the hole to find Larry still grinning as when I descended into the little earthy home. Ernest soon struggles back to the surface with his canes.

Twilight is falling over the rolling hills, the barn and the sheds housing the 1946 plane and 1930 Chevrolet, as we retrace the narrow path by the foundation of the burned house. I'm a bit torn about leaving this wonderful old man. I feel relaxed and at peace here. This is a most welcomed change from the tensions on the wagon train and the violence at the Indian mission today.

When we arrive at the trailer, Ernest opens its door. His eyes beam with new hope.

How about a Milky Way? Will you eat a Milky Way with me now?

Could I have it for later? I say. Then, when I eat it, I'll think of you.

Ernest laughs as he pulls a frozen Milky Way from the freezer, the sensual calendar girl staring at us from the wall, forever ready with America's best spark plug. I put the cold candy bar into my pocket.

Thank you for showing me your home.

I hope you'll come back someday, he says, leaning on his canes. Maybe next time you can stay for a while and have an Eskimo Pie.

Ernest is so warm, gentle, and simple that I almost feel like giving him a hug as I leave. He certainly has given me one whether he knows it or not.

Larry and I get back into his truck. He eats an Eskimo Pie with passion, the chocolate dripping down his chubby fingers. He insists on driving over to show me where he lives. Larry stops the truck in front of an old plain country house. I see the mailbox where Ernest's grocery list arrives each week.

What a wonderful place to live, I say, eyeing the old house as it sits overlooking the Kansas prairie.

It's where I grew up. I guess I'll die here, too.

You seem happy about that.

Larry, licking his chocolate from his fingers, nods. He drives me back to the wagon train as night falls. As I start to leave his truck we shake hands. He gives me one final grin and heads back to his home.

I crawl into Charlie's wagon and get into my sleeping bag. The wagon's cold and dark, but I feel warm inside. I like the wind, rocking the wagon and flapping the canvas covering. The stars shine and everyone else is in the campers for the night except for David. I'm almost asleep when I hear gentle harmonica music coming from his wagon. The tune is a bit sad, but not without hope. It puts me to sleep as I envision the Rabbit Man, happy down in his hole.

CHAPTER
ELEVEN

 I'm the first one up at the wagon train the next morning. I crawl from Charlie's wagon just as the sun is rising and a mourning dove coos, its song gentle and soothing.

I stroll into town and have coffee and breakfast at a café. The waitress looks at me with eyes warm and inviting and I find myself wishing that I could hold her. For all the people I'm around on the wagon train, I'm starting to feel an increased loneliness. As I sip coffee and finish breakfast I write in my journal, pouring my thoughts and feelings onto the paper as if it were a friend—forever listening without judgment or defense.

I return to the wagon train to find everyone hurrying about as they feed, water, hitch, and saddle the animals. Charlie is tying a red ribbon around Jack's tail.

Open a beauty shop, Charlie? I tease.

Lily, holding the reins as she sits in the wagon, offers a smile. Charlie almost does the same, but spits tobacco juice to the ground.

Mule kicked me, says Charlie. This ribbon's to warn people that he's a kicking mule.

Are you okay?

It left a big blue mark on my thigh, moans Charlie.

He wouldn't kick you, says Lily, if you didn't jerk on him from dawn till night. That hurts his mouth.

If he kicks me again, snaps Charlie, I'll see how he likes a two-by-four across his back.

That's not right, Charlie, says Lily, and you know it.

I'll decide what's right, Charlie almost yells.

Lily lowers her head as she shakes it and Charlie continues to fasten the red ribbon around Jack's tail. Their fussing seems to border on emotional violence and I don't find it any more inspirational than I do seeing Jack get jerked on with the reins. I don't want to ride with them today.

I wander over to David, who brushes his mules, hitched to his little green wagon. The tiny American flags stick from the harnesses.

How's the limp today, David?

Better, but my neck and back are sore.

That was a bad fall you took.

Yes, says David, but I'm so glad none of those kids was hurt. I had trouble sleeping last night for thinking about what happened. I think somebody threw a rock or something. I've put kids on my mules' backs for years. They never did that before.

Everybody was lucky, I add. You offered for me to ride with you sometime. Could I do that today?

Yes, says David. I'd like that. I'll show you how to drive my team.

The wagons are soon lined up and Ted, the trail boss, lifts his hat from his head and swings it.

Wagons hoooo, he shouts, lowering the hat to his head and kicking his spurs into the great sides of his horse.

Ted and his horse lead the wagon train from the meadow and onto a dirt road. The blonde on the palomino is at his side. They seem like close friends. I've made eye contact with her a few times and she intrigues me. Sometimes I catch her looking my way. Then, when she spots me looking back, she turns her head. Ted saw this one time and I became uncomfortable with what I saw in his eyes. It reminded me of myself when I was a teenager and wanted people to think I was mean and tough. I hope I only imagined that is what I saw in his eyes. It saddens me to see that in anyone, and especially grown men who are older than myself.

When I look into David's eyes I see compassion and wisdom, qualities I admire. As we roll down the dirt road across the Kansas prairie he hands me the leather reins to his mules, Gold and Silver.

There's not a whole lot to driving them, says David. Pull to the left to go that way and the same for the right. Pull straight back and say whoa for them to stop. If they slow down too much just let the reins fall on their backs. Sometimes Silver will get lazy. If he does, just tap him a little on the back end with the whip. He'll listen. It's mostly just getting the feel for it.

The leather reins in my hand gives me a new joy. I savor the mules' power and how easily they heed my pull to the left or right.

As we head northwest, across Kansas toward Nebraska, most of the original Oregon and Pony Express Trail has been closed because farms on the Trail have fences. Ted drove the Trail some weeks ago, however, to map out our route as close to the actual Trail as possible. From time to time we stop to behold a rock monument sticking up from the ground three or four feet. They've been posted here to honor the Pony riders who risked their lives and galloped at breakneck speeds to get the mail through, and the pioneers who struggled westward in covered wagons in hopes of a brighter future. Each time we spot one of these sites I can almost imagine myself back in those days, and it gives me a jolt of excitement. I wonder if the other riders on the wagon train are feeling this, too. I look at David, who seems lost in thought.

I heard you playing your harmonica last night, I say, pulling Silver a little to the left for him to stay in line with Peter's wagon in front.

You did?

You sounded good.

My father taught me how to play, says David. He learned when he was just a boy living in Holland. He could play the bones, too. It used to send chills down my back to hear what he played. He used bones from a bull we had raised. My brothers and I used to take turns running across the field to see if he'd chase us. I tripped one day and he came charging. I barely made it up an apple tree before he got me. My brothers thought it was funny. They refused to get his attention so I could get down. I stayed in that tree till almost dark. I guess it seems small now, but I never trusted my brothers the same again after that. And every time my father played the bones I saw myself up in that apple tree waiting on the sun to go down. But I loved to play the harmonica for my first wife. We met at a square dance. We went for a walk down by this pond. We were young, and well, you know how that is. I wasn't a big talker, but I felt confident when I blew the harmonica. After we were married, she said it was my playing that first night down by the pond that helped win her heart. We were married twenty years before she died. Then I married my second wife. She lived on the next farm and she and my first wife were best friends. I'd be lost without her now. When I phoned her yesterday after I fell, I got a lot of my strength back just hearing her voice.

She sounds like a rare person.

She is, says David. You're a pleasant person to be around.

I like getting to know you, too. I've had trouble communicating with some of the others in this group.

They don't talk to me much either, David admits.

As the day goes on and I drive David's team down the Trail I'm feeling more and more at ease. It's almost noon when we're coming down a dirt road at the bottom of a high hill covered with tall green grass waving in the constant wind. Then, as if the earth itself opened up, a herd of fifteen or twenty buffalo comes charging over the hill. Their massive bodies and horns are magnificent in the sunlight. The horses and mules jerk their ears skyward as the buffaloes' hooves create thunder on the hillside. We stop the wagons to gawk and there's wonder in our faces at such a sight.

I always wanted a rug made from a buffalo, says David, to lay before my fireplace. It's a shame we almost killed all of them.

I hear the herds are coming back.

Yes, says David, in time, maybe.

The wagon train rolls on again and the buffalo disappear as we take the next bend. When we come to a farmhouse with a windmill twirling, we stop to water the animals and ourselves. I hear Josh starting to sing a playful song as we gather around the old well pump beneath a giant oak. The red garter and turkey feather still decorate his cowboy hat as he entertains.

I don't know, he sings, but I've been told that she was sweet as a peach on a summer day. Warm and wet and soft in the center. My cousin said I'd find one just as good under the tree down in the ditch. But all I found was an old black bitch.

Ted and Peter, standing by the pump, begin to laugh along with Josh. I eye David, who doesn't crack a smile, but simply wipes sweat from his forehead. Maybe my sense of humor needs sharpening, but I don't find it very funny either.

You only know nigger songs? says Ted.

No, sir, boss, grins Josh, I knows colored songs, too. But I have more fun with my nigger songs.

I want to know where that ditch is with that old black bitch, laughs Peter. I's be liking sweet peaches.

Ted, Josh, and Peter now look my way as if my name has just been called at an important meeting. It's my turn to be present and accounted for. I fill my canteen from the pump.

Good water, I say.

I screw the top on my canteen and head back to the wagon with David. I take the reins and the wagon train soon moves on down the dirt road, but I keep thinking about what happened back at the pump. Growing up in Alabama, I heard "nigger" talk for as long as I can remember. I didn't know any blacks and I never wondered much if what people said about them was true. Then, at the age of seventeen when I thumbed to New York to visit my sister, I got a ride with a black man and his wife. They fed me and treated me like I was a friend or son and I began to wonder just how many things I had heard about different kinds of people were untrue. I felt a new kind of strength—different from lifting weights, fighting, or arm wrestling—as my mind opened to consider such questions.

I'm made uneasy by the racial slurs back at the pump because they strip away the dignity of all races. And that kind of talk begins to make me feel an outsider. It makes me want to be cautious about revealing what I think and feel to these people on the wagon train. As if hiding what I believe will make my journey with them easier, make them think I'm a good ol' boy, just like them. Some of my Cherokee ancestors in 1838 hid their identities to avoid being put in stockades and marched to Oklahoma on the Trail of Tears. Because they concealed the truth of who they really were, they got to stay in the mountains where I was born and raised, but I wonder what those lies did to their minds and hearts.

Still, I refuse to let those words at the pump get me down. My faith in the goodness of people is too strong to fall prey to such a frail trap.

That evening we arrive in Seneca, Kansas, near the Nebraska border and camp in a field near another 4-H Club barn. The locals are to serve us a free dinner, and a country and western band will play beneath the stars.

You did good with my mules today, David tells me.

I had a good teacher.

I saw a pay phone back a couple of blocks, says David. Think I'll call my wife and make sure she's feeling okay. Want to walk that way?

Yeah, I've got a call to make myself.

We walk into Seneca past an old church with a towering steeple. Its lawn has just been mowed and the moist grass fills the tiny town's air with the smell of spring. We arrive at a pay phone outside a café, where David phones his wife. When he hangs up, he's wearing a big smile.

She okay? I ask.

David nods. She's started making a new quilt. She's designing it with a wagon on the Oregon Trail. I'll wait on the church steps while you make your call.

No, I say. Go on back. After my call, I'm going down to that plowed creek over there and look for arrowheads.

He nods and leaves for the wagon train. I dial the number of my sister Sandra in Phoenix. She answers.

Having fun? she asks, and I think how good it is to hear her voice.

I'm becoming friends with an old man, I tell her. I drove his team today. Some of the others on the wagon train aren't exactly what you'd call mind-expanding experiences. I'll get to know them in time, though. I called to see if Ken had heard the results of his tests.

The pause that follows is a bit spooky. Ken has been her husband and my friend for over thirty years. He and Sandra have given me four nieces and nephews, and since I don't have children, that makes them all extra special. He went to the doctor last week after struggling with chest pains for a couple of weeks.

He has lung cancer, says Sandra, her voice cracking.

I care greatly for Ken, but I love my sister like no other

person on earth. The tone of her voice haunts me, for in it I can hear that it is only a matter of time till Ken dies.

Maybe I can come down and see Ken, I say, hoping that he'll still be alive by the time I reach the end of the Trail.

That would be wonderful, says Sandra. Ken will be touched that you've called.

When I hang up the receiver, I walk down to the plowed field on a creek to look for arrowheads. I cannot shake the sad news. I walk out into a meadow, far away from any houses, and start to chant in the manner of my ancestors, hoping to purge myself of sorrow and find new strength. But my true feelings refuse to rise and what comes from my mouth is as feeble as the beat of a heart. Something is blocked deep down inside and this scares me.

I head back into town across the plowed field. Something white and about the size of my index finger lies in the dark soil. I pick it up to discover that it's a quartz crystal. My Cherokee ancestors believed that such a stone had healing powers. I rub the earth from it and spot tiny swirling dots of red inside it. I hold it up for a closer look and the red looks like a ruby-throated hummingbird in flight, speeding through falling snow. I slip the small treasure into my pocket.

It's almost dark when I get back to the wagon train. Dinner is being served outside where the band plays and locals square dance to celebrate the wagon train rolling down the Oregon Trail.

I take my pack from Charlie's wagon and walk to a lonely elm at the edge of a field. I unroll my sleeping bag and crawl inside as the wind blows and the limbs sway.

As I look up at the stars, I feel overwhelmed by loneliness, so far from my sister, unable to help her husband. And while I lie on the hard ground thinking how small and insignificant I am, one man out here on the prairie, I can almost hear the hoofbeats of a lone Pony rider as he passes by the herd of buffalo, the water pump, the field where the crystal hummingbird lay. He probably never dreamed he would lead me here.

CHAPTER
TWELVE

As the wagon train rolls toward Nebraska I alternate running and walking with riding with David in his wagon. He is still the only one I feel close to in this group so far, and if that doesn't change soon I may head out on my own. I don't like feeling like an outsider. I want to belong and be part of people's lives. I want to have some meaning.

As we exit Marysville, Kansas, and move down a paved county road over the rolling hills I hop into the wagon with David. I open my pack and pull out the diary of Sir Richard to see what he found on this leg of the journey in 1860:

> Passing by Marysville, in old maps Palmetto City, a county town which thrives by selling whisky to ruffians of all descriptions, we forded before sunset the "Big Blue," a well-known tributary of the Kansas River. . . . The soil is sandy and solid, but the banks are too precipitous to be pleasant when a very drunk driver hangs on by the lines of four very weary mules. . . . At 6 P.M. we changed our fagged animals for fresh. . . . At Cotton-wood Station we took "on board" two way-passengers, "lady" and "gentleman," who were drafted into the wagon containing the Judiciary. A weary drive over a rough and dusty road, through chill night air and clouds of musquetoes, which we

were warned would accompany us to the Pacific slope
of the Rocky Mountains. . . .

That evening the wagon train approaches the Cottonwood
Station that Sir Richard wrote of in his diary. I drive the team
as David is asleep in his little bed in the back of the old green
wagon. He had trouble sleeping last night and is tired today.
His aged body gently rocks as the wagon rattles down a dirt
road toward Cottonwood Station, also called Hollenberg Station, which serviced both the Pony Express and the stage
lines with horses, food, water, and lodging.

The old wooden station sits atop a small hill overlooking
Cottonwood Creek. The station is made of rough-sawed lumber with windows and three doors. As the wagon train gets
closer to the old building I see two chimneys sticking from
the roof. Some say that it's the only truly original Pony Express station left standing today. It's named after its founder,
G. H. Hollenberg, who came from Germany. He tried his luck
at striking it rich in the gold fields of California, but gave up
and came here to build a ranch. He was also the local post-
master.

Are we there? says David, lifting his head from a pillow in
the little wagon's bed.

Almost.

My mules give you any trouble? he asks.

No. Did you have a good nap?

Yes, but I dreamed of the time my father made me stay
with my brother after he was married. I had to cut his wheat
for free. I did more work than he did and that wasn't right. A
man needs to be fair.

Ted leads the wagon train onto the grassy field behind the
old building. The tiny town of Hanover, Kansas, is only two
miles away and dozens of locals—dressed in clothes like
those worn in the 1860s—have gathered to celebrate the ar-
rival of the wagon train. It now numbers only three wagons

and eight riders on horses because some have already left and gone back to their homes. Sally, the crabby drill sergeant who organized the wagon train, tells us every day that more wagons will join us. But they don't appear and with each passing day her puffy white face hardens a little more. Her wagon train dream appears to dangle by a single thread. She and Kathy, Peter's wife with the red fingernails and *Cosmopolitan,* rarely ride in the wagons now. They go on ahead in a camper and await us each evening at the next campsite while they watch TV and try to sell Oregon Trail T-shirts. I'm not sure how much longer their hearts can endure the excitement.

Want me to water the mules, David? I say.

Do you mind? he asks, crawling from his wrinkled bed. I'll feed them.

I water Gold and Silver and walk over to the old station. The front door is open and dust floats in the sunlight as I enter. I like the smell of the old lumber. A narrow staircase, looking more like a ladder than anything, leads to an attic. I climb it and find exposed wooden beams about as big around as my arms. Plaster is falling to the floor and a piece of wood, almost as big as the crystal quartz I found yesterday, lies under a window. I pick it up to wonder at, holding a piece of the past in my hand. This is where the Pony rider slept after his long, hard ride. If I close my eyes, I can almost hear the hooves of the horse as he races toward this old building. I can also hear the rider as he collapses here at my feet onto a bed after riding nonstop for a hundred miles. This was a "home station," that blessed place where the rider could turn his *mochila* over to the next rider. He would sleep and then leap atop a fresh horse the next day or night to carry the mail back to his starting point from the day before.

The stagecoach lines had stations about every thirty miles along the Trail. But since the Pony Express needed a station every fifteen miles for the rider to change horses, more stations were built. Some were little more than square log or rock buildings, containing a table, chair, bed, and cookstove. A corral was built next to the building and usually as close to a creek or river as possible to save on the labor of hauling water. In the desert areas water sometimes had to be hauled to the stations by wagon. One hundred forty stations stretched between St. Jo and Sacramento to service the Pony Express.

While the Pony riders certainly deserve the most glory for the daring risks and constant challenges they faced to get the mail through, they could not have done it without those who tended the lonely stations, cared for the horses, and fed the riders. I wonder if those humble stationkeepers had any idea of their worth in helping build the American dream to connect East and West. Sometimes people don't realize how important they are because their jobs on the surface seem so small.

Maybe I should place this little piece of wood back on the attic floor of the "home station" where I found it, but I don't. I want to take it back home to my cabin on the hill to remember this journey for as long as I live. I slide the piece of wood into my pocket and ease back down the steep, ladderlike stairs to go outside.

The horses and mules have been unhitched and unsaddled and the locals—dressed in Old West attire—wander about the wagons as if to breathe in the spirit of the journey. Sally and Kathy sit at a card table with the T-shirts and badges for sale. So far there's no line.

I take my pack from David's wagon and place it in the back of Charlie's wagon. I dig into that pack to pull out my journal, when two boys walk my way. Their faces are as open and warm as the face of the Rabbit Man.

This your wagon, mister? asks the older boy, who looks to be about six years old.

No, I say. I just ride in it sometimes. This is where I sleep, if I don't put my sleeping bag under a tree.

Are you a cowboy? he asks as the other boy looks on with timid eyes.

No, I'm part Cherokee. I loved to play cowboys when I was your age, though.

I like Indians. We study them in school. This is my brother. Is that your backpack?

Yes, I say, lifting it for them to see. It's my home for a few months. I have a tent inside.

Me and my brother have a tent. Sometimes we sleep in it in the backyard. I wish I could do what you're doing. I don't like school.

I didn't like school my first year either, I say, feeling a kindred spirit with this kid. I wanted to be outside.

Yeah, the boy nods.

Ted hurries from around the side of the wagon as if an emergency were at hand. He always seems to have more energy than he knows what to do with. He stares down at the two boys.

How you girls doing today? his voice thunders.

The older boy stares at him and the younger one steps closer to his brother. Both faces look just a bit anxious. I feel protective of them and ease my boot atop the tongue of the wagon to come between them and Ted.

You girls ain't talking today? says Ted, his voice even louder than before.

I become a bit disgusted with Ted as I catch the worried looks on the boys' faces. Then it sinks in with sadness that he doesn't realize that he is scaring them. I want to break the tension.

This is our trail boss, I say. He rides a horse out front to lead the wagon train.

Ted stands towering over them and the boys look up at the

giant. Ted finally turns and walks away. The older boy watches him till he disappears around the wagon.

He has a little trouble knowing what to say, I explain. He thought he was being funny.

My uncle talks like him, says the boy. He doesn't understand that kids have minds.

A man in his thirties wearing blue pants with grease on them comes our way. On his shirt is written BILL'S SERVICE STATION.

These boys bothering you? smiles the man.

Not at all, I assure him.

The boys step closer to him and he rests his hands on their heads. Their faces glow.

No, says the father, they're pretty good boys. Your mother has dinner ready. We better go.

Bye, mister, says the older boy, his eyes a bit sad. I wish we could stay longer.

Yeah, I say, me, too.

I envy the warmth between the father and his sons. I watch them get into their car and drive away and I feel very alone. No, more than that. I feel a bit freakish on this wagon train. I'm more than a bit concerned that I don't simply slip the pack on my back and take off on my own down the Trail.

CHAPTER
THIRTEEN

I've been with the wagon train for almost two weeks when we reach Oak, Nebraska—population seventy-five or a hundred, depending on whose wild story you believe. We park the wagons in the tiny town square, where six picnic tables sit beneath trees. Many locals wander over to get a look at the horses, mules, and wagons. History is made when one of them actually buys an Oregon Trail T-shirt from Sally. I was wrong. She can smile.

From Oak the Trail meanders across the southern part of Nebraska to Wyoming except for a dip down into the extreme northeastern part of Colorado, into the town of Julesburg. On a map that dip looks a lot like a V. I'm studying that map in Oak as I sit in the back of Charlie's wagon, when a man wearing a cap with JOHN DEERE written on it appears.

The man with the beard tells me you're interested in the Pony Express, the stranger says.

That must've been Charlie you talked to, I nod.

Well, if you go down that road over there for a couple of miles you'll find a marker for the old Pony Express station called the Little Blue. If you go look at it, you might want to hunt the field next to it. Sometimes you can find pieces of china and window glass. They're from a Mormon wagon train that was destroyed by the Indians. I think it was headed to Salt Lake City.

Thanks for the tip, I tell him.

Yep, says the man, wandering away.

I head down the dirt road into the prairie. Eight or ten crows fly overhead and disappear into a grove of towering cottonwoods along a creek. A rabbit hops from the weeds into the road and sits for a moment before it runs back to where it came. I've walked almost two miles when I find a dead black snake in the road. The sun has started to dry it out. I ease my boot against it. It is as stiff as a piece of wood. Still, its black skin shines with some rare beauty.

I take only a few more steps when I spot the marker for the Little Blue Station. It's only a concrete slab sticking from the weeds. There's no trace of even the building's old foundation.

The field next to it, however, has been plowed and I walk to it with hopes of finding pieces of the Mormon wagon train that was destroyed by the Indians. The soil is a rich brown and moist. I like how my boots leave tracks in it. They remind me, however, how fleeting my own history is on the earth. The wind and rain will soon take them away to wherever such things go.

I become excited when I spot a piece of china in a clod of earth. The piece is the size of a quarter. I don't pull it from the dirt just yet, though. I want to savor the find. It has been here for over 130 years and I hesitate now to separate it from the earth. When I do pull the piece of china free, I feel a bit sad, for I think of the Mormons and wonder if some of them were killed by the Indians here in this very spot where I stand.

I search the plowed field for almost an hour and find seven pieces of china and window glass. Excited by these little historic treasures, I walk back to Oak with a new eagerness in my step.

I find the wagon train group seated at the picnic tables.

The locals have furnished free food and everybody eats as if in celebration. I sit by Peter and his wife, Kathy.

How's the food? I ask.

Peter continues to chew. I'm convinced that the kid who once rode that pony to the middle of the pond is still inside Peter somewhere, but it's pretty hard to find. I certainly don't want him to act like a kid. I'd just like to see him drop his guard and stop acting so tough.

The food's good, says Kathy. Especially the baked beans.

Look what I found. I pull the pieces of china from my pocket. They're from a wagon train that was attacked by Indians. One of the locals told me where to find them in a plowed field.

As they eat, their eyes glance at what I consider curious little treasures. But not a single word—no, not even a grunt—comes from Peter or Kathy. This lack of response makes me feel unwelcome.

Guess I'll try some of that food, I say, easing the broken china back into my pocket, where I now wish I had kept it to begin with.

I get a plate of food—the folks in Oak are mighty fine cooks—and look for David. He's not seated at the picnic tables and I wander over to his wagon. I find him in bed.

You okay, David?

No, he says. Not really. I got the flu or something.

Could I bring you something to eat?

Thanks, he says. But I'm not hungry. I called my wife. She thinks it's just a twenty-four-hour virus. She always tries to make me believe the best. She has half the Oregon Trail quilt done now. Her sister came up from Kansas City and helped her with it. Think you can ride with Charlie and Lily tomorrow? I better not hitch my team. Guess I'll just load the wagon and mules onto my trailer and move ahead to the next campsite. I had hoped to travel for four or five more days, but if

I'm not better in a couple of days, I'll head home. I miss my bed. My wife.

I'm sure I can ride with Charlie, I say. But I think I'll leave the wagon train tomorrow. I'm feeling pretty closed in.

Why don't you ask Ted about riding his spare horse? David suggests. You said you wanted to do some riding.

Yeah, but . . .

Sleep on it, says David.

You better rest. Anything I can get for you?

No, says David. But you want a drink of whiskey with me? I'm about to have one.

I nod and David pulls a bottle of Jack Daniel's from under his bed. He takes a drink right from the bottle. He rubs the mouth of the bottle with the blanket on his bed and gives me the bottle. Even if I didn't drink whiskey, I'd have a snort with this old man. I hope I have his sense of peace and love of life when I get to be his age.

Here's to your wife, I say, and raise the bottle to my lips.

David places the bottle back under his bed and lays his head back on his pillow. He looks so tired that I hope he does have only a twenty-four-hour flu. He closes his eyes and I study his wrinkled face for a moment. I can almost see his wife with a needle and thread working on his quilt till he gets home.

The next morning I crawl from Charlie's wagon and stuff my sleeping bag into my pack. I'm surprised to see Ted hurrying my way. His broad shoulders stick out.

You want to ride one of my horses today? he says.

I find this offer too much of a coincidence after just speaking with David about it last night. I figure he suggested to Ted that I ride his spare horse.

Yeah, I say. I guess. Which one of your horses?

Comanche. He's still learning, but he handles pretty well. Have you done much riding?

Some. Well, no, not a lot. I was kicked in the head by a horse when I was five. I've always been cautious around horses since then.

He's saddled already, Ted tells me. Why don't you ride him some before we leave and see how it goes.

Even if David did suggest to Ted that I ride his horse, he seems to have a warmer tone than I usually hear when we talk. Things may be looking up. Why, I just might go hog-wild and buy a T-shirt from Sally to go with my wagon train badge, forever on my hat.

He neck-reins, says Ted, as I climb atop Comanche. You know what that is?

Yeah, that's what my sister's horse did.

Well, says Ted, try him out. If he won't go, take your fist and knock the shit out of him.

I ride Comanche around the town square and he handles with ease. I must confess that my excitement about this trek is increasing by the minute now. It's not simply that it feels good to be on a horse, but I now have new hope of truly getting to know Ted. Maybe Josh and Peter will open up more as well. Charlie? Well, I've accepted that Charlie has little time for anything or anybody except his mules, his wife, and his rock collecting. Oh, yes, and his tobacco chewing and spitting.

Ted leads the wagon train out of Oak and we soon ride down the dirt road I walked yesterday. The sun-dried black snake appears and so do eight or nine crows atop a cotton-wood down by the creek. I see my footprints in the plowed field where I found the broken pieces of china and window glass. I feel like I've taken a giant step since those tracks were made.

In only a few miles I begin to trust, but not take for granted, that Comanche will obey the slightest weight of the leather reins against his neck. I do begin, however, to feel a bit confined by the boundary of the wagon train. I'd like to take off across the meadow to my left. I ease my heels into the horse's sides and he begins to gallop down the road until I stop him next to Josh riding his horse.

Well, says Josh, you're one of us now. Did you hear the news about Wyoming? That state still hasn't okayed the wagon train getting to cross. It claims that the wagons need special insurance. I don't care if we go around that whole state myself. I read about three men there who hold people down while they punch out their eyeballs with their thumbs.

I'm not sure I believe that, I say. I got a ride from the Kansas City airport to St. Jo with a guy who said he had a wonderful time in Wyoming.

For the second or third time today the blonde who rides the palomino beside Ted each day—her name is Anne—turns to look my way. This time I wave at her and she doubles back on her horse to ride beside me. Josh takes her place on his horse next to Ted. Ted looks back at Anne and me as if to say something, but changes his mind.

Well, grins Anne, do you feel like a cowboy now that you got a horse?

I'm not sure about that. But it's a nice change from walking and riding in the wagons. Have you always been a horse person?

Oh, yes, ever since I was a little girl. One day the teacher asked us to draw a cow and I drew a horse. I had plastic and wooden models of horses scattered all over my bedroom. Sometimes when I awoke in the night, I thought they were alive.

Maybe they were inside your imagination.

Yeah. She smiles as if having an imagination that was still very much alive.

Ted turns to eye us. He isn't smiling.

You and Ted must be good friends? I ask.

We are. But that's all we are. He can't tell me who to talk to. Not anymore.

I don't understand.

We used to be married, she explains, sadness in her voice.

I was married once, I say. A divorce is a painful thing. At least it was for me. But I didn't feel the whole hurt till months later. Guess I tried to deny it. That was over twenty years ago.

The human heart, she mumbles. It never lets us forget.

Yeah, I grin, lucky me, huh?

No, she says, that's interesting. A lot of men aren't aware of their emotions. Well, I shouldn't say that. I only know that a lot of the ones I've met haven't been. Or if they were they sure kept it a secret from me.

Lily told me that you're a telephone operator in Memphis.

Yeah, Anne sighs. For fifteen years now. It pays the bills. I'd rather live on a farm, but it's a hard way to survive.

How'd you meet Ted?

On a CB, she says. I have a set at home and talk to people sometimes. Well, I used to. Ted and I got to talking one day and we discovered we both loved horses. I agreed to meet him for lunch. I didn't know he was driving a truck for a living. Anyway, when I finally saw him on a horse I fell for him.

You can't ride a horse everywhere you go, though, can you? I tease.

No, she grins. You sure can't.

Ted looks back over his shoulder at us and pulls his horse to the side while Josh leads the wagon train forward. When Anne and I catch up with Ted, he reins his horse in next to ours. He gives Anne a look of disapproval, then he eyes me.

How's my little nigger making out on my horse? he smiles.

His smile does not match his hardened eyes and I'm put out by his remark. If he's trying to be funny, he surely recalls that I didn't laugh back at the water pump when the racial slurs were celebrated. If he's simply trying to belittle me in front of Anne, she must think he's making a fool of himself. A part of me wants to strike out and level him to the ground, but that would only lower me as well. I try to find strength and dignity.

I like your horse, I say. I appreciate you letting me ride him.

Yeah, says Ted, his face becoming perplexed. He's a good horse.

Ted kicks his silver spurs into the horse he's on and gallops on ahead of the wagon train—there're only two wagons now —to join Josh, the brass bell on his horse jingling. Anne and I study each other for a moment as if we've just seen a most peculiar shadow on the ground and we wonder what cast it. Then she kicks her horse in the sides and gallops to the head of the wagon train to ride with Ted.

CHAPTER
FOURTEEN

The rest of the day I ride Comanche at the end of the wagon train by myself. When we arrive on the outskirts of Deweese, we camp behind a farmhouse overlooking a great meadow with a river meandering through it. Towering cottonwoods line the banks. High overhead circles a lone hawk.

I'm happy to see David in a chair in the backyard of the farmhouse. His mules, Gold and Silver, graze nearby.

Feeling better, David?

Some. How'd it go on the horse?

It added a little excitement.

The people who live at this house, says David, are cooking chicken for us tonight.

That sounds great. I think I'll walk into town and see what it's like before we eat.

Don't blink, smiles David, you'll miss it.

Town is about a half mile away and I walk across railroad tracks to get there. There's only one building open and it's a café and bar. I go inside and order a whiskey, then another one a couple of minutes later. It feels good to relax. The last few days my body has been stressed. My neck is stiff. My shoulders and lower back ache.

Want another one? offers the bartender.

Sure. I pay for the third whiskey.

I take a sip and go to the rest room. I splash my face with

water and the coolness is refreshing after riding in the sun all day. I'm thinking about what happened with Ted today—his "nigger" remark—when I look into the mirror to see if I've washed away the day's dust and dirt. I'm startled by what I see. There's no radiance in my face. No spontaneity. No emotion in the eyes. My God, it makes me think of when I was a teenager and I stood before a mirror to practice not showing any emotion because I thought it would make me appear strong to others. Is this what I've been doing the past few days without realizing it? Have I gotten so bottled up and discreet that I'm vanishing? And now, here in the bar, I'm drinking to numb the alienation I'm feeling? I leave the bar without finishing the third whiskey.

I arrive at the back of the farmhouse to find everyone seated near a picnic table that is set with plates, forks, and knives. I'm hungry and take a chair between David and Anne, who offers a subtle but tender smile.

This is some beautiful country, says Peter.

Sure is, agrees Josh, the turkey feather and red lacy garter still adorning his cowboy hat.

I went through a stretch today that made me think we were in a John Wayne movie, Peter adds.

Now he was a *real* man, Ted's voice thunders.

I understand that in his last years he showed incredible strength, I say. He'd had his stomach removed and had to be very gentle with himself. A real switch from his fantasy Westerns.

What'd you mean? asks Josh.

Well, I say, in real life you don't always come out on top. You can't settle everything with your fists. None of us will ever know what a real inner fight John Wayne had to survive. Movies don't show it, but it's stuff going on inside that really determines who you are as a man. The macho games men play only go so far before they become thin and self-defeating.

The eyes of the women become curious, as if wanting to hear more. But the look on the faces of Ted, Josh, and Peter make me think I've said too much already. I feel out on a limb.

I wish more men thought about these things, says Anne, turning to Ted. It might make them be more open.

Yes, Lily nods, as if to herself.

The way Ted continues to eye me makes me uncomfortable. I'm relieved when the woman who lives in the farmhouse comes out her back door with a big plate of chicken.

It ain't fancy, she calls, but it's hot and there's more on the stove. Dig in.

The sun sets as we help ourselves to the chicken. In the great distance a coyote begins to howl.

I awake in the middle of the night from a bad dream. The wagon is shaking so much that I fear it will overturn at any second. The wind howls with such force that I'm convinced a tornado is approaching. The others are in their campers on the hill next to the farmhouse. I'm down in the meadow in Charlie's wagon near the river. Even David is in his camper tonight.

The towering cottonwoods bend and shake in a tremendous frenzy as the howling wind grows stronger. I slip into my jeans and hurry from the wagon to scout the boiling clouds for the twister.

A limb crashes from the tree and lands only a few yards away. My hair blows wild as twigs snap and one flies into my chest. Another hits my face. I want to run to safety, but I'm not sure where. The howling gets louder and louder as I continue to seek the tornado in the clouds.

But then the wind begins to calm. Most of the limbs of the cottonwoods slowly find themselves still in one piece. A light comes on inside David's camper at the top of the hill and I wander that way to where the horses and mules are tied. Jack looks massive in the night and I wonder how his mouth is holding up from Charlie's continued jerking on the reins. When Comanche spots me, he whinnies. I stop to look at him, remembering that he was in my dream.

David sticks his head from his camper.

That was some wind, he says.

Yes, I thought we were goners.

I walk back down the hill to the wagon and crawl into my sleeping bag.

The next morning I rise later than usual. I get dressed and head up the hill. I spot Ted saddling Comanche.

What time are we leaving today? I ask.

Why? Ted's tone seems agitated.

We are some thirty feet apart and he bolts my way with his massive shoulders held back. His huge hands are cupped into half fists. I'm perplexed and a little startled. Why is he angry? He stops only a foot before me and stares as if *I* have offended him somehow. It concerns me that I consider punching him in the gut to lay him out, but his tone is so hostile that I feel put on the defensive. I try to maintain control and tell myself that he may not even be aware of his tone or body language. He's simply upset about something that has nothing to do with me. I lower my eyes to avert this puzzling confrontation.

I was going into town for some coffee, I explain. I just wondered if I had time.

Oh, he says, backing off a bit. Well, why don't you ride Comanche?

Okay . . .

Shit, says Ted, I'll have to shorten the stirrups for you some.

No, I'll be okay without them.

I climb into the saddle. I now realize that it's foolish not to adjust the stirrups so I can reach them, but I don't.

He hasn't been away from the herd before, says Ted. Make him go.

This strikes me as a bit odd that I'll be the first person to try to take the horse from the herd. I just hope he doesn't stop and give me the opportunity to make a fool of myself before the others.

Giddup, I say, and Comanche starts from the farmhouse lawn. His ears go skyward and his massive body is tense, I can feel it between my legs. As we move down the road his head is almost quivering as he looks left and right and left and right as if to make certain that he is safe and no tractor tires or mailboxes are becoming monsters to spook him. I'm concerned when I see two children—a boy and girl of about six and seven—standing by the side of the road with books in their hands, awaiting a school bus. I haven't forgotten the horrible stampede at the Indian mission, where kids were almost killed.

That's a big horse, shouts the boy, stepping forward.

Yes, I say, don't come to him. He's not used to being away from the other horses. He's nervous.

Comanche moves on past the children and I'm relieved when we get into town and I climb down from the saddle. I tie his reins to a tree limb outside the tiny post office and go inside the bar and café from last night for some coffee.

When I step back outside again, Comanche swishes his great tail and whinnies. I go to him and rub his great nose and head before I mount.

We head out of town and his body becomes tense again. He throws his head from left to right as his ears stick skyward. I had hoped that the two children would be gone by now, but they're not. They still stand on the side of the road. Now they're throwing rocks at a mailbox.

Don't do that, I say. You might spook my horse.

They stop throwing rocks, but when Comanche spots the other horses back at the wagons, he jerks the reins and lowers his head—jolted by some inner storm. It is as though some part of that howling wind in the night has hidden in his muscles. With his head still lowered, he shoots forward with such thrust that he throws me backward. Without my boots in stirrups, it's all I can do to stay on. My hat is jerked to the back of my head as I press my knees into his sides for balance. We race out of control down the road as the two children drop their books and run for safety. I'm torn between a bizarre kind of thrill and a very real fear. My heart is pounding and I wonder if I can stay on his back and what he will do when he reaches the wagons. I finally get my balance enough to pull back on the reins, but he continues to race like a wild horse driven by madness. His hooves thunder. I jerk again on the reins and hold them back without showing any mercy on his gums and lips, pinched by the hard steel bit. Finally, he slows and begins to walk again. My heart is still pounding, but I feel some new sense of pride. At least I'm in one piece. Still, I don't deny that the kids or me could've been seriously hurt. While I admire the strength and daring of the teenagers who rode for the Pony Express, I'm certainly no longer a kid myself. I cherish my forty-plus bones.

When Comanche and I arrive at the wagon train, I drop from the saddle. Funny, but I feel a little closer to the horse now and I feel I've redeemed myself after all those years of fear since being kicked in the head by a horse when I was five.

I spot Ted pouring oil into the motor of his truck.

He tried to run away, I say. But I got him back under control.

He simply eyes me and continues to pour the oil. I'm wondering what to say next when Anne appears from her camper.

Out for a morning ride? she asks.

Ted let me ride him into town. It saved me having to walk. He tried to throw me.

She looks at Ted holding the oil can. Then she turns to me in disbelief.

Ted didn't do that to help you. She lowers her voice. He did it to see what would happen.

You saying he wanted me to have trouble?

She opens her mouth to speak but stops short. In the moment that follows it starts to sink in that Ted's motives may not have been pure when he wanted me to take the horse into town. At the same time, I'm remembering the dream I had last night. Maybe it's just a coincidence. Maybe not. But I dreamed that I was riding Comanche when he became a runaway.

Just be careful, Anne says, and turns to saddle her horse.

CHAPTER FIFTEEN

That evening the wagon train arrives at Fairfield and we set up camp in the city park. I find a café to have dinner. The food and service are so good that I decide I'll buy breakfast for everyone on the wagon train in the morning. Yes, that's what I'll do. I'll reach out to them, rather than withdraw. This thing with Ted? Well, that's his problem. I'm surely strong enough to stay above such nonsense.

The next morning I get to the restaurant early to make sure the waitress has tables pulled together for everybody.

Could you go ahead and put some pastry and pots of coffee on the table? I ask. They'll be here soon. I think.

I'll be happy to, says the waitress. You're with that wagon train? That sure sounds like fun. Waiting tables gets pretty old.

Last night when I mentioned my idea to the other folks we agreed to meet at eight o'clock and it's already ten past. No one has arrived and this makes me uneasy. Finally, David appears at the door, smiles, and enters. He sits across from me.

See anybody else? I ask him.

Oh, yes, they're all coming, except for Charlie and Lily. I didn't understand why. Something about him working on his wagon. Lily doesn't do much without him.

Yeah, I nod, trying to hide my disappointment.

The door opens and all the others enter to sit around the table. Only David and Josh remove their cowboy hats. Ted and Peter wears theirs as if to keep away a sun that isn't there.

I'm glad y'all came, I tell them. I just wanted to thank you for the rides and some of the meals you shared with me.

Where should I start taking the orders? the waitress asks.

Maybe start with the women? I suggest.

Hey, says Ted, leaning his cowboy hat over the table. You know how to tell when a queer has a hard-on?

The waitress looks at me and rolls her eyes as the men, except for David, laugh as if their sides might split. This is not the first "queer" or "nigger" or "Jew" joke I've heard on the wagon train, but it bothers me more since I had invited these folks to eat with me. I really believed that I could make something special happen by bringing us together. I was wrong. I'm not as tough and strong as I thought I was inside. Instead of now saying something to change the tone of the table I find myself recalling that a good friend of mine is gay and that he was beaten up two or three times when he was growing up in Oklahoma. One of those beatings knocked out his two front teeth. I find it difficult to separate Ted's joke from that violence against my friend because he wasn't like most of the other boys.

When breakfast is over, everyone thanks me and leaves. I pay the bill and wait a couple of minutes for the waitress to box up some pastry that was left. When she hands me the box we make eye contact, but nothing is said. I think she's kind of figured out that I'm disappointed and leaves me alone with my thoughts.

David won't drive his team today because he still feels ill. He'll be moving ahead in his camper to the next town to wait for the rest of us to arrive late this afternoon. With this in mind, I leave the restaurant and head for the wagon train to ride with Charlie and Lily. I'm over a hundred yards from their wagon when rain and hail begin to pour from the dark, swirling clouds. I start running and hop into the wagon. Water drips down my nose as I hand Lily the box I've been carrying.

It's some pastry that was left over, I say. It's pretty good. It's fresh.

You didn't have to do that. Lily's voice is tender.

No, says Charlie, his eyes warm. You sure didn't.

I appreciate your having let me ride with you some the past two weeks, I explain. I'll be leaving the wagon train at the end of the day. I have something I want to give you before I forget it.

I reach into my pocket, pull out the crystal quartz, and hand it to Charlie. His face softens as he eyes the rock.

I found it back in Seneca, I tell him. You have to look close, but a ruby-throated hummingbird is flying through a snowstorm. At least, that's what it looks like to me. It's for your rock collection.

Charlie studies the crystal and wonder lights his face. A subtle grin even flashes across his mouth, its corners tobacco-stained. He slips the bird crystal into his pocket.

Thank you. I don't have one like it.

I watch the hailstones bounce off the backs of the three mules as Charlie, Lily, and I try to protect ourselves under some cottonwoods. We sit in silence and I get to thinking of the trip that lies before me. It's hard to believe that it's been only two weeks since I left St. Jo. I feel as though more has already happened than I bargained for and not all of it pleasant. I feel discouraged by the elements of violence, disrespect, and bigotry in some of these wagon train folks. A part of me wants to give up and head home. But if I do that I won't be able to look myself in the eye. I must overcome this depression and challenge myself to keep searching for the adventure I hoped for when I packed for this journey. To do that I'll have to find new strength and faith in myself and my fellow man. Frankly, I'm not so sure that I can. But if I don't try with all my heart, I will have failed the spirit of the Pony riders and others who took a leap of faith when they set off to encounter the unknown in the Wild West—and in themselves. More importantly, though, I must not fail the kid inside me who once risked his life to thumb all over America in search of himself, adventure, and knowledge as if it were as natural as breathing.

By late afternoon as we pull into Hastings, Nebraska, the hail has stopped, but now a thunderstorm brews. We find a park at the south end of town and unhitch the animals. I ask Anne to give me a ride into town, some ten miles away, so I can get a motel room, since I won't be staying with the wagon train tonight.

Okay, she says, a little regret in her voice. If that's what you want.

I put my pack in her truck as it begins to pour. We can barely see to drive, though the windshield wipers go as fast as they can.

Would you tell David bye for me? I ask. I looked for him, but he wasn't around. I think he stopped to have some work done on his old truck.

I'll tell him.

He's crazy about his wife. She's making him an Oregon Trail quilt. Showing the Trail in red cloth. Anne?

Yeah?

What's with Ted?

She frowns as her hand wipes the moisture from the inside windshield. She rubs her hand on her jeans.

I don't know, she says. I'm not sure he even knows. Sometimes when we were married, I'd try to hold him. He wouldn't let me. He said it wasn't natural.

She stops the truck at a motel. I start to get out, but turn to

Anne for a last good-bye. We reach over and hold each other for a few seconds. A subtle but inviting moan comes from deep inside her. It isn't easy for me to let go.

Finally, I get out of the truck with my pack and Anne drives away as I stand in the rain.

I pay the motel clerk and go to my room. How odd to be surrounded by four walls after two weeks in a wagon and on the ground in my sleeping bag. The bed—a *real* bed—looks mighty fine, though. Pillows and clean sheets are a luxury.

I savor the shower. I've always found water helps wash away bad feelings as well as dirt, and this time is no exception. It's also reassuring to be inside where it's warm and dry while the storm continues. Thunder booms and blowing rain splashes against the window.

When I start to crawl into bed, I spot the wagon train badge on my hat. I take the badge off and start to throw it into the trash can. Instead, I place it in my pack beside my journal, where I've stored so many thoughts and feelings.

I crawl into bed and turn off the lamp. Lightning flashes yellow and the room flickers. I pull the second pillow into my arms. I'm tired. I've come only about 350 miles so far. Over 1,700 miles await me. But as I tell myself that I am now free of the wagon train and its restrictions, I begin to feel a little hope. I close my eyes and fall asleep as the pouring rain becomes a gentle drizzle.

CHAPTER
SIXTEEN

Along with being in love, one of life's great gifts is to awake rested in good health and have the road ahead of you. This is what I'm thinking as I crawl from the motel bed. When I pull back the curtains, I find that the rain has stopped and the sky is clear.

As I get dressed in the small, quiet, and private room, it begins to sink in deeper that I am now on my own. I will decide what I do and how much time I spend doing it. I am my own trail boss and my own wagonmaster. This new sense of freedom already makes me feel better about the journey, but as I've often found with freedom, a loneliness is sure to follow close behind. I feel him at my heels.

I grab coffee and breakfast at a café across from the motel and hit the Trail. It's a wonderfully warm spring day as I head for Kearney, Nebraska, which is two or three days by foot. I hope to reach the Platte River by dark.

Farms are scattered about the countryside and there is a moist, rich smell of newly plowed fields in the air. The ground will soon come alive with sprouting corn. Windmills tower between houses and barns, blades turning in the breeze, gears squeaking. Cows stare at me as barnyard chickens scratch and peck the ground.

The true Pony Express Trail has fences running across it through this part of Nebraska, and so I walk alongside a county road as near to it as I can get. Farmers in trucks slow

down when they spot me. Some wave. Some grin. A few
stare as if trying to figure out what I'm up to. I wave at all of
them.

In three hours my feet hurt. Yes, I walked and ran part of
the time on the wagon train, but there's a big difference between a mile or two here and there and mile-after-mile-after-
mile now. My pack is getting heavier with each step. Sweat
drips down my face. From time to time, I remove my hat and
the breeze cools my head. If I think too much about having
half of Nebraska and five states left to go to complete this
trek, it becomes overpowering. Thank goodness I learned
from walking the Trail of Tears that a long journey such as
this should only be viewed a day at a time.

I stop by a creek and sit in the shade of a cottonwood. I'm
taking a drink from my canteen when I discover a little black
beetle climbing a fallen leaf. I pick it up and the bug walks to
the edge of the leaf. He stops as if to ponder the distance
between him and the ground. I lower the leaf and he walks
onto the earth and disappears behind a rock the size of my
head, bordered by weeds. Hundreds of ants come and go by
a hole beneath that rock.

I take off my hiking shoes and socks to the glory of blisters.
A flock of crows call out from a treetop less than a quarter of
a mile away; I cherish their squawking songs. I open the
corkscrew on my knife and pop the blisters, sinking my swol-
len feet into the cold creek. I force myself to keep them in the
water for five minutes, though it's mighty chilly. As I sit beside the creek I spot a male pheasant sitting on a fence post,
his red, green, and bluish feathers remarkable in the sunlight.
He isn't the first pheasant that I've seen on the journey so far,
but he is the closest I've been to one and he seems so at
peace that nothing in the whole wide world could bother
him. When I begin to put on my socks, however, the sight of
my feet seems to jolt him. He bursts from the top of the fence
post to flutter across the creek and disappear in a grassy field.

This might be a lesson to heed. If I later come upon a mountain lion or a bear in the Wyoming or Utah mountains, I can simply show my toes to protect myself. I put back on my shoes and move on. My feet still hurt.

I only walk a half mile, however, before my feet are a bit numbed from the pounding. I have a second wind and push on till I come to the same creek again, which meanders before me. A field has been plowed and I go down to it to look for Indian and pioneer artifacts.

A frog leaps from the bank to splash in the water as I wander along the creek. I'm making my way through some pretty thick vegetation when I realize with a start that I'm in the midst of thousands of marijuana plants, standing almost knee-high and wavering in the warm Nebraska wind. Then it dawns on me that this probably isn't a dope patch, but the offspring of plants from the 1800s when hemp was a major crop in the Midwest. It was used for making ropes and canvas for masts of great sailboats as well as for the coverings of the very wagons that followed this Trail. William Waddell himself—one of the three Pony Express founders—owned a hemp warehouse. I wonder if anyone is aware of this field and keep my eyes open for an illicit farmer lurking in the plants. I appear to be alone, though, and follow the creek for as long as I can.

That evening as the sun goes down I spot the Platte River. It's a perfect spot for tonight's campsite. I'm more than ready to stop walking for today, too. I'm exhausted and the pain in my shoulders and back is soothed only when I'm distracted by my burning feet. Somewhere along the way my shoes became cushioned torture chambers.

I'm not only happy to remove the pack from my back and stop walking, but also to drop the plastic bag I've been carrying from my tired hand. It's held a cleaned chicken since I bought it over an hour ago. I found it in a store that also sold pickled eggs from a jar by the cash register. I chose not to excite the clerk by saying anything but I wondered what kind of green bug was floating near the red pepper among the eggs. Needless to say, I left those pickled eggs for customers who might have more exotic tastes than my own.

I build a fire and begin to roast the chicken on the end of a stick. While the chicken cooks, I pitch my faded-green nylon pup tent in the grass under a massive cottonwood. The earth is soft here and the wire stakes ease into the ground without a moment's hesitation, as if I'm a welcome visitor. When I packed for this journey, I discovered that I was missing one of the stakes so I made one from a coat hanger. My mother brought it and a pair of pliers to me in my bedroom. Her constant kindness and consideration are sometimes humbling to the point of painful because they make me recall the times I have not been as thoughtful to her as I could've been. I can't begin to imagine what life was like for many of the orphaned Pony riders without a mother. I wonder if they ever lay awake at night and pondered who their mothers were and tried to imagine their gentle faces. While a boy may have been expected to reach physical manhood by the age of sixteen back in 1860, I doubt that his heart had yet become as callused as his hardworking hands. How comforting it is to me, here on the vast prairie, to envision my mother and know that she is alive and well.

Some juice drips from the cooking chicken into the fire. It hisses as it lands and tiny streams of smoke rise. I smell the meat and my mouth begins to water. Except for eating an apple back at the pickled-egg-bug store, I haven't had anything except water since breakfast. I'm starved.

I burn the roof of my mouth as I try to gobble a piece of the roasted bird, but it's worth the pain. It's dark now and dinner is seasoned with the stars. Between bites—if I don't chew—I can hear the river flowing. I float around the bend, imagining all that lies downriver. I think I see a light in a farmhouse in the distance and wonder if a family there sits around a table for dinner. When I let my imagination drift further, I see a woman sitting alone at the table. I wonder if she's dreaming about leaving the farm to meet a man on the Trail, camping out by an open fire.

There wasn't a single campfire while I was on the wagon train, and this one seems special. The night air is cooling and I add another piece of dead cottonwood atop the blaze. I take the published diary of Sir Richard F. Burton from my pack and begin to read by the firelight. But I'm too tired and who do I think I am anyway, Abraham Lincoln?

I feel at peace with the river and stars, but I can't help but think of my parents back in the Appalachian Mountains of North Alabama. I reach into my pack and remove the leather pouch. I open it and take out the hawk-wing bone-whistle, five inches long. I gently blow into the whistle and it creates the discreet sound of a hawk like the two that often circle high over my cabin. The faint song helps put me in touch with that part of myself that is home. I gently blow again into the bone to send my prayer back to the mountains where my family lives. I ask for my parents' health and long lives as well as for my own strength and safety as I continue down the Trail.

I blow the hawk-wing bone-whistle again into the night. It is music that only I will hear. Unless, of course, the Great Spirit chooses to lend a kind ear.

CHAPTER SEVENTEEN

I walk along the Platte River for two days and it leads me straight into Kearney, Nebraska. I'm ready to rest by this time, and I need to wash my clothes. The smell of sweat and woodsmoke may not be everybody's cup of tea.

I get a cheap but clean and comfortable motel room. While my clothes wash at a nearby Laundromat, I soak in a tub of hot water. Ah, yes, this feels just as good as I imagined it would. I step from the water refreshed and my feet, though still sore, are starting to harden.

It's Friday night and it's been days since I've spent more than several minutes with people. Then it was just to buy food or refill my canteen with water. Wanting company, I stroll over to the motel office and ask the clerk if there's an interesting place in town for visitors like me.

Depends on what you call interesting, he says. Two blocks down the street the church is having a potluck dinner. All you can eat for four dollars. Or you can go to the Fireside Inn, where there's entertainment. That's where I go on Friday nights. Has a good cross section of people.

Thanks, I say. I'll give it a look.

It's a warm spring evening in Kearney as I walk across town toward the Fireside Inn. Dogs wag their tails and I sniff the smell of fried chicken drifting from the window of a house. An old woman sits in a wooden rocker on her front porch as she drinks a glass of tea. She holds herself with a certain charm and grace.

Nice evening, I tell her.

This is the best time of year, she nods, taking a sip of the tea. Back in the winter when the snow was blowing, I didn't think it would ever get warm again.

You have a pretty yard. I eye red and yellow tulips.

Oh, well, it used to be before my husband died. The flowers don't grow like they did when he was around. He had a green thumb. They wilt when they see me coming.

She is in her late seventies, but her smile has that youthful quality that makes anyone attractive. I smile back and as I walk on I hear her chair begin to rock, the wooden porch start to squeak. It fades into the song of a mockingbird sitting atop a wooden fence at the street corner. The mockingbird flies off when two boys approach on bicycles.

It's another six blocks to the Fireside Inn. As I come near the door I hear loud music inside. I don't like loud music. Somewhere between the age of thirty-five and forty my ears started leaning away from thunder and toward drops of rain on a tin roof. I am, however, still prone to turn up the volume when I hear Mick Jagger trying to wake the dead.

I open the door and enter the Fireside Inn. On the stage is a woman of about twenty or twenty-one who is shaking her body as if God or the devil himself has just entered her flesh to celebrate every inch of it. She wears tight short shorts made of faded jeans and her breasts are covered with a black lace bra while her lips are thick with bright red. As she squirms to loud music, her black leather boots pound the floor. From time to time, she bends over to touch her toes and reveal a hole in the jeans over tight hips, her naked skin peeking out at the audience of shouting cowboys and farmers.

I'm surprised to spot an empty seat at the bar and head that way. I take a seat and the man beside me nods.

Hi. I place my elbows on the counter.

The man—weighing around two hundred and fifty pounds and standing over six feet tall—eyes my biceps, bulging from under my T-shirt. I hope he doesn't feel some kind of competition. I seek conversation, not confrontation.

This place is packed, I shout above the music as the stripper pulls her shorts from her thighs.

Yeah, says the man. There's a farm equipment show in town. People are here from all across the state.

The stripper is drawing shouts from the crowd as she dances onstage. She taps into my lust, but she also makes me a bit sad as well. Her face is not filled with passion and romance, but that cool, glazed look of a phony salesman. Still, parts of her sell themselves.

The bartender has a head as bald as a watermelon. The red neon light over him reflects from that head. He sets a shot of whiskey on the counter for me and I start to pay him.

It's taken care of. He points to the giant next to me. Mike got it.

Thanks, I say, shaking Mike's hand. My name is Jerry. I'm from Alabama. I'm retracing the Pony Express Trail on foot.

You look like you're in good shape, he smiles, eyeing my biceps again. I'm overweight now, but I played two Orange Bowl games. I had a chance to play pro ball, too, but I got married instead. Don't think I regret it because I'm in here. I love my wife and I got two beautiful girls. I just got a lot on my mind and need to relax a little. I planted two thousand acres of corn today and I'm worried about it coming up. We still need more rain.

I farmed one summer, I say, thinking how comfortable I feel talking to this man. I raised watermelons and sugarcane. I didn't get rich, but I loved watching my crops grow. I was my own boss and that means a lot to me.

You got that right, Mike agrees. I couldn't work for the other man now.

The crowd goes wild with shouts and hollers as the stripper picks up her panties and other clothes from the stage. She runs past Mike and me and disappears into a back room. I now understand where the Fireside Inn gets its name. Would someone kindly turn down the flame?

I tell you what, says Mike. I live over in Lexington. You'll be passing right through there. Here's my phone number. Call when you hit town. We've got a guest room and can put you up for a day or two. You can meet my wife and girls and I'll show you my farm.

I appreciate it, I say, tucking his phone number into my pocket. I'll be looking forward to it.

This invitation strengthens my confidence and the whiskey goes to my head. Across the room I have been eyeing two women who sit at a table. One has red hair and from time to time she looks my way. Soft music begins to play and couples head for the dance floor.

Think I'll try my luck, I tell Mike as I slide from the barstool.

The redhead? Mike asks.

Yeah, I'm a sucker for fire.

I walk across the room and ask the redhead if she would like to dance. She studies me for a moment and then glances at the woman seated across from her as if to make sure she's doing the right thing.

Maybe just once, she says. I'm expecting someone.

She stands and eases into my arms. I feel her body heat through her clothes as the fingers of my right hand hold her lower back. I smell her perfume as we dance and it makes me want to pull her nearer. She isn't beautiful, but it doesn't matter. She is soft and warm and I'm just lonely enough to savor a kiss that doesn't involve lips at all, but simply the delicate closeness of two strangers.

When the song ends, she returns to her table, where a man now sits. They laugh and put their arms around each other. I feel out of place and head for my seat at the bar, only to discover that Mike has vanished. Now I really feel out of place in this loud, smoky bar.

Mike said to be sure to call him, says the bartender. He went home.

I go outside and start walking for the motel. I hope that the old woman I passed earlier this evening will still be in her rocking chair on the front porch. I would enjoy listening to her tell a story or two. I liked the tenderness and warmth in her voice when we said hello.

But when I get to the house where the old woman sat, I find only the rocking chair in the moonlight. The red and yellow tulips growing in the yard begin to quiver as the wind blows and I walk on.

The night air is cool now as I head for the motel room and I slip my hands into the pockets of my leather jacket. I feel a lump inside the lining and my fingers dig around till they find a hole in the right pocket. I'm surprised to find the Milky Way I got from the Rabbit Man. I pull it from the lining. It's been smashed flat at one end but I unwrap it anyway, and eat it among the stars as the moon follows me to my door.

CHAPTER
EIGHTEEN

In the winter of 1860 the Pony rider William Campbell almost lost his life as he rode with his *mochila* down the Trail to Lexington along the Platte River. He was caught in a blizzard so fierce that his horse could barely lift his legs through the snow where drifts were three to six feet high. The blowing snow was blinding both horse and rider and the Trail was buried. Campbell's only hope was to follow the tops of weeds that he recalled had grown along the route. They quivered only inches above the howling wind to finally lead him home. He rode twenty-four hours straight through that snowstorm to make certain the mail got through.

Another time on this stretch of the Trail to Lexington, that same tough and determined Pony rider came upon a pack of twelve wolves. They attacked his horse and he spooked, jerking sideways and kicking at anything that moved. With his silver spurs jingling, it was all Campbell could do to stay atop the horrified horse. The growling wolves grabbed at his legs with their ice pick–sharp teeth. Finally, the horse found his footing and raced down the Trail to leap a creek and escape.

Haunted by the attack, Campbell later returned to that section of the Trail and poisoned the carcass of a buffalo. Days later, he returned to find the bodies of twelve dead wolves. He skinned them as the sun went down, packed them on his horse, and carried them to a friend, a Sioux squaw.

Make me something from these skins, he told her. Something that will last.

The Sioux pulled the skins from the horse.

Come back in one moon, she said.

A month later Campbell went to see her. She entered her tepee and returned with a magnificent robe made from the wolfskins. He put it on over his shoulders and it dragged the ground as he walked as if he were a king. When he mounted his horse and raced away, the robe lifted in the wind like the wings of an eagle.

As I walk down the Trail along Route 30 from Kearney to Lexington I can't help but wish that I were living back in 1860, before all these cars and trucks passing me were invented. I'd even like to hear a pack of wolves howl at the moon as I sit by a campfire. Then my fantasy fades as I imagine the wolves being starved and attacking me. If I died on the Trail, how would my parents and two sisters handle the grief? Would they even ever know what became of me? I wonder if Campbell pondered who would've missed him if he had died in that snowstorm or wolf attack.

In 1932 William Campbell was the last living Pony rider. He died that same year in Stockton, California. In his last months, when he could barely walk, I like to picture him slipping into the robe to dream of his days of danger and glory along the Trail.

I'm certainly not wearing a robe by the time I've walked from Kearney to Lexington, but I'm ready to slip from my pack. The little town, bordered by railroad tracks and towering grain elevators, is only four or five square blocks big. The sun is setting and birds sing in the trees. What a fine place to spend a couple of days. It makes me feel welcome here to know I have a place to stay with Mike and his family.

I set my pack on the sidewalk and dig into my pocket for Mike's number. The paper it's written on is damp with sweat, but there's no problem in reading his writing. I drop a quarter into the pay phone and dial his number. A woman answers. I like her warm, friendly tone.

Is Mike in?

Just a minute.

Hello, says Mike.

Mike, it's Jerry.

Oh, he says, followed by nervous laughter. How are you?

I'm fine, I say, already finding it a bit hard to continue the conversation because my instincts tell me that his laughter is laced with regret. I just got into town and thought I'd give you a call like we talked about.

Yeah, it was good talking to you the other night. I'm caught up in work right now, but if you're around for a day or two, give me a call.

Okay, I tell him, knowing that I won't.

I hang up the receiver. I understand how he could've invited me to stay with his family after a few drinks and regretted it later. There's no hard feelings, but I am disappointed. I've been on the Trail for three weeks now and it would feel good to stay in a home.

I lift my pack and walk down the sidewalk. I enter a café and pool hall called Lakoda—Sioux, in English—to get something to eat. The bartender points at my pack and then at me.

I saw your picture in the paper, he grins. This trip must be the time of your life.

As I eat a sandwich the bartender and I get acquainted. His name is Tom and he is in his late twenties. His exceptional warmth and enthusiasm are most welcome, especially after not getting to stay with Mike and his family. A stranger in town always likes a friendly face.

I was in the infantry for four years, Tom explains. I've done skydiving and hang gliding. Every time I've leapt off a cliff to glide I've felt like a new baby was born. I'm really glad you came in.

What do you mean?

It's got me to thinking. What am I doing here behind this bar if I love adventure so much? I came to this town in the first place because I fell in love with a woman who lives here. I've really been feeling caged lately, and I'm not even sure if we still love each other. I need to prove to myself that I'm still free. Couldn't I come along with you for a few days? It would be like medicine to me.

It's not often that I make a new friend, but Tom seems like someone I could trust and talk with. And just thinking about it makes me recall my two teenage buddies, both dead now. I could use a buddy on the Trail, I think.

Let's try it together for a few days, I offer my hand. When can you leave?

All I have to do is get somebody to work my shift, says Tom, his face beaming. The boss is looking for a second bartender now, but I shouldn't have any trouble getting a waitress to fill in for me. I should have it all worked out in an hour or so and we can leave in the morning, if that's not too soon. I'd really like to get out of town.

That's perfect. I'll find a place to pitch my tent for the night and come back in a bit.

There's a homeless shelter just three blocks away, if you don't mind staying with Mexican hobos. Iowa Beef Packing just opened and some are in town trying to get work.

Fine, I used to spend a lot of time in Mexico. I speak Spanish.

Tom directs me to Haven House and I slip into my pack to head that way. It is a two-story building that was once someone's home. Trees border its right wall and eight or ten bicycles are lined up out front. Two Mexicans sit on the steps, smoking cigarettes.

I go inside the building and I'm surprised at how clean and homey it is. It smells good, too, as if the food cooked here is done with loving care. The curtains have been ironed and the windows washed.

I enter a little office and fill out an application to stay at Haven House. *How long have you been homeless?* it asks.

You can stay as long as five days, says the woman who interviews me and checks my application. If you need to stay longer, we can discuss it. Do you need anything special in the way of diet or medicine?

No, I say. Just a bed and a place to shower is plenty, thanks.

I start upstairs when I spot a tall, skinny man with his two front teeth missing. He is watching *The Dating Game* on TV. Half of the button at the top of his shirt is cracked and red paint spots his sleeve. A folded envelope sticks from his shirt pocket.

How's it going? I ask him.

Not too bad. He turns my way.

How long have you been here?

A couple of days. You think this show is real?

I guess, I say, thinking how far he and I are from being invited to appear on *The Dating Game.* Do you like it here?

It's okay for now, he says, trying to hide his mouth with his hand, as though ashamed of his lost teeth. I left home back in North Carolina over a month ago. I was thumbing to Montana where I got a construction job lined up when a circus picked me up and offered me a job. I was promised $150 a week, three meals, and told I'd only have to work four to six hours a day. But I got $105 and only two meals. I had to work all day and a dog wouldn't have liked where I had to sleep. Some of the people were nice, though. I liked the clown. He was a good clown with two little girls who were acrobats. He could stack chairs and stand on them, too. The animals, I loved them. But that's why I had to leave the circus.

I don't understand.

The animal trainer, he says, hit an elephant one day with

an iron bar to make it go to its knees. I couldn't take it. Stuff like that gets to me.

It gets to me, too.

Does it? says the man with a hint of hope in his voice as he lowers his hand from his mouth for the first time. I'm headed on to Montana when I leave here. I'm supposed to start off doing labor, but the man said if I did good he'd teach me how to be a carpenter. I'd like to learn how to make things from wood. I helped my grandfather build a barn one time when I was little. He wrote my name and his on the side of it. I didn't do much more than hand him boards and nails, but he told people we both did it. I didn't know my daddy. He killed a man when I was only four years old and ran away. My grandfather was real good to me. When he died, his place was sold. The new owners tore down the old barn, but I got the board with our names painted on it. They didn't care. They burned the rest of the wood and sold a building lot where the barn had been.

Where's that piece of wood now? I ask.

I took it to my brother in Durham. He put two little hooks in it and hung it on the wall in his garage. He said I could have it back when I had a home of my own like he does. I'm going to build me one if I learn how to become a carpenter. How far you think Montana is from here?

Maybe five or six hundred miles, I tell him, feeling my heart go out to this man and wondering if he'll ever make it.

I hope that job is still waiting on me. Sometimes it's hard to get a ride hitchhiking. These Mexicans hop the trains, but I'm afraid I'd end up in Los Angeles or somewhere like that. I like to know where I'm going.

I'm going to take a shower, I say, and find my bed.

Maybe I'll see you at dinner. We're having hot dogs. You can have more than one, if you eat it all.

I head for the stairs as the pretty woman on TV picks Date Number Three, who likes to ski, cook, and drink good wines in the French countryside. The man without his two front teeth watches her with awe, as if he wishes he had been picked. When he catches me studying him, he smiles but quickly hurries his hand back over his mouth. As I look into his homeless eyes I can't help but see his grandfather's old barn going up in smoke while the board with their names painted on it hangs in a dusty Durham garage.

CHAPTER
NINETEEN

I enter the upstairs room to my left, where I find six bunk beds. On the bed by the opened window, curtains blowing in the Nebraska breeze, is a man with a book over his face. His shoes stick over the edge of the bed. Both have holes the size of dimes in the soles. He lowers the book to reveal dark eyes. They aren't happy.

What do you want? His accent is Mexican, his tone harsh.

Hello, I say in Spanish. I'm looking for my bed.

He grunts and points at the bed to my left. I set my pack there and get out clean clothes so I can take a shower. I'm about to leave the room, when the Mexican sits up.

Hey, he says.

His lips part as if to speak, but he stops himself, seeming to grope with a decision. I tell him my name and offer my hand. He accepts.

Me llamo Río. Sorry I gave you such a hard look when you came into the room.

No problem, I say. I don't always feel like talking to strangers myself.

Where did you learn to speak Spanish?

In Mexico, I used to thumb there a lot. I stayed with friends up in the mountains who spoke only Spanish.

I just got into town on a train yesterday from Salt Lake City, he says. I'm broke and I can't get hired at the meat-packing plant for another two weeks. They say it's hard work anyway. You do the same thing over and over so much you start to talk to yourself. I had a good restaurant job in Salt Lake City. I speak five languages: Spanish, French, Italian, broken English, and fluent bullshit.

Are you a good bartender? I ask. I was just in Lakoda and heard them talking. They're looking for a bartender. I'm going back later. If you want to come, I'll introduce you to Tom, who works there. Maybe he can help you before he leaves town with me tomorrow.

Yes, but don't go too much out of your way for me. I don't like people who try to get close to me. It's a promise I made to myself three years ago back in New Jersey when my five-year-old daughter was killed. Don't think of asking how. I've been a hobo ever since and that's the way I want it. I come and go and nobody gets to me.

I've been thinking about hopping a train myself. I've never done it except once when I was a kid. The train had to slow down almost to a stop when it got to a curve near the creek I fished in. I ran to grab the ladder and a string of perch kept swinging against my leg. I only rode it for a half mile or so before it got to going faster. I got scared and jumped off. I fell on the fish.

Make sure you have a partner if you do, he insists, his tone warming. I had one back in Salt Lake City when I first tried to leave for here. I was drunk and fell on the tracks. If it hadn't been for my partner, I would've been run over by a train. I cracked two ribs when I fell. They're still sore. The woman downstairs offered to tape them, but I don't want anybody poking around on me.

Is your partner here at the shelter?

No, says Río, laying the book down. I ended up leaving Salt Lake by myself. He got drunk again and I crawled into an empty milk tank. They didn't get it all washed out. It smelled like soured milk. I can't even put cream in my coffee now.

I'm sorry about your daughter. I like kids a lot.

I don't want any more, he says, his voice almost cracking before becoming hard again. How soon are you going back to that bar?

As soon as I take a shower.

I'll be downstairs waiting on you.

They're serving hot dogs, I tell him.

Again? Maybe somebody will give me their fries for mine.

Río and I skip the Haven House hot dogs and fries and head toward Lakoda. The evening sky flutters with swallows just above the treetops. Three Mexicans on bicycles roll past us as we say hello.

They've worked in the meat-packing plant all day, Río tells me. Did you see how tired they looked?

Yes, I worked in a factory one summer in Los Angeles. I couldn't stand it. I went back to Alabama and started college.

I have two years of college, he says, but it doesn't help much in getting a job. Maybe one day I'll go back and finish. It would be nice to return to Mexico with a little class and money. My brothers are still there. They have big families and it's all they can do to make it from week to week. They seem happy, though.

The more Río talks, the warmer his tone becomes. It's reassuring to watch his defenses drop. It also makes me more excited about Tom leaving with me for a few days because I'm reminded how much fun it can be to get to know another man.

Río and I turn the corner and enter the Lakoda. I see Tom seated at a booth near a pool table where balls bang and crash. He holds a pen and writes on a piece of paper as if his very life depends on it.

That's Tom over there, I point in his direction. I'll introduce you when he gets through with whatever he's doing.

I'll go ahead and get an application from the waitress. You can bet that's part of it.

I take a chair while Río fills out an application. I can't keep my eye off Tom. He continues to look obsessed as he writes. He knows that I'm here, for we've already made eye contact. Some fifteen minutes later, he comes from the booth with the paper in his hand.

I phoned my girl, he says. She said I could go for a couple of days, but I can't find anybody to work my shifts. Shit, man, I'm just stuck here. I'm a prisoner. I wrote this poem about how I feel. Would you take it with you so at least a part of me gets to make the trip? Could you do that?

I read the poem in which he pours out his heart and soul to echo what he just told me. I fold it and place it in my wallet. Without him, I have more freedom on this journey, but I'm sad that he isn't coming.

I'll take your poem, I say. If I make it all the way to San Francisco, so will this part of you.

You'll make it. His voice is laced with both regret and hope. I got to be alone for a while and try to understand why I don't leave here anyway.

Tom sighs and walks out the door. Río lifts his pen from the application and eyes me.

Everybody's not meant to be free, he says. They just want to dream about it.

He begins filling out the application again as I leave the Lakoda. I return to the homeless shelter and go upstairs. It's just now getting dark and I'm the only one in the bedroom, where plastic bags of clothes stick from under two of the six bunks. I dig into my pack and pull out my journal. I fill the lines with Tom, Río, and the toothless man from North Carolina. It seems that we all may have something in common. We've all put ourselves in positions that make us live on the edge. While this often creates intrigue and suspense in my life, sometimes I think I would trade it all for the security of love.

At dawn I awake to a dream about walking through a new cornfield for as far as the eye can see. It makes me think of home because it is a ritual to plant corn with my father in the garden and check the soil each day for the first sprouts. This dream stirs a sweet pain deep within. Sweet because I have a home to return to, pain because it is so far away. This does not make me want to go back home now. It just makes me recall how wonderful it will be at the end of the journey. I accepted long ago when I was a teenager and began working out and pushing myself to my limit that pain was part of life. Of course, thoughts and feelings can't be set into a rack as easily as a barbell.

The birds begin to sing and I crawl from bed to get dressed. I'm putting the pack onto my back when Río raises his head from the pillow.

If you hop a train, he says, don't be stupid and fall. The wheels, they can cut off a leg before you know it.

I'll be careful, I tell him. Good luck with the job at Lakoda. Tell Tom I said good-bye?

He nods and lowers his face back into the pillow. The curtain dances in the breeze of the opened window as I go downstairs and out the door. It's not yet dawn and the trees flutter with birds. A train whistle blows in the great distance. I'm thankful I don't have to go pack meat into a can. On the shelter's steps sits the man from North Carolina who worked for the circus and built the barn with his grandfather. He smokes and drinks a cup of coffee.

Leaving for Montana today? I ask him.

I'm thinking about it, he says, sipping the coffee. But I can stay here a few more days, if I want to. This ain't a bad town. I just wish I could speak Mexican.

As I study his eyes, lonely and vulnerable, I can't help but wonder if he'll get trapped here in the shelter and ruin his chances at learning to become a carpenter in Montana.

The hobo named Río might teach you a few words, I offer. Just give him a little time to warm up.

I'll ask him, says the man, sipping the coffee.

The first orange and yellow rays of the sun come through the trees and across the great cornfields as I walk past the grain elevator. A windmill rattles as it turns in the breeze and a train slows to a stop. I wonder if a hobo is arriving to take my bed. I move on down the Trail.

CHAPTER
TWENTY

The Platte River winds through Nebraska for mile after mile, its clear, cold water a constant companion on my journey. I have been walking for several days along the Trail when I arrive in the town of North Platte. I'm excited to be here because this is where the ranch and Wild West Arena of Buffalo Bill, a Pony rider, have been preserved. I'm also happy to be getting close to where the Trail dips down into the northeastern part of Colorado; that spells comforting progress for a man on foot.

I walk several miles north of town toward Buffalo Bill's home with the hope that the management might let me sleep there, where my childhood hero once lived. Ever since I saw a photograph of Buffalo Bill, standing like a giant in his buckskin jacket with shoulder-length hair falling from his cowboy hat, I believed that he had super strength and abilities. I also thought that all big people, adults, knew everything there was to know. I couldn't wait to grow into a man so I would know it, too. Some lesson in patience this has turned out to be.

The sun is going down when I spot the home of Buffalo Bill, a great Victorian house surrounded by a white picket fence. Behind it stands an enormous barn. The grounds are manicured. I almost feel like I should take off my hat and bow.

When I get to the fence, however, I'm disappointed to see a sign that says *CLOSED*. The grounds won't reopen till the morning.

I'd like to take a shower, but it's a long walk back to a motel and I think it might be fun to camp overlooking my childhood hero's home. Twilight is falling as I walk across a meadow to a grove of trees. The moon appears as I push the last tent stake, made from the coat hanger, into the moist earth. I build only a very small campfire for fear someone passing by on the highway might be alarmed by flames and phone the police.

The home of Buffalo Bill is a shrine in the moonlight. When I was a kid, I wanted to own the fringed leather jacket he wore. Just like the cape Superman sported, I was certain that such a jacket would enable me to leap from horse to horse as they galloped down hills and over the prairie. I had a dream I never told anyone about wearing that jacket. I wanted to wear it at a circus where I was shot from a cannon to land on the back of a great white horse. The audience was to be spellbound as I then circled the arena before them, waving my hat as the fringe on the jacket waved in glory.

It's almost embarrassing to look back at the hero worship that a young boy holds for some bigger-than-life legend. But I guess I was like other kids, admiring the strength of Superman, the courage of Buffalo Bill. I suspect that the young Pony riders had heroes, too, whose footsteps they longed to follow in. There's something wonderful about aspiring to be strong, tough, and brave. But sometimes I worry about what happens if a boy grows to be a man and never learns to let his emotions grow as well. Many of the men I've met so far on the Trail seem to have closed themselves off from their feelings and that delicate sense of awe and wonder about being alive, which they surely once celebrated when they were children.

Only a few days ago, in Gothenburg, I visited three fifth-grade classes where the boys and girls were very much alive with wonder and awe, their feelings not yet hardened as I had seen in some of the folks I met on the Trail. I told the children about my journey—as well as my cabin, which began as a tree house—and asked them to write letters for me to carry to San Francisco as I make my way down the Pony Express Trail. My old worn backpack is acting as my *mochila*, and it's stuffed with almost a hundred of the kids' letters. (I have not—as yet, anyway—started to believe that I'm a horse and running fifteen miles an hour, as the Ponies did in 1860.)

Each night around my campfire I allow myself the luxury of reading one or two of those letters. I dig into my pack now to get one. I asked the kids to write what they liked or disliked about America and what they would change about it, if anything. A few of the kids' pencils were suffering from spring fever; they seemed stuck to the desks. I suggested that they imagine that their fathers had left home in Nebraska and gone to the Gold Rush in California. They were to write a letter convincing the fathers to come back home. As the moon rises higher over Buffalo Bill's Victorian home and my little fire flickers beneath the trees, I now read one of those letters:

Dear Daddy,

I miss you so much. Mama and me are working hard to feed the pigs. I hope we are doing it right. Almost all the crops are gone from a tornado that came through. Please come home. We don't need gold. We will be rich with love. Our cow died and now we have no milk. Baby brother is sick and might die. He needs to see you. Mama always talks about you at night. Sometimes I have to leave the room. Come home soon, Daddy.

If I got this letter while I was in the goldfield, I think I would hurry home and wonder why I left to begin with. I fold the letter and place it back into my pack as the flames from the campfire die down into glowing coals. I crawl into the tent and get inside my sleeping bag. A breeze blows and the nylon tent slowly flutters like the canvas on a covered wagon. I fall asleep, dreaming that Buffalo Bill is driving a team of horses pulling that wagon through the moonlight.

The next morning I am awakened by the cooing of a dove. It's a couple of hours before Buffalo Bill's home will open to the public. The fresh night air has made me hungry, so I pack my tent and walk to a café for breakfast and coffee.

When I finally get to enter the famous home, I can't stop myself from hurrying from room to room, my eyes wide with wonder and excitement. *This is where Buffalo Bill himself lived* keeps running through my mind. *This is where a legend ate, slept, dreamed, laughed, cried, and made love.* Parts of rooms are roped off to prevent anyone from touching the furniture. But I reach over one of the ropes to let my fingers run across a rocking chair where my hero once sat. It begins to rock back and forth and I love hearing it squeak. The room seems to be coming alive and I almost expect to turn to the doorway and behold Buffalo Bill himself, towering over me like a giant. On the walls are pictures of him and his Wild West Show, and his eyes seems to watch me as if at any moment he might wink and let out a laugh loud enough to shake the whole musty Victorian house. I'm so thrilled to be here that I imagine that I'm living back in the 1800s.

Buffalo Bill—William Frederick Cody—the most famous of the Pony riders, was born February 26, 1846, in Scott County, Iowa. Nine years later his family moved to Kansas Territory, where Buffalo Bill learned to ride and shoot with the neighboring Kickapoo Indians. With a keen ear for language, he began to speak their tongue as well as that of the Sioux and other tribes.

He was only eleven when his father was killed in a dispute over slavery; his father thought the blacks should be freed. To help support his family, Buffalo Bill went to work for Alexander Majors, to be a messenger between wagon trains headed for Utah. He writes about that experience in his book *Buffalo Bill's Life Story:*

> I went to Mr. Majors, whom I always called Uncle Aleck, and asked him for a job. I told him of our situation, and that I needed it very badly for the support of my mother and family.
>
> But you're only a boy, Billy, he objected. What can you do?
>
> I can ride as well as any man, I said. I could drive cavayard, couldn't I? Driving cavayard is herding extra cattle that follow the wagon train.
>
> Mr. Majors agreed that I could do this, and consented to employ me. I was to receive a man's wages, forty dollars a month and food, and the wages were to be paid to my mother while I was gone.

At the age of fifteen, after working for Mr. Majors as a messenger and cattle driver with the wagon trains for four years, Mr. Majors hired Buffalo Bill to become a Pony Express rider on the Trail west of Julesburg, Colorado. He was later transferred to the Wyoming section of the Trail and once rode from Red Buttes to Rocky Ridge and back again to cover 384 miles, setting the longest ride on record.

In 1864, three years after the Pony Express had folded, Buffalo Bill joined the Union Army. During this time, on a trip to St. Louis, he fell in love with Louisa Frederici.

When Buffalo Bill left the Army, he became a stage driver for Ben Holladay's Stage Company. Following his marriage to

Louisa in 1866, he built a hotel called The Golden Rule, but it failed, as did a town named Rome, which he and his business partner, Wild Rose, built in Fort Hays, Kansas.

Buffalo Bill got his nickname when he was in his early twenties and went to work for the Kansas Pacific Railroad. His job was to supply meat to the construction crews, and he used a .50-caliber Springfield rifle to shoot twelve buffalo a day. Special wagons followed him to haul the meat back to the camps. He once got into a contest with another sharp-shooter named Billy Comstock to see who could kill the most buffalo in a single day. Comstock got forty-six. But Buffalo Bill killed sixty-nine.

After the Custer Massacre the U.S. Army took unmerciful revenge on Native Americans in the Dakotas. Buffalo Bill was hired by the Army as a scout and fighter against the Sioux there. When he killed Yellow Hand in a knife fight he scalped him. He was apparently so proud of having taken the Indian's hair that he sent it to his wife, Louisa, here at his Victorian home in North Platte.

When I heard this story at the age of seven or eight, I didn't want to believe that my hero would kill and scalp one of my distant kinsmen. I had seen pictures of Buffalo Bill standing side by side with Indians and I thought they were friends. From that point on I stopped dreaming about wearing his leather-fringed jacket.

Still, as I now wander from room to room and find more old faded photographs of Buffalo Bill and his Wild West Show, I can't help but be impressed by his great legend, extending all the way to Europe: Queen Victoria herself invited the charismatic Buffalo Bill to England to see her. She's said to have told people that he was "the best-looking man" she had ever seen. Back home, here in North Platte, his wife, Louisa, was enraged with jealousy over the attention given to him by the queen as well as thousands of other female fans. I'm not sure how justified Louisa's suspicions might have been, but Buffalo Bill sued for divorce in 1904. He lost the suit, though, and stayed married until his death in 1917.

At his request, Buffalo Bill was buried just above Denver, Colorado, on Lookout Mountain. I've been to that spot and it overlooks a valley where a herd of buffalo roam.

I leave the grand house and go to the enormous barn, which once held Buffalo Bill's prize horses. I am the only one here just now and some of his saddles are displayed. I ease my fingers around the horn of one and it seems to give me strength. The leather's smooth and smells warm and rich. There's a nick near the top of the horn and I wonder if a belt buckle worn by Buffalo Bill himself scraped it there as he rode in his Wild West Show. I look about the barn to make certain that no one has entered to see me. Then I grab the horn and swing up onto the saddle as if I'm on a bucking bronco. Closing my eyes, I find myself once again wanting to wear that leather-fringed jacket as I race around the arena and wave my hat at the wild and joyous audience.

CHAPTER
TWENTY-ONE

I wouldn't mind having a pony to carry me down the road west along the Platte River because my feet are burning more with each forced step I take. Still, seeing Buffalo Bill's home has lifted my spirits, and my load seems lighter as I head for Julesburg in northeastern Colorado. The Trail then leads northwest back into Scottsbluff, Nebraska, near the Wyoming border.

By the time I reach Julesburg, even my buoyant spirits can't disguise the fact that my body is aching all over. My neck and shoulders are stiff, and even my eyes hurt. I'm running a fever. I hope that I'm just tired from all the walking, but I fear I may be coming down with some kind of virus. I tell myself I can lick it before it goes any farther.

I get a room at the Grand Motel, not so grand with red paint peeling from the old broken neon sign. I can't brag on the worn room I'm given, either. But the owner has made over a dozen birdhouses that hang from trees just beyond my window, and their beauty, as birds come and go, makes the aged furniture and torn carpet easier on the eye.

I wash my face and take a couple of aspirin. I dig into my pack for the diary of Sir Richard Burton for some distraction. In 1860, he met Joseph Slade, who was hired to clean up Julesburg at the time of the Pony Express. He killed the town's founder and outlaw, Jules Reni, and cut off both his ears. One he nailed to a fence post and the other he carried in his pocket. Some say he made a watchcase from it. This is what Sir Richard wrote in his diary when he met Slade and his wife:

> . . . [she] was like women in this wild part of the world generally—cold and disagreeable in manner, full of "proper pride," with a touch-me-not air. . . . Her husband was the renowned Slade. . . . This pleasant individual "for an evening party" wore the revolver and bowie-knife here, there, and every where.

As I close the diary on this ear collector, Slade, I wonder what today's sheriff is like in Julesburg. I go to the motel office to see the clerk.

Do you know the sheriff? I ask him.

Everybody in town knows him, says the clerk. That's Gene Mikelson. We call him Mean Gene.

His office nearby? I wonder, intrigued with the sheriff's nickname.

Yeah, says the clerk. But you'll probably find him at the café across from the hardware. Two blocks that way.

I walk toward the café in the middle of town, which is only three square blocks. Eight or ten cars and trucks are parked along the curb and only an old man with a cane walks down the sidewalk. At the corner, a dog chews on a bone. It isn't a ghost town, but it sure seems kin to one.

I enter the café to the sound of rattling plates and the smell of frying bacon. I'm surprised to see some twenty or thirty customers sipping coffee and talking up a storm. I'm even more surprised to spot a giant man with a big silver star headed for the door I start to close.

Excuse me. Are you Sheriff Mikelson?

That's right. They call me *Mean* Gene. Who are *you*?

Mean Gene stands as tall as Matt Dillon in *Gunsmoke.* He's

in his sixties and he may be as rough and tough as his nick-name promises, but there's a warm light in his eyes. I explain what I'm doing, how far I've come along the Pony Express Trail.

Could I buy you a coffee? I offer.

I'm full of coffee, says Mean Gene. But I'll join you for a few minutes.

We sit at a table by the window. The waitress brings me coffee and a menu, but I'm too sick to eat. Sweat drips down my face.

Are you really mean? I wonder aloud.

Hell, says Sheriff Mikelson, I don't know. Some say yeah. Some say no. I'm getting tired of being a sheriff, though, I can tell you that much. I've done it for forty-one years now. I'm ready to spend some time alone. I want to go camping. This town used to be alive at night. People sat outside and talked to each other. Now they stay home and watch television. If I visit somebody and the damn thing is on, I walk right out the door. My walls are covered with awards, but they don't mean a thing. What I want is community action. Hell, people are just interested in making money today. I had two kids smash some tractor windows the other day when they should've been home. I don't know what the world's coming to. Did you know that right here in Julesburg was where Buffalo Bill's Wild West Show had its last performance before the banks foreclosed on it?

Mean Gene takes off his glasses and rubs his tired eyes. My head is pounding. I need to lie down.

Looks like you need some rest, I say. I'll not keep you.

It's more than that, says Mean Gene. My wife and I have company for a couple of days and I need to get back home to see them. If you stick around town for a couple of days, I'll be free. We can talk some more and I'll show you around.

He moans as he gets up from the table, towering over me with his big silver star. I leave the café as he does. He gets into his patrol car and drives off. I wish that he could leave his job and go camping with me for a few days. I wish I had the power to pull people out of their routines and onto the Trail. I guess it's true that we all like to see parts of ourselves in others, and it's the adventurer I seek.

When I get back to the motel room, I collapse on the bed. My fever is going up and sometime in the night a train whistle blows to jolt me awake in the middle of a nightmare. A hobo has cut off both my ears and I am in the sheriff's car with Mean Gene as we drive around Julesburg trying to find them.

The next morning I awake feeling better. At least the fever seems down and I have my ears back on my head. Common sense tells me to stay in bed, but it's hard to accept that my body is being overpowered by something I can't even see. I want to talk with Mean Gene some more, but the thought of being cooped up in this room for a couple of days to await him doesn't suit my fancy. I pack my bag and hit the Trail.

It's a beautiful spring morning, but I walk only a couple of miles before I'm soaking wet with sweat. I feel like I've been trampled by a herd of wild horses. My head is pounding again. I was foolish to leave Julesburg.

I decide to forge ahead, though, and try to thumb a ride. There is very little traffic. I'm relieved when a pickup truck stops. It's driven by a man with his wife and two kids who are headed all the way to Scottsbluff. I crawl into the back of the truck, which is covered with wheat straw. It makes a soft bed as we roll down the road, but it doesn't make the pain in my body any less.

Only miles east of Scottsbluff, we roll on past the famous Chimney Rock, which marks the end of the prairie. Pioneers carved their names into the base of the rock as they moved westward. But just as they have become dust, most of the names have been eroded by wind and rain.

We arrive in Scottsbluff and I get a motel room on the outskirts of town. I collapse on the bed and turn on the TV with hopes of escaping my body. The movie *Alien* is on and the monster show seems so safe and contained in the magic box. Now if I could only place this virus in there as well.

The next day I'm better. By the day after that I feel I have found salvation. My body, mind, and spirit are back together. I'm so thankful to have strength and energy again that even breakfast in McDonald's seems like a luxury. Besides, it would be naive to pretend that McDonald's hasn't become as American as apple pie along the Pony Express Trail. Will the day come when I am dust and someone will retrace the original fast-food sites to see what America has become?

After breakfast, I head west on Highway 26. The red bluffs and hills overlooking Scottsbluff are a sight for sore eyes. I'm more than ready to leave the prairie.

That evening has the most beautiful sunset I've seen so far on the journey. Maybe it only seems that way because it's been such a good day after being sick. Then, too, I'm less than fifteen miles from the Wyoming border, and that excites me. I just hope they arrested those three men Josh talked about on the wagon train who were said to hold men down while they pushed out their eyeballs with their thumbs.

It's twilight as I spot an abandoned farmhouse with an old barn near the Platte River. I read in the diary of Sir Richard Burton that he had to sleep in a haystack at a station near Fort Laramie, and I'm tempted to see if the old barn will offer me a bed of hay.

I walk down to the old wooden building and go inside to find its hallway already getting dark. It's a bit spooky, and I take my small flashlight from the pack. It lights my way as I climb the ladder, missing two rungs.

I almost fall backward in fright when a pigeon flutters from a rafter and disappears into the dark. The loft, however, is perfect for sleeping. There's plenty of hay and the loft door is open to the stars. I slip into my sleeping bag and feel a bit like a kid with a secret. No one knows that I'm here, and what the welcoming mountains whisper is not about me.

CHAPTER
TWENTY-TWO

The next morning sunlight comes through the barn loft door and cracks in the boards. I feel as though I'm in a cathedral as this golden light falls across the hay, dust rising as I crawl from my sleeping bag.

As I get dressed I peek through the barn loft door to spot a truck slowpoking down Highway 26, its headlights glowing in fog rising from the Platte River. The truck is hauling cattle, and they bellow as if worried about where they're going.

I go down the ladder and find footprints in the dirt of the barn floor. I wonder whose they are till my sleepy brain recalls that they're mine.

It's cold this morning and I build a fire down by the river to make coffee, warming myself by the smoky flames while the water heats up. The river treats me with a surprise when I discover a crane wading around the bend, its long, delicate legs no wider than my fingers.

Ever since I was a child, I've searched the skies for a glimpse of a crane. When I walked the Trail of Tears, I considered the cranes to be my spirit guides, watching over me. When I was a child, I went hunting with my father and two other men. I saw a crane fly over the treetops and it filled me with wonder, it was so graceful and proud. I was horrified when the other men raised their guns and fired. The crane fell to the earth, dead. The men cut a wing from it and placed it in the game pouch of a hunting jacket where a dead rabbit was stored as well.

As I raise a cup of coffee to my lips the crane wading in the Platte River leaps from the water. It makes me happy to watch it fly so free and disappear into the soothing and quiet fog.

The word *Wyoming* comes from two Delaware Indian words meaning large meadows, and it takes only a day's walk along Highway 26 to reach the state line. As I head toward Casper, to the northwest, I follow country roads along the Trail, which still follows the Platte River.

Every few miles these large meadows roll with buttes as high as the hill where my cabin awaits me back home in the Appalachian Mountains. It's quiet here, without the roar of cars and trucks, ringing phones, and the blasts from human herds in the streets. It's easy to keep a clear head out here. Except for down by the river, this stretch of land is barren of trees. There, in the great distance, I spot a swirling funnel of dust called a dust devil, fifteen feet tall. It seems alive and appears to be looking for something or someone as it rushes across the earth to suck more dust and dried blades of grass up into its determined and pushy path. Then, as if giving up the will to live, its swirling slows and finally stops to become no more than a cloud of dust drifting over the land.

I spot my first antelope at the base of a butte. He raises his head and studies me as if to decide if I'm an animal or just another dust devil that will soon vanish like all the others. Then his whole body seems to become as fast and fluid as the Platte River. He leaps into the air and gallops across the land, a delicate trail of dust chasing after him. As if looming from the earth itself, two more antelope now appear to run in the same direction. When they are almost out of sight, they stop and look back, their trails of dust floating toward them.

I build a fire from dead cottonwood limbs on the bank of

the river to cook dinner. Back in Scottsbluff, I mixed a bag of spices—garlic, basil, oregano, red pepper, and a pinch of curry—in a herb store. I now add some to a small pot of rice as a crow calls out downstream.

I place my fingers to my nose and sniff the spices. I want to recall preparing this meal on such a beautiful spot because the time will come when I'm too old to walk the Trails and perhaps such a memory will help amuse me and keep me company.

The lid on my small pot begins to rattle as the smoky flames do their good deeds. Up till now I have used a plastic spoon to eat the meals I cooked. Now, however, as the rice simmers, I sit by the fire to carve a spoon from a piece of cottonwood. It is softer than pine and the type of wood that many Indian tribes used to carve their toys and totems. I carve the head of a crow in the handle of the spoon. I see nothing wrong with eating with a bird in my hand.

I take the pot from the flames and remove the lid. It has overflowed and broth has baked to the side of the pot. As usual, I don't wait long enough for food to cool and I burn my mouth with the first bite of rice. But it doesn't matter. As I sit by the river, savoring this spicy meal I've made, I know I wouldn't trade it for a cool bite of caviar in a swank French hotel.

I become tired and lazy after the meal. The sun is setting and the fire is going out. This is a good spot to camp for the night, but the beauty of a nearby butte and its challenge to climb it call me. I want to see what it's like to sleep there on it, closer to the stars, as I look out over the Wyoming country-side.

It's about two miles to the nearest butte and when I finally get to its base, it's almost dark. As I look up at the butte it appears much steeper than I had thought, some nine or ten stories tall. Looking for the easiest route up the hill, I circle its base. I'm about to start up it when the bushes shake. I'm relieved to see only a rabbit hop into the moonlight.

Climbing the butte, I fall to my knees but catch myself with my hands against the earth. When I finally reach the top I have a greater reward than I ever dreamed. I feel on top of the world as I behold the river snaking through the moonlight, while the Milky Way seems so brilliant with stars that I could almost reach out and touch it with my fingertips. In the great distance, I spot a tiny light in what I assume is someone's home. When a coyote calls out from the darkness it sends welcome chills down my back and up my arms. High on this butte, I am King of the Mountain.

I don't put up my tent tonight. I simply slide into my sleeping bag so I can behold the stars and feel the fresh air. From the leather pouch, I take my hawk-wing bone-whistle. I place its tip to my lips and blow gently. Its soft song blends with the breeze to sing across the great open land.

The next day I watch the butte fade into the distance as I walk over to Highway 26 to try to thumb a ride to Casper, which is fifty miles to the northwest. Boy, could I use a hot shower about now.

I have to wait for over an hour before a car stops. It's a 1968 Buick. When I get a close look at the driver, I'm not sure I want to go with him. His eyes are bloodshot and his clothes are wrinkled. His backseat has been turned into a bed. The brown-stained pillow has no linen. He eyes me with equal caution.

How far you going? I ask.

Montana, he says, eyeing my sign, which is made from the back of one of the children's letters from Nebraska. I'll drop you off in Casper.

Thanks, I say, placing my pack in the backseat.

I get in and he says his name is Carl. We start down the

road. Two empty paper cups from Hardee's roll about on the floorboard at my feet and Carl sips a third cup of coffee.

You had coffee this morning? he wants to know.

Yeah, I say, thinking it's considerate of him to ask. I had coffee where I camped.

I've decided that Josh on the wagon train had his information scrambled about the guys who were removing eyeballs. I think they have been doing dental work instead, for Carl— like the homeless circus worker—is missing his two front teeth. Maybe it's not really so odd to find these ivory holes on the Trail, for folks out here in the wilderness don't seem too concerned about putting on the dog. It certainly saves time brushing.

Carl isn't too big on chewing the fat at first, but when I say that I've been on and off the road since I was seventeen, he loosens up.

I'm living out of my car right now, he tells me. I hit the road when I was only fifteen. I grew up in Boston, but when I got back from Vietnam I landed in Wyoming. I met a woman at the bus station in Rock Springs and married her. It was the pits, though. She drank a lot and started screwing around. I left her five years ago and been bouncing around ever since.

How do you support yourself? I ask, recalling that I almost joined the Green Berets to go to Vietnam when I was eighteen, angry, confused, and disillusioned with my girlfriend, who was seeing someone behind my back.

Whatever, he says. Wash dishes, brand cattle, shovel horseshit. It all adds up to work. The last two days I was docking sheep. Cutting their balls off. I'm headed to Billings, Montana, now. I'll probably have to do some work between here and there to buy gas. I already blew most of the docking money. When I first got back from the war, I was a cop over in Medicine Bow, but it didn't pan out. I hope you know you're in the best state in the union. Only shithole in the whole state is Glendo. The population is fifty-two and every-body sticks his nose in the next person's business. I tried to make a go of it there, but it was a waste of time.

I camped on the lake there a few days back, I say. When I had breakfast in town, I heard some railroad workers talking about the local badass, called Jimmie. Did you know him?

Know him? I put the son of a bitch in the hospital. I was in the bar when he tapped me on the shoulder and said he didn't like Yankees. I told him I didn't like rednecks and punched him in the mouth. I took out five teeth at once. I wouldn't have hit him so hard, but he called my wife ugly. She was ugly, but . . . He was okay if he wasn't drinking. Same with my brother down in Florida. I just got back from there a few weeks ago. I had to go down and punch him.

All the way to Florida to hit your own brother? I say.

I went there from Boston, says Carl. Our father had died and my brother didn't even phone. I drove down and broke into his house and waited on him till he came home. When he walked in, I came from behind the door and punched him out.

You back on good terms now? I ask.

We're always on good terms, he says. He just needed a little reminder of what's right and wrong. He gave me a job for two weeks after that.

Carl drops me off at a service station three or four miles south of Casper. If I were his brother, I think I would be tempted to check behind my door each time I came home. Indeed, violence is the last force I care to be around just now. I've been on the road for several weeks and I'm feeling a bit vulnerable and exposed to the world. I seek warmth, tender-ness, and the celebration of life—not its destruction. I hope that Casper, like a home station for a Pony rider, will prove to be a good place to rest and get a second wind to continue on down the Trail.

CHAPTER
TWENTY-THREE

It's a beautiful summer day in Casper as I head for downtown to look for a motel. I've been in the wilderness for so long now that it's almost culture shock to see restaurants and stores and people on sidewalks. A woman with long legs comes from a department store and I smell her perfume. It's so sweet and sensual that I almost stop as if I've stepped into a tropical garden.

I get a room for eighteen dollars at the Greek Motel. It's clean and cozy, but eight or ten houseflies buzz around as I get caught up in a game of Dodge the Swatter, my right arm swinging here and there like a prize fighter. Carl might be impressed with my speed, I think, as I flatten one behind the door.

When I at last emerge from the hot shower, I slip into shorts and take my Trail clothes to a Laundromat. While they wash I explore Casper and find a little Italian restaurant. I like the menu posted in the window and peek inside to see tables with candles and flowers. I wish I had someone to toast with tonight when I return to have dinner, but even dining alone in such an inviting spot stirs romance within me. I'll toast the Trail and imagine that it does the same.

Thinking about eating often brings to mind my family because the meals were a special time when my parents and two sisters came together to talk and enjoy each other. When

I get back to the Laundromat, I phone my sister Sandra in Phoenix. What a comfort to hear her voice.

How's the trip going? she asks.

I'm a bit road-weary, I say. But that's part of the challenge. I think a couple of days here in Casper and I'll get rested. How are Ken's treatments coming?

It doesn't look good, she says. The doctor thinks it has spread from his lungs to his brain. They're running tests.

This news disturbs me. It's only a matter of time now till Ken will die. I'm concerned that I may not finish the journey in time to see him alive again and this leaves me somewhat torn. A part of me wants to leave the Trail so I can see him. But if I do, it'll be hard to come back and the spirit of the journey would change.

I hate to tell you this, too, says Sandra, but I think you should know . . .

I don't want to hear more bad news.

Carolyn called a few days ago, Sandra continues. Sean is dead.

Dead?

Yes, says Sandra, suicide. He hung himself.

I'm shocked. Sean, a friend, was twenty-three and lived in Seattle with his single mother, Carolyn. Sandra was living in the same house till only a few months ago. I stayed the month of May there in 1990 and slept in the same room as Sean. It had been years since I slept in a room with another male, and it was curious to see how he had decorated his room with pictures of heroes from fantasy magazines. He was bright and gifted, but had recently failed to make it though basic training in the Army. He couldn't climb the walls. Haunted by this, he sometimes confided in me.

I realize this macho stuff is bullshit, Sean had told me. But I can't stop thinking about it. I hated the sergeant and we were always at each other's throat. He had the brain of an idiot. He knew I was smart and it bugged him. It was all such bullshit, but I became obsessed to prove to him that I could make it through boot camp. I got to try twice, but I couldn't make it over that damn wall. I tried with everything I had. I just couldn't do it.

My heart went out to him. I knew what I had gone through as a teenager trying to prove myself. I understood his need for the heroes he had taped to his bedroom walls. I once did the same thing. It takes a long time for a man to accept that the only real hero he can count on is the very human one within himself. I wonder if Sean was having trouble accepting that he couldn't live up to the heroic images taped to his bedroom walls.

It might mean a great deal to Carolyn, says Sandra, if you gave her a call.

Maybe I'll do that, I say, thinking I don't really want to because of the pain. Is Ken home?

Yes, but he's asleep.

When he wakes up, will you tell him I said hello? My voice begins to crack.

Sure, says Sandra. Are you okay?

I think so.

When I hang up the receiver, I'm a bit dazed. I take my clothes from the dryer and head back to the motel. As I walk that way I try to make sense of the news about Ken and Sean. It seems so unreal that I find myself staring at cracks in the street as I walk. I go a block past my motel before I realize where I am.

I drop my clothes onto the motel bed and phone Carolyn. The rings go on and on and I'm about to hang up when she finally answers.

I still can't believe it's happened, says Carolyn. Sean was a little down about his girlfriend because she had just told him she was pregnant. I didn't know till then that he had had a child from when he was married back in Denver that he and his ex-wife gave up for adoption. We were sitting at the kitchen table talking about this when the dog ran away. I went out to look for him and when I got back I found Sean had hung himself. He was already blue. I tried to bring him back, but it was too late. He left a new poem on his bed. A couple of days later I discovered that his girlfriend wasn't pregnant at all. She had told him that to play with his mind. This is all such a nightmare. I called the police station to try to get Sean's clothes back, but someone had stolen them. Then the next day the coroner's office phoned to say I should come down and get the rope he used.

When I hang up the receiver I go outside, where twilight is settling over trees. Casper Mountain, only a few miles to the west, towers over the town. I walk toward it as though it might take away part of my mounting sadness.

I walk about Casper as night falls, but I can't get away from myself. I go into a liquor store and buy a bottle of tequila to take back to the motel room. I do shots till I begin to feel numb, then stretch out on the bed and fall asleep as a fly buzzes in the dark.

My head hurts from the tequila and I feel guilty that I drank it to try to deal with yesterday's news. I take the bottle from the nightstand and drop it into the trash can as I head for the bathroom to drink a glass of water and take a shower.

I step outside and the Wyoming morning air is fresh and clean. I'm surprised to find a black bird-dog puppy playing with my feet. His long hair is slick and healthy and I bend over to rub him. He licks my fingers and jumps into my hands.

I look up to discover a wiry little man in his fifties with determined eyes walking toward me. His exceptionally powerful voice resonates as he speaks a language I do not understand. The puppy runs to him.

Is he yours? I ask.

The curious stranger again speaks in a tongue I do not recognize. He picks up the dog and we both stroke him.

I'm sorry, he says. I sometimes forget when I am speaking Lakoda instead of English. My name is Bill Norman. This is my dog, Dixie. In Lakoda his name means Tepee Beggar.

You don't look Sioux, I tell him.

No, not on the outside, he says. But I grew up with them. I spoke Lakoda before I knew English. My mother's milk dried up and my Sioux grandmother nursed me. In Sioux my name is Meadowlark. If the inflection is changed only a bit my name becomes Boy. This is a good thing, as I think you may already know. A man who has lost the boy has lost the man.

It intrigues me that he just said what I have thought a great deal about on this journey. He smiles as he continues to stroke Tepee Beggar.

My name is Jerry Ellis. My Cherokee name is Crane at Creek.

Hmm. He thinks it over. A Meadowlark and a Crane. This is a good thing we are meeting. I was about to have a prayer meeting on the floor in the motel lobby. Would you like to join me and a friend there? There's coffee.

Fascinated by Meadowlark, I follow him into the tiny lobby of the motel, where we sit on the floor. The old Greek who owns and operates the motel gives me a cup of coffee. The clerk, a friend of Meadowlark, is about my age and joins us. The prayer meeting is, for my own taste, among the best kind —we simply talk about our lives and reveal ourselves as though time on earth were limited. I start to tell them the news I got yesterday concerning Ken and Sean, but talking about it makes me so uncomfortable that I change the subject.

You grew up in Wyoming? I ask the older man.

Out here, says Meadowlark. It means . . . well, there is no English word for it. *Out here* in Lakoda means something like wherever the eye can see. The U.S. Government has given it boundaries the eyes don't know.

He tosses three coins on the floor between his legs and chants a song in Lakoda. Tepee Beggar curls up on the floor beside him as if to listen.

I am chanting a Buffalo Prayer, he says. For the Sioux, everything came from the buffalo. You and I have not met by accident. We smelled each other in the wind.

He starts chanting again and this time it is louder and richer, as if he has opened his heart for a more private song to come forth. The sound is doing something to me I don't understand. It is making me drop my innermost walls, which I didn't realize until this moment were up. I begin to feel some overpowering pain and sorrow. Then it dawns upon me that I have not chanted since that second day on the wagon train, when I was nearly overwhelmed by the bigotry at the water pump and the news that Ken had cancer; only a small, timid voice came forth. I haven't chanted since then, even though that is what I have done for years to gain strength. Now, as Meadowlark continues chanting, I feel myself coming more alive deeper inside. The sorrow I now feel makes me want to cry, which I have not done in several years. Have I tried to bury my loneliness and feelings of rejection on the wagon train deeper than I realized? Has the recent breakup with my girlfriend in Denver been pushed down that far as well? Has the news of Ken and Sean jolted my innermost core? I'm relieved when Meadowlark stops chanting. I don't want to feel this much at once.

Tepee Beggar springs from the floor and runs outside. Meadowlark scolds him in Lakoda till the puppy stops to lick water from a puddle.

He knows what he needs, says Meadowlark.

Are you staying here at the motel? I ask.

Yes, says Meadowlark. I drift into town every moon or two, spend the night, and play a little pool. I used to be a lawyer, but I don't practice anymore. I have a cabin back up in the hills where I find more peace than a town has to offer.

He takes the three coins from the floor and sticks them back into his pocket. Tepee Beggar runs back into the lobby and jumps into his lap. He eyes his watch.

I'm to meet someone down the street in a café, he says. Want to come?

I want to explore the town, I say, thinking that I need time alone to deal with the emotions that the chanting stirred within me. But let's walk together as far as we can.

He locks Tepee Beggar in his motel room and we start down the sidewalk. It dawns on me that even for a couple of blocks, I am walking the Trail with someone. This feels good and I wonder how Tom is doing way back in Lexington, Nebraska. His poem is still snug in my wallet.

Meadowlark and I part when we come to the café where he is headed. As I walk down the sidewalk I'm still shaken by our meeting and the unexpected prayer meeting he invited me to. Then, from behind me, I hear the Sioux language spoken again. I turn to see Meadowlark running toward me and shouting in Lakoda as if an emergency were at hand.

I'm sorry to have shouted at you like that, says Meadowlark. But it was the only way I was sure of reaching you.

There is some great urgency in his eyes. It seems natural to place my hand on his shoulder. He does the same to mine and looks into my eyes unlike anyone has ever done before.

I am Brother to the Serpent, he says. Now *you* are Brother to the Serpent, too. No, he adds, do not question this now. When the time is right, you will understand.

He chants as he lifts his hand from my shoulder and heads back down the sidewalk. All that I was feeling back on the floor at the prayer meeting comes back in full force. I am about to cry again and I don't want anyone to see my eyes. I turn the corner to avoid a man and woman pushing a baby stroller my way.

I consider myself a very down-to-earth person and I'm skeptical of metaphysics or anything that smells too much of that world. Still, I cannot deny what is happening any more than I can afford to deny my Cherokee roots. Something is trying to be released inside me.

For the first time since that second day on the wagon train I begin to chant as I walk across a field on the outskirts of Casper. Pain and sorrow rise from my gut and up through my chest and out my mouth in a most private song. It is as though I have been dangling by a thread to the Great Spirit, listening to my inner voice in the faint tune of my hawk-wing bone-whistle. As I walk on across the field my chant becomes a little louder, my body a bit lighter.

CHAPTER
TWENTY-FOUR

When I get back to the Greek Motel that night, I knock on Meadowlark's door with hopes of getting to know him better and finding out what a Brother to the Serpent is. I knock again, only to be disappointed that the door doesn't open.

The next morning I discover that Meadowlark's car is gone, and that prompts me to hurry to the motel office.

Did Meadowlark check out? I ask.

Yeah, says the old Greek who runs the motel. He left for the hills early this morning. I'm not sure where he lives. You staying another day?

No, I say, I guess I won't, since Meadowlark left. I looked at my map last night and Alcova Lake is only a few days away. I think I'll head that way and camp on the water and do some fishing.

Casper Mountain borders town to the west with such beauty that God must've been in good spirits when He breathed in that direction to create it. I walk the Trail between that mountain and the Platte River as I pass Fort Casper.

The river seems more powerful here than anywhere I've seen it so far as it twists and turns and boils in some pockets, as if hoping to suck drifting limbs down to its muddy bottom. The towering red cliffs along the water are jagged and antelope graze near the gulches. They study me with caution till I pass and they become part of bushes and boulders. A buzzard circles overhead, a dark, lonely creature in the sky, scouting the earth's carnivorous menu of deer, antelope, and jackrabbit.

I reach Alcova Lake and I've never seen anything like it in my life. I stand staring out over it and know that even the great Mediterranean Sea can't top it. Surrounded by hills and desert, the water is blue and green, splashing against the shore as the Wyoming wind sweeps across the land. As I walk closer to the lake, as big as a town, the sun reflects from it in such a way to make the water appear alive with gold and silver light looming from its depths. When a large fish jumps from the surface and lands back in the water with a big splash, I become so excited that I almost stumble over a rock. For all I know, I am seeing a mirage. Why aren't the banks jumping with people to celebrate this great gift of earth?

I bought a rod and reel for two bucks at the Salvation Army Thrift Store in Casper and some lures, hooks, and sinkers at a yard sale. With the worms I get at the marina, I cast into the lake with certainty that I'll catch a beauty, like the one that splashed the water only minutes ago.

My baited line lands in the lake some forty yards from the bank, where I stand ready to jerk when I get a bite. But some twenty minutes later nothing has touched my bait except for the wind, and who can catch that? I set my rod and reel on the ground and sit beside it. It's not always easy to wait for what's beneath the surface.

Every time I go fishing I recall when I was a boy and my father and I took our rods and reels to walk to a nearby creek feeding into a lake.

You stay here at the creek, said my father, and watch your float. I'll walk down to the lake and try my luck there.

I watched him walk to the lake, but eyeing my float soon got old. I sneaked up behind him to surprise him at the very moment he began to cast a giant plug with eight dangling hooks. One caught me in the ear as he jerked forward. The big plug, a green minnow with yellow spots, dangled from my ear as we walked up the road toward our house. We had to get pliers to cut the hook in two and pull it on though my ear. It didn't hurt to have a hook in my ear as we walked, but the look on my father's face was painful. Anytime my sisters or I got hurt he got angry. I didn't understand till I was grown that he got angry because he hated so much to see us hurt. He just didn't know how to show us it was love, not anger. That made him act so funny. Yes, sir, men sure do have trouble with emotion sometimes.

Sage is plentiful in Wyoming, and its dried, twisted trunks, as thick as my wrists, make ideal firewood. I gather some near the banks of the lake and build a fire to cook a vegetable soup of fresh onions, carrots, and potatoes. Sea gulls cry out as they float over my smoke and I throw them pieces of bread. I welcome such guests who sing songs in the sky.

After lunch, it's a treat to have a cup of coffee back at the marina. Sipping it, I daydream of returning to my line where a big one is hooked. But getting back to that line, I find that the fish here are even rarer in this lake than could be dreamed. They not only have pulled in my rod and reel but they've come from the water and taken my paper bag of lures, hooks, and sinkers as well as the worms. They also wear shoes. I hope the guy who took my gear is proud of himself for pulling off such a daring robbery. Lucky stars, my pack went with me to the marina. It would've been hell to have had my journal swiped as well and lost so many memories of people from this journey.

That evening I sit by the water and reflect on my travels, writing it down in my journal. I still can't say that all the sadness is gone about Sean or the approaching death of Ken, but my confidence is growing after the encounter with

Meadowlark. I'm feeling freer to feel and more optimistic that I'll meet more people I like. It's not for me to judge if our meeting was a coincidence or an act of the Great Spirit, but I continue to be thankful for it. For that matter, here by this beautiful and soothing lake, I have been counting my blessings for this entire journey so far. I'm over halfway to San Francisco now, and I'm still in one piece. I made it through the flu and no lunatic has shot me or stabbed me as I camped at night, no car or truck has run me down as I walked along the road so far. I've lost several pounds from all the walking and my leg muscles are in excellent shape, though my feet do still hurt like hell from time to time. I can't truly say that I'm feeling on top of the world about all my experiences on the wagon train, but I forgive those who were cool toward me or wanted to see me harmed or humiliated. I also forgive myself for starting to hide my true thoughts and feelings. It forced me to learn more about myself and I always welcome that, even if it sometimes isn't so flattering. I accept that I sometimes don't like being part of a group. I'm a bit of a misfit in the world, a romantic loner who sometimes must endure great loneliness. But right now, as the sun sets over Alcova Lake, I don't feel lonely at all. Rather, I celebrate my aloneness. I'm at peace and the gulls, drifting over the water, lift me into the sky with them. Oh, if only I could always be so light.

I've camped on Alcova Lake for two days now, and on the third day I walk to the marina for coffee and breakfast. Kyle, the marina owner, has let me bathe for free in a little cabin near the water and I enjoy talking with him and his nephew, Steve, who helps him run the restaurant. Steve is pouring me more coffee this morning, when I become curious about a conversation that he's having with Kyle.

When are we leaving for the branding? Steve asks.

It'll be a couple of days yet, Kyle tells him.

What's this branding? I ask.

It's an annual event, Kyle explains. The calves are rounded up and branded. All the ranchers take turns helping each other. It's an important time because it brings neighbors closer together.

Are these real cowboys?

Yes, most of them grew up on ranches. Cowboying is their whole way of life.

I'm tempted to see if I can go to this branding and meet these cowboys, but after some of the narrow minds I found on the wagon train, I'm not so sure I want to get burned again. Still, those on the wagon train seemed to be living out an Old West fantasy instead of being genuine cowboys. Maybe these guys are for real?

Any chance you could call those cowboys, I ask, and see if I could help them brand?

Sure, Kyle agrees. I know one of the foremen and his wife. I'll phone him right now.

When Kyle returns from the phone, he is wearing a smile. It makes me hopeful.

Everything is set, Kyle tells me. Bob Musfelt said you were welcome to come. He and his wife, Tammy, will put you up for the night.

Steve gives me a lift in his car some 10 miles down the road to the Pathfinder Ranch, which is named in honor of the explorer John Frémont. The sign hanging over the entrance is enough to make a man tip his hat: A steel cowboy sits atop his horse with a rope around a calf, and beneath them hangs the giant head of a steer with horns three feet long. It swings back and forth in the wind as Steve and I drive under it.

The Pathfinder Ranch has over 140,000 acres, which is 20 square miles. Steve has no idea where the branding is taking place on this vast ranch, and we can't find anyone home at the ranch houses. It looks like I'll have to be all by my lonesome till the cowboys come home for the night. Finally, though, we spot two women in a pickup truck and wave them down.

Any idea where the branding is? I call out to them.

Yeah, says the driver, it's about fifteen miles back in the mountains. We're headed that way now. You needing a ride?

I hop into the dusty, banged-up truck with the two young women and we head down a dirt road. An antelope leaps from the sage and crosses our path to race over prairie dog holes. It vanishes as we roll on and come upon a truck stuck in the mud. Two women and two children are trying to push it free. We get out to help, but it does no good.

We better leave it for later, says the driver of the stuck truck. They're waiting on the food. If we don't hurry, my husband will come looking for us.

I see fear in her face and we quickly unload the baskets of food from their truck into ours. I'm about to hop into the back with the kids and one of the women, when a third truck approaches. It's driven by a man who looks plenty pissed, and the fear in the woman's face increases. I never like to see one person fear another, and it especially bothers me if I see a man frighten a woman. He eyes me as if he wonders who the hell I am and what I am doing here. I begin to wonder if I've made a mistake in coming to this branding.

CHAPTER
TWENTY-FIVE

We move on down the dirt road for another four or five miles and nothing man-made can be seen save for our truck and the one driven by the stuck-in-the-mud husband. His wife's face has now become relaxed and this makes me feel more at ease about joining these folks at the branding. I take a deep breath of the fresh air as I behold the landscape, so beautiful that it seems that Lake Alcova itself has followed me to become the sky, with its wild and inviting blues and greens. A new sense of freedom rushes through me and I become excited to meet the cowboys who run this ranch.

A tent appears upon the vast horizon and hundreds of cattle and fifteen or twenty saddled horses gather behind it. Some fifty to sixty men, women, and children line up at a chuck wagon where a man with a red mustache stands over a grill to slice pieces from chunks of beef as big as the picnic baskets we unload from the trucks. The women now take baked beans, potato salad, and bread from those baskets, and the hungry cowhands look on as they hurry to get plates and forks. They grin as if everything is about to become right in the world.

I'm directed to Bob and Tammy, who offered to put me up tonight. She seems just a slight bit cautious, but Bob appears as happy as can be to meet me. I like the way he shakes hands. Just firm enough, as if he wants to show his strength without bragging.

Thanks for offering to put up a total stranger, I say.

You're no stranger, says Bob. Kyle recommended you and that's all I need. We'll get back to the branding after lunch. Won't you have something to eat?

I get some baked beans, a piece of bread, and a cup of coffee from a half-gallon pot. Bob introduces me to the others and I join them to eat under the tent, black clouds boiling in the west over the Seminoe Mountains.

We were out on the ranch just a few days ago, says Bob, and a storm caught us. A twister dropped down and hail started falling everywhere. I was pretty spooked. We drug our saddles from the horses as quick as we could and put them over us. I was glad when the hail stopped. The twister disappeared back into the clouds.

You didn't tell me about that, says Tammy.

I didn't want you to worry, says Bob as his fingers gently touch her hand.

An old man sits alone in a pickup. His door is open and he watches the cattle as if he's concerned that they might run away. I wonder about the blood on his hands, but more than that I wonder about the blood around his mouth and on his cheeks. He wears dark shades, a cowboy hat, and boots with his jeans tucked inside them. I wish I could see his eyes.

I see you got an electric branding machine, I remark to Bob, drawing my attention away from the old man. Is that what most ranches use now?

Most of them, says Bob. It makes an awful racket, but you don't have to worry about your branding iron cooling off like you do when you build a wood fire. You have to watch about tripping on the wires, though. Some people can't afford to buy an electric branding iron and the open fire sure is nice if it's a cold day. It's a good way to clean up old fence posts.

Boy, that was good food, he adds, wiping his mouth with his hand. You ready to brand some cows?

I'm willing to try, I say. I've never done it before.

As if a sudden spirit moves us, everybody leaves the tent and hurries into the corral, where the cattle huddle and bellow. Is all hell about to break loose? Cowboys hop atop their horses, and the gasoline generator for the branding iron begins to roar. It's a powerful sound and the cattle pick up their ears. Lariats twist and twirl through the air to snatch the hind legs of calves. The cowboys then wrap the ropes around the saddle horns, and the horses, as determined as soldiers, march forward to drag the bellowing calves through the dust and out into the open.

Each calf, as big as a mountain lion or bulldog, is flipped onto its back by two cowpokes. I join forces with Jay Stevenson, who was born and raised on this great ranch. His father was once the owner and his brother is now boss. While I pull the rope tight and up to my shoulder to throw the bawling calf off balance, Jay grabs his head to throw him to the hard, dusty ground.

Guard your teeth and eyes, warns Jay.

When the calf hits the dirt, Jay twists the animal's head while I shoot my left foot over the kicking hind leg. My two arms now grab the other leg, its hooves as sharp as the claws of a steel hammer. The animal surges with fear and its strength doubles as I hold tight, hoping to avoid a free-flying jab to the face.

While Jay and I try to hold the bellowing creature in the straitjacket of our hands and legs, another cowboy presses the red-hot branding iron into its hide. Smoke rises from the burning hair as a fourth cowpoke clamps a tag into the ear. A fifth helper—a boy of only eight or nine—approaches the calf with a gallon container strapped over his shoulder. A clear plastic tube, the thickness of a pencil, stretches from that container to a hypodermic needle, which the boy holds in his steady hand. He squats beside the animal and inserts the tip of the needle into its hip.

What he's doing? I ask Jay as we both struggle to keep the calf still on the ground.

He's inoculating the calf against diseases, says Jay.

When the boy removes the needle and backs away from the animal, the old man with dark shades and blood around his mouth hurries over with a bone-handled pocket knife in his rough, wrinkled hand. With lightning speed, he slices the balls off our beefy friend. It all happens so quickly that I don't notice what he does with them. Perhaps he swallows them or drops them in his pocket, to be divided among us later.

Let me release his head first, says Jay. Then you let go of his hind legs. It'll be safer that way.

When we release the calf, it runs back to the herd to seek its mother. Towering over me, Jay offers his hand and pulls me upward. His grip is strong and sure and it feels good to have a partner. While I may not pound my chest like Tarzan from having helped knife a calf, I do feel some surge of tribal connection to these cowboys. We work toward a common goal.

I was watching you, a cowboy grins at me. You held that dang calf like you thought it might turn into a bear.

It tried to kick like one, I smile.

You're strong, says Jay. Most people don't get the hang of it that fast.

No, says the cowboy who teased me. You got the muscle for it. We just like to play with newcomers a little. If we don't have some fun from time to time, we start to get too hard on ourselves and each other.

There's branding and gelding going on all around us and Jay and I soon begin the wrestling ritual again. Even women throw the calves to the ground. One is in her fifties and I like watching her strong arms at work and the determined look on her face. Her younger partner fascinates me even more. She wears dark shades and a pink cap. She's slender and graceful in such a way that she almost seems out of place out here. I wonder why she keeps glancing my way.

That I am almost trampled by a runaway horse pulling a calf from the herd is a point not worth belaboring. You learn to jump and roll in a split second here or get the hell out of the corral. The chairs are over in the tent for those who simply want to watch.

By the end of the day I'm tired from wrestling calves, but I like the peace it gives me. I've often found that hard physical work relaxes the body and clears the mind.

When all the calves have been branded, we mount horses and head for The Buzzard, a house with a giant kitchen and several dining tables, some five miles away.

The horse I ride does not have the spark and personality that Comanche did, but I feel on top of the world as I ride across the land, thick with sage, with the cowboys I've worked and joked with all afternoon.

Say, mister, says a huge cowboy on a horse, hurrying toward me to ride alongside, I sure am sorry I almost trampled you earlier today. My horse don't usually spook like that. He must've gotten a good look at my old ugly face.

No harm done, I say, thinking he's kind to mention it. It let me know I can still run when I have to.

You can sure jump, too, mister, he grins. I thought for a second you'd jump right out of your skin.

You worked on this ranch long? I say, becoming more amused.

He uses a pocket knife to cut a piece of tobacco and slide it into his mouth. His cheek bulges as he closes the knife blade and drops it into his pocket.

I don't work here at all, he says, almost choking as he tries to chew the piece of tobacco. I live down in Texas. I just come up once a year to help out for a few days because I like to see my friends here and look at these mountains. I don't know, it just somehow fills me up and makes me feel young again ever time I do it. I guess it's just something you're born with.

He offers one of the most beautiful and innocent smiles I've seen on this journey, and tobacco juice drips down the corner of his mouth. It's almost run to his chin when he rubs it on his sleeve.

It washes out, he says with an apologetic tone.

He then grins, nods, and kicks his horse with his spurs to make it race toward two other cowboys on horses some fifty yards ahead of us. As the horses' hooves rise and fall, they sling dust into the Wyoming wind, and I imagine for a few glorious and magical moments that they are the hooves of a horse ridden by a Pony rider back in 1860.

When the tobacco-chewing cowboy slows his horse to join his two friends, I look to my right to discover the slender woman with the shades and the pink cap. She rides her horse with such smoothness and grace that she seems to float through the air. When we arrive at The Buzzard and gather around the tables to eat dinner, she takes a chair across from me.

Mind if I sit here? she asks, setting down her shades and removing her cap. Her long hair falls over her shoulders.

No, I say, liking her clear and curious eyes. Please do.

What I really want to do is pick your brain.

Why *mine*? I say, feeling flattered but put on the spot.

You're a writer, aren't you? I wondered what you write.

People and places, I say. Thoughts and feelings. Things that happen along the Trail.

The two worlds, says the cowgirl. The internal world and the external world.

You must be a writer yourself, I say, or want to be?

I can't express myself very well. I try to put down what I

feel inside sometimes. I write poems sometimes about being a woman, a mother, a cowgirl.

The cowboy next to her pokes her with his elbow.

Tell him who you are, he says.

Oh, she says, lowering her head. You just shut up.

Who are you? I ask, my curiosity building.

I'm sorry. My name is Tanya Stevenson.

She's a world champion bareback bronc rider, the cowboy tells me.

No, says Tanya. It's nothing. I love to read, but my husband, Otie, doesn't like for me to. He thinks it's a waste of time.

Wait a second. You're a champion bronc rider?

Bulls, too, says the cowboy. She could ride a tornado.

I won the Women's Professional Rodeo Bareback Championship in 1979, 1980, and 1989. In 1979 and 1980 I won the Bull Riding Championship. My mother, Jan Yowen, who helped me brand today, is also a champion bull rider. Look what you're doing. You're getting into my brain instead of me getting into yours.

I'm a better listener than I am a talker, I say.

Bob, my host for the night, sits to my right while his wife, Tammy, sits next to him. Whatever the caution was I saw in her face when we met has vanished. She eyes me with warmth and openness. I feel just a bit naked when I discover that the entire table of some ten people has stopped talking to listen to Tanya and me. We are the pin heard hitting the floor.

You know what Tanya said about Otie not wanting her to read? says Bob. I feel the same the same way when Tammy reads. Except I don't think it's a waste of time. I just want the attention instead of the book getting it.

I admire your honesty, I tell Bob.

Yeah, laughs one of the cowboys, but he's more interesting when he tells a big lie.

Tanya's husband—he wears white feathers in his cowboy hat—turns thirty-six today and a birthday cake with a candle atop it is now placed on the table. Otie is blowing out that tiny flame when the ranch boss hurries into the room. He carries a ten-year-old girl in his arms. Her head hangs and her blond hair dangles toward the floor.

My God, says a woman hurrying to her feet. What happened?

The horse got me, Mama, says the little girl.

They were playing in the barn, says the ranch boss.

I'm sick, Mama, says the girl. My stomach hurts.

The girl is placed on a couch near the tables. Her mother puts a washcloth on her head and I'm concerned that the stomachache signals a possible concussion. But the nearest doctor is sixty miles away in Casper and nothing is said about him. One of the older cowboys goes over to the girl and sits on the edge of the couch. He puts his hand to the washcloth on the frightened child's head.

Well, I'll tell you, honey, he says, we all get knocked around and stepped on a little in life. But we get back up and keep going, don't we?

Yes, says the girl. That's what Daddy says.

Yes, that's what we do, says the old cowboy. We get back up and go on.

I still can't help but worry that the girl has been injured more seriously than anyone is saying.

Don't worry, Tanya tells me. She'll be okay. I'm a mother, and kids can take more knocks than we think possible.

Tanya takes me to the barn where the girl was trampled. It's here that she stores some of the saddles she won riding broncs and bulls. In her house, across from the barn, she shows me her gold and silver medals housed between the spokes of an antique wagon wheel that now serves as a coffee table with a glass top. Now that we are alone Tanya's face and eyes have taken on some new light, as if she's happy for us to have a few minutes away from the others. I guess most of us have a need to meet new people in new places with different thoughts than our own and imagine what it would be like to live like they do. I'm happy again to recall that I can come and go as I like along the Trail.

When Tanya and I come from her house, I spot Bob and Tammy standing by their truck and I head their way.

You looking for me? I say.

Yeah, says Bob, we're ready to leave.

Is the girl feeling better? I ask Tammy.

Yes, says Tammy, and so is her mother.

I climb into the truck with Bob and Tammy and we drive away from The Buzzard. As I watch Tanya wave good-bye, I look at her strong hand, a hand that sometimes holds a pen, sometimes a wild bronc. I feel drawn to her, a woman unafraid of even the poetry in her heart.

CHAPTER TWENTY-SIX

I hold the Native American belief that in the long run, man cannot own the earth. It owns us and always proves it in the end. But as Bob, Tammy, and I drive over a ranch containing twenty square miles of mountains and meadows, I must confess that I have a bit of admiration for the man who holds the deed to this land. In the next breath, however, I think of the homeless who own nothing but the clothes on their backs and sleep in cardboard boxes. If I owned this great ranch, I wonder if I would have the compassion and courage to give some of this land to them and help them build little houses.

Bob stops the truck, overlooking a lake. The water is held back by the Pathfinder Dam, built in 1909. We get out and walk a narrow pathway onto it. Save for a single coyote calling in the distance, the air is moved only by our breathing. The rusty remains of a crane used in building the dam over eighty years ago stands like a giant skeleton to honor those who worked here. All have become dust by now.

This is where I come sometimes, says Bob as he eyes the lake in the sunset, to be alone and walk and think.

I didn't know this, Tammy tells him. It's the first time I've ever been here.

It makes me feel good that they are now here together on the special spot. It makes me feel even better when Bob eases his arm around Tammy's shoulders.

I want to have my own ranch, says Bob. Doesn't have to be anything this big, but something that's mine. We tried it a few years back, but the winter was so rough my cattle froze. Then I made picnic tables for two years while Tammy worked as a guard at the Wyoming Women's Prison. The people I ranch with are good people, but the owner lives back in St. Louis. He's a little out of touch with what really goes on out here. He seems more interested in trying to impress visitors he brings than he does in caring for us who run the ranch. He bought those fancy longhorn steers to fence in near the ranch entrance so they'd be seen when people arrive, but they're good for nothing else. That big dance hall he built across from where me and Tammy live is nice, but I think the workers needed the money more. What can a little man say to a big banker? I'm not complaining so much as I am just looking forward to having my own place one day.

Don't worry, I tell Bob. You'll have it.

I hope you're right. A man can put more of himself into what is his.

We crawl back into the truck and move on across the land, thick with sage. It's almost dark when two sage chickens flutter from the ground to disappear into the twilight. We stop at a single grave no longer than my leg. Bob tells me it's the grave of a child who ate poisoned meat that was meant to kill coyotes. It's eerie now to hear a coyote call from the darkness as we stand looking at the old tombstone.

Cottonwoods tower around the little picket-fenced house where Bob and Tammy live. Rushing to greet them, three dogs wag their tails as if at last the day is complete now that their masters are home. When Tammy opens the screen door, twenty to thirty moths fly into the air, scattering in all directions against the moonlit night.

We had some kids over to stay a couple of nights ago, says Tammy. Their mattress is still set up in the living room and you can stay there.

She leads me to the living room and the mattress on the floor looks just right for a good night's sleep. Bob and Tammy's daughter, Jaime Lea, is thirteen months old and she is staying with their family till the branding is over later this week. Her box of toys—stuffed dogs and cats—sits between the mattress and the fireplace. I like how homey it is here.

Do you like popcorn? Tammy asks. I'm going to pop enough for the three of us.

Bob insists that I take my shower before he does. He claims that he has a couple of things to do before he can bathe, but I don't buy it. He just wants to make me feel at home.

What a treat to get clean in the shower after wrestling cattle in the dust. I come out of the bathroom to smell the bowl of popcorn Tammy has set by my bed. She and Bob have to get up at three in the morning for the branding and say good night.

Stay for a few days if you like, Bob urges me. Help yourself to anything in the kitchen.

They disappear into their bedroom and I dig into the popcorn. I'm so grateful to have the choice of sleeping or getting up when they do to help with another day of branding. I can stay for days or hit the Trail at noon. Not knowing just what I'll do makes sleep rich and life long.

When I awake at seven the next morning, Bob and Tammy have been gone for hours. I get dressed, make a fresh pot of coffee, and cook an egg sandwich. It's a great luxury to have a whole house to myself and I'm tempted to stay another day, but yesterday things at the branding went so well that I don't want to chance tarnishing the picture.

I write a thank-you note for Bob and Tammy and set it on the kitchen table, a bottle of Hunt's ketchup holding it in place.

My well-worn pack on my back, I head down the dirt road

toward the Pathfinder Ranch sign where the giant steel cowboy is lassoing a steer. Four—no, *five*—antelope stare at me
from the side of the road, then burst into a gallop, creating
dust behind them. The dust veils the sun, still red and orange.
I feel so good that I don't know what to do and break into my
own Eagle Dance. With my pack on my back, I dance in a
circle and let my arms flap like wings. My legs raise and
lower me, and my neck and back arch in a fluid motion, as if
I am part snake. The five antelope stop to stare at me as if
trying to figure out what I am doing. One thing I'm sure of is I
don't try to figure it out. I just know that it feels good and, for
the moment, that's enough for me.

The Trail winds on past Independence Rock, where more
pioneer names are carved in stone. This section of Wyoming
is wild and rugged and there are more antelope than there
are people. I spot my first golden eagle, sitting on a dead tree
near The Three Crossings Station on the Sweetwater River.
He looks as peaceful as a hummingbird on a red rose, but I
can see that his beak and claws could tear through flesh like
a razor when needed. I wish him long life, but if I could find
one of his brothers dead on the Trail I would gladly take a
wing bone to make a whistle to add to the hawk-wing bone
in my leather pouch. When I release a loud Cherokee chant,
the eagle leaps from the dead tree and soars toward the
mountains.

At the intersection of Highways 135 and 287, it is a great
joy to find a small grocery store. I go inside and buy some
supplies. A bottle of cold beer is paradise.

Two miles down the Trail, I climb a butte and sit on its
edge, letting my legs dangle over Wyoming. Many miles to
the west a lightning storm puts on one of the greatest shows
I've ever seen. It's easy to imagine that the flashes are veins of
fire in God's chest and He's feeling such passion that He
doesn't know what to do but explode with light. I wouldn't

want to be any closer to that storm, but I like the sharp edge of excitement it puts on the horizon.

I leave my pack at the base of the butte and roam the bank of an ancient creekbed with hopes of finding fossils or Indian and pioneer artifacts. Purple flowers and moss spot the ground as a prairie dog runs into a hole where a coyote seems to have once dug in vain. I bend over to pick up one of the flowers when I'm jolted by the sight of the skeletons of two great buffalo. They are huddled together as if they froze seeking each other's warmth in a snowstorm. How did they get lost from the herd, or were they a herd of two? Some of the mane is still strong and thick, as if it refuses to give up the ghost. I take a handful of the buffalo hair and place it in my pouch. When I get to the Utah desert, I plan to carve a pony from the limb of a cottonwood. I will use the hair for the tail and mane of that pony.

I slip into my pack and move on down the Trail. The lightning storm to the west continues to feed the sky and earth with yellow fire, but I find myself looking back to the spot where I found the two dead buffalo. I hear the thunder their hooves once made. From where I now stand I can barely see their massive heads and white ribs sticking from the ground among purple patches of moss and sage. As I walk on toward the next town they fade into the earth, as if becoming dust before my very eyes.

CHAPTER
TWENTY-SEVEN

Remember in the Old West movies how when the cowboy hits the end of a cattle drive or a long ride across the desert he races into town and pays to take a bath in a big wooden tub? You can hear him moan in great delight as someone pours clean, warm water over him to wash away all his dust and worry. That's how I feel when I get a motel room in Lander, Wyoming, and take a shower.

One of the first things I see when I leave the motel room to eat some lunch is a poster advertising Old West Days in the city park today. It promises demonstrations in arrowhead making, weaving, knife and tomahawk throwing, and gold panning. I find all these things interesting, but I'm especially excited about the gold panning, because it was the Gold Rush of 1849 that sent Americans into a frenzied race to California to strike it rich. Being so far from home left them starved for letters from family and friends, and this inspired the need for the creation of the Pony Express.

I study the poster's map to see how to get to the Old West Days in the park and walk that way. The town is filled with towering cottonwoods and some of the pea-size pods on the trees have already opened; cottonlike fibers float in the summer air, as if seeking a woman's soft, blowing hair to land in for comfort. The mountains to the west are snowcapped, but the lower elevations are covered with great patches of purple flowers. They become brighter as I approach the park, at the base of a mountain.

The Old West Days in the park is a fine sight to behold. Men, women, and children gather to eat from a chuck wagon pot hanging over an open fire. It smells like chile to me, spicy and rich. Eight or ten men are dressed in the furs of coyotes, beavers, and deer. One of these Old West mountain men wears a necklace of bear claws. His beard is over a foot long and a hunting knife hangs from his belt, decorated with red and blue beads. He carries a muzzle-loading rifle, and his clear eyes have such a sharpness that I bet he could shoot a fly off the nose of a rabbit fifty yards away. Only a few feet from this mountain man sit two women, operating a loom to make cloth. Next to them, under a tree, an Indian chips stone with the tip of a deer antler to shape an arrowhead.

A stream, no wider than a small woman's waist, runs through the center of the grassy park, and several people have gathered to watch a man stand in the water as he demonstrates how to pan for gold. He is over six feet tall with broad shoulders and a big mustache. He wears glasses and red suspenders. His hat is as faded as mine. When I approach him to join the others and savor his experienced hands on the pan, he begins to study me.

That wraps up this demonstration, he says with a voice I find rich and warm. Next one will be in thirty minutes.

He steps from the little stream as the crowd thins. I'm disappointed that I arrived as the demonstration was ending, but it gives me an opportunity to talk with him. I try to catch his attention.

What can I do for you? he asks, setting his pan next to a plastic two-gallon bucket that holds dirt containing gold he used in the demonstration.

I explain about my journey down the Trail and why gold was so important to the creation of the Pony Express. He listens carefully, as though to weigh every word.

It would mean a lot to me, I say, if you could take me to pan for gold back in these mountains. I'd like to see what the real thing is like.

I'll tell you, son, he says, the last time I talked to a writer he wrote a story and got all the facts mixed up. That didn't bother me as much as his attitude. He only had bad things to say about America and that got under my skin.

I'm sorry you got burned, I say. I know how that feels. When I meet people who have only negative things to say, it makes me wonder what happened to them to think that way. I love life myself. I can't say I find America to be perfect, but for the most part I think it's a wonderful country.

He takes off his hat and wipes the sweat from his forehead, sitting down at the picnic table only a few feet away. When he eyes me again, his eyes have warmed a little.

What'd you say your name was? he asks.

Jerry Ellis. I offer my hand. I'm from Alabama.

I'm Sam Peterson, he says, taking my hand. If I took you to pan at one of my spots, you think you could keep its where-abouts a secret?

Yes. I look him straight in the eye. I think I could arrange that.

The old prospector finally offers me a subtle but welcome grin. He places his old faded hat back on his hot head.

You meet me here tomorrow at two o'clock, he tells me. We'll try our luck back down on Beaver Creek south of here at Atlantic City.

That night I check my map and discover that Atlantic City is south of Lander some twenty-five miles down Highway 28, which crisscrosses the original Pony Express Trail. That's the highway I'll walk when I part with Sam after panning for gold. I also see from the map that I'm almost across the state of Wyoming, its border not that far from Salt Lake City.

The next afternoon I slip into my pack and head for the

park to meet Sam. I load my pack into his truck and we leave Lander.

I didn't mean to bite your head off yesterday, when we first met. I was tired and—

I understand, I say. Sometimes it's hard to trust a total stranger. How long have you been prospecting?

I'm sixty-three and a retired miner. I've looked for gold my whole life. It gets in your blood. Gold fever is very real. Aren't these mountains something? I think God was having wife trouble when He created them. He threw trees and rocks everywhere.

I find that men and women the age of Sam have, for the most part, matured and mellowed to such a degree that they offer not only wisdom but also a certain abandonment that makes them fun and easy to be around. In other words, they have dropped ego and bullshit. The Big Roundup is getting too close for them to play games with themselves.

Back in 1948, Sam tells me as we speed down the highway, my daddy found a young man sick on the Pony Express Trail. He had come out on a horse from back East looking for excitement and all that. But he came down with spotted tick fever. Daddy took him home and put him in bed. It looked like he would die, but three weeks later he pulled out of it. His father owned a car dealership back in Chicago and offered Daddy a new Chevy at cost for being so kind to his son. So Daddy and me caught the train all the way to Chicago and drove that new car back home.

Sam and I take a dirt road off Highway 28. A few cabins are scattered here and there. In the severe winters, only two people stick it out, Sam tells me. He has a home in Lander as well as a cabin here.

Right through here, he explains, is where the gold vein runs for seven miles. Millions of years of erosion has washed some of the gold into Beaver Creek. Now let's go over this again. You promise not to tell anybody where this spot is I'm taking you to?

I promise.

We go to his cabin first. Sam takes great pride in showing me the head and skin of a black bear on his wall.

I was out elk hunting, says Sam, when I heard something on the trail behind me. I turned just as this big black turned to smell my partner hunting back behind him. I got lucky and one shot killed him. He was good eating, too. I put this cabin together myself from two I bought and tore down. It was to be my dream house, but me and my wife now spend the winters down in Arizona. I found a three-ounce nugget there in the desert with a metal detector. Oh, but this cabin, it makes me a bit sad but I may sell it. If I've learned anything in my life, it's that everything changes. Even a man's deepest dreams.

Sam pulls out a drawer and sticks his giant hand inside. He removes two wires twisted together about six inches long. He grins at me.

Know what they are? he asks. Pieces of the original telegraph line that replaced the Pony Express. I found them myself over on the Trail.

Could I hold them? I ask, wishing they were mine.

I take the twisted wires and they're as valuable to me as gold. It fills me with excitement and mystery that in my hands I hold a piece of this country's history. It makes me just a bit sad, though, that the "lightning wires" meant the death of the Pony Express, with its daredevil riders. It's a typical but curious twist of human nature that Americans got so used to getting the mail across the country in ten days on the Pony Express that they began to want to get it faster and faster. This gave increased momentum to stretching telegraph wires across the Great American Desert. Only a few weeks after the Pony Express had thrilled the country with its speed, Congress stepped into the picture and passed a bill offering a subsidy of forty thousand dollars per year for ten years to the company that would connect East and West by "talking wires." The right to cut poles and take other natural materials from public lands for construction was also granted. Bids to build the telegraph line were submitted to the secretary of the treasury, and in the spring of 1861 construction crews began work on the telegraph lines in the East and the West. Twenty-five poles per mile were called for. A contest between the crews was set in motion to see who could cover the most ground. It's ironic that the death of the Pony Express was delivered by the Pony riders themselves, racing past the wires and crews stretching them, for they brought news of just how far the telegraph rivals had progressed each week.

Ready to find that gold? Sam asks as he places the telegraph wires back in the drawer where he got them.

We crawl back into his truck and head down Beaver Creek. Wooden buildings crumble to the earth where mine shafts once deepened with hopeful diggers.

This is not so good, says Sam. The snow has melted more than I thought and raised the water over the spot where I usually dig. We'll get out here, though, and try it.

Sam puts on rubber boots that come up to his knees. He wades out into the creek with a long shovel. I offer to do the hard work, but he won't listen. Maybe the very way the shovel enters the earth brings good luck.

Even if we don't find gold today, says Sam, just look where we are. We got sun; mountains; fresh, clean air, and a beautiful stream. What I'm doing now it digging down to false bedrock. Gold gets caught in clay and that's what we're after. Right here behind this big rock is a good place to look because it prevents the stream from washing it away.

His tone makes gold seem like a creature that lives and breathes as much as man. It hides in veins and behind big rocks. It listens and sniffs for man and bites him on the ankle to fill his soul with gold fever. As Sam fills my pan with clay and rocks from the stream I begin to wonder if I haven't already gotten a taste of the venom from the air itself. Gold, gold, *I want gold*. Nuggets as big as marbles. Baseballs. Basketballs.

Gold is heavier than other metals, says Sam. It will sink to the bottom. Work the pan round and round and get the lighter stuff to wash out. When you hold the pan down in the water like this, it's called the Australian method. Hold it up out of the water like this and it's called the Alaskan method. See all these dark stones? They got iron in them and that's a good sign. You find gold with iron. Look, look there in the bottom at what you got.

Sam is so excited that he almost slips on a wet rock to fall into the creek. He grabs his shovel just in the nick of time to save himself.

I take a closer look at the pan and discover three or four flakes of gold, shining a pale yellow in the sunlight. Sam now shows me how to take each flake of gold from the pan by easing the tip of his finger to it, as if he were doing heart surgery with a delicate instrument. Once the flake sticks to the finger he places the gold speck to the mouth of a tiny bottle filled with water. When he turns the bottle upside down, the water falls against that finger to wash the gold from Sam's skin. Sam screws the cap back on the bottle and holds it toward the sun so we can wonder at the gold, resting in the water at the bottom of the bottle like some sunken treasure.

As Sam and I continue to dig and pan the stream we just may decide to take over the world with our riches. Within an hour we have enough gold to buy a small box of crackers. If they are on sale.

The sun is starting to set when Sam and I leave Beaver Creek. We crawl back into his truck and move on out of the hills till we come to the old Oregon Trail, the ruts from the wagon wheels still visible. A Pony Express marker, as big around as my arm and made of concrete, sticks four feet from the sage-covered earth.

Let's get out for a while, says Sam, opening his door.

We walk on down the Trail till we come to a plaque honoring a mass grave of eighteen Mormons. They were members of a handcart company who froze to death in a snowstorm as they marched toward Salt Lake City in the 1850s.

The plaque says they died right here, says Sam, but it makes no sense that they would have sought shelter in this spot. See that cliff just over there? That's where they tried to save their lives. I have found pieces of their carts with my metal detector.

Seeking freedom from bigotry, the Mormons began the long and harsh journey West out of St. Jo and Independence, Missouri. Many were so poor that they could not afford wagons, so they walked and pushed handcarts. One such walker was Thomas Dobson, who became a Pony rider in Utah. When he emigrated with this family in 1856, he walked *barefoot* all the way from the Sweetwater River, near where I found the two dead buffalo, to Salt Lake City.

As Sam and I stand overlooking this place where so many died, the wilderness's great, gentle silence seems to honor them. This tranquillity, however, is shattered when a gunshot rings out across the land, echoing off the surrounding mountains to fill the twilight with an eerie jolt. Standing in the open like this makes me feel vulnerable and my heart begins to pound. I turn to Sam to find his eyes now charged with fear. A second shot explodes to echo louder and I quickly search the land to seek whoever holds the gun. Discovering only approaching darkness, I become alarmed that some drunk or lunatic may hold us as human targets in the cross hairs of some disturbed fantasy.

Where are those shots coming from? I shout.

I don't know, says Sam, his look worried.

The next few seconds I feel frozen as fear builds in me. When a third shot rings out, Sam and I look at each other and begin to run for the truck. When we hop inside and slam the doors, I feel a little protected—but my heart is still pounding, my mind racing. Sam starts the motor and we take off up the dirt road. Neither one of us speaks, as if we're holding our breaths to make certain no bullet shatters the windshield.

Some fifteen minutes later, I'm calming down as we get back up in the mountains near Beaver Creek by Atlantic City. It's almost dark when Sam takes me to a campsite I noticed when we arrived this afternoon. The stars are coming out as I hop from the truck with my pack.

I hope you'll come visit me one day. I swing the pack over my shoulder. We'll go pan for gold in Dahlonega, Georgia.

I've heard about that deposit, says Sam. I've always wanted to try it.

You got my address.

You just may hear me knocking one day, Sam promises.

He grins and the red taillights of his truck disappear into the darkness as I enter the campsite. I'm the only one here and I pitch my tent among a grove of aspen. I took a tour one time with a forest ranger in Colorado and he said that each aspen in a grove is connected by its root system. If a man took a knife and cut a piece from one, then a dark spot would appear on all the other connected trees in the same place of the cut. I've thought a lot about that story and I can't help but wonder if people are connected in a similar way. How one person treats another must have something do with how that person treats the next. I wonder if sometimes we don't stick it to the next guy because we felt somebody stuck it to us. If someone is gentle and loving to us, maybe we want to pass that on as well. I've always thought that trees had wisdom, stretching from down in the earth to the very sky itself.

I'm about to crawl into my tent when I recall the big black

bear on Sam's cabin wall. His teeth and claws were long and sharp enough to tear me apart. I take my food supplies from my pack and hang them in a tree, far from my tent.

I crawl into the tent and slip into my sleeping bag. I curl up and savor my own body heat as I remember that I lie atop a gold vein seven miles long, thoughts of these riches dancing in my head as I drift into deep sleep.

CHAPTER
TWENTY-EIGHT

The aspen leaves are still a young and tender green and they quiver in the morning breeze as I break camp. I walk only a couple of minutes till I discover fresh moose tracks in the dirt. They are as big as a horse's hooves and I'm tempted to see how far I can track the owner. I decide, however, to make tracks of my own and push on down Highway 28.

I carry my inflatable sleeping pad rolled up and tied to my pack with a leather strap, and when I stop to take a drink of water from my canteen I discover that the pad is coming loose. I untie it with thoughts of securing it and set it next to my pack so I can first take another drink of water. I am at the top of a hill, however, and the wind blows the rolled pad down the hill. It bounces over a ledge and lands some eight or ten feet lower against a rock, some seventy or eighty feet from it to the base of the clifflike hill.

I start down toward the pad through loose rock and dirt when all of a sudden my footing gives way. I slide like any fool till luck helps my feet catch the same rock as my pad. Luck or no luck, however, I feel frightened. It is not a straight drop-off to the bottom, but if I fall from here I stand a good chance of tumbling into a broken arm, leg, or neck. So here I am, caught in the middle. It is ten feet back to the top over a fragile surface, or seventy feet down to Broken Bone City. All of this for a piece of plastic you blow air into. Please, no applause. Not everyone can be as smart as me. Now, in an Old Western a cowboy could whistle for his horse to drop a rope down the hill or lower his tail to pull his master out of danger. I can certainly whistle, but unless my pack has a secret it's been keeping from me, it won't budge even if I whistle "The William Tell Overture."

Hoping for the best but fearing the worst, I take a deep breath, lift the pad, and throw it up next to my pack. It begins to slide and a couple of stones roll toward me, an avalanche in the making. But the pad slows to a stop and no more rocks head my way, though I can't be certain that gravity won't play a dirty trick at any second and send the whole hillside down to pay me a most uninvited visit. I finally get the nerve to step forward. I become startled as my foot starts to slide backward and I fall toward the ground, my hands slamming against dirt and rocks. Like a madman, I begin to claw the earth as I squirm my way to the top.

When I reach my pack, I stand to find blood dripping from my hands, tiny, sharp pebbles embedded in the palms. But they hardly hurt and I'm so relieved to make it to safety that I roll a big rock down the hill just where I have crawled from. It crashes to the bottom, knocking others down along with it, and I rejoice in the-path-not-taken.

Still a bit startled, I decide to take a break from walking and remove my pack so I can sit under a tree. The wind has started to blow and I take off my hat to feel the air against my sweaty head. My palms are stinging a bit from the pebbles that pierced them when I fell, and I open my canteen to pour water over them. What a joy now simply to stretch out in the sun and feel the very solid and level ground beneath me.

As I continue to laze in the sun I spot Green River in the great distance, meandering across the land, which seems timeless without buildings or telephone poles. Thinking about time, and how things often change over the years, makes me wonder what Sir Richard Burton experienced when he traveled through here on a stagecoach in 1860. I dig into my pack for his diary and read:

> . . . We had now fallen into the regular track of Mormon emigration, and saw wayfarers in their worst plight, near the end of their journey. We passed several families, and parties of women and children trudging wearily along: most of the children were in rags or half nude, and all showed gratitude when we threw them provisions.

How easy my trek now seems compared to what the Mormons faced back in 1860. As I read on in the diary I learn that Sir Richard soon reached Salt Lake City. This makes me want to arrive there as well, because a part of me longs to behold city lights and wonder at strangers' faces, my loneliness looking me in the eye yet once again.

Except for some three hundred miles by wagon and horseback, I have mostly walked so far. But I promised myself I would allow the luxury of an occasional ride. When I reach the Utah border, I make a sign on the back of a letter from a fifth-grader back in Nebraska, go to the road, and hold out the sign saying SALT LAKE CITY.

An hour passes and hundreds of cars and trucks shoot past me and my sign. I'm relieved when a small pickup finally stops. The driver looks to be about twenty-three, his eyes so intense that I suspect he is high. I hope it is from travel and not from speed or booze. I open the door and wait to hear his tone of voice as I sniff the air for beer, whiskey, or grass.

How far you going? I ask him.

San Francisco, he says. My band has a gig out there. I'm from Washington, D.C. The way you were standing made me think you had a purpose.

I'm retracing the Pony Express Trail.

Cool, he says. I'll take you on into Salt Lake City.

He opens the back of his truck and I place my pack inside. On the side window, finger-written in dirt, is FRISCO or DEATH. We get into the cab and hit the road.

My name's Fred, he tells me. I haven't talked to anybody in three days. I was writing in my journal when I saw you standing there.

You write in your journal and drive at the same time? I ask.

It's not as hard as you think. You just have to keep the pen on one line while you keep the truck between two other lines.

I keep a journal myself, I say, glad that he's not trying to steer and write at the same time now.

You do? he says. That's a coincidence. You been to California before?

Yes, I used to live in L.A. and San Francisco.

I've never been before, Fred admits. I'm a little scared. I just hope my car makes it. My band, Birds in the Wind, just got a recording contract in Frisco. We got a club to play, too. We do industrial music and try to reach workers, but we get a lot of the late-night leather crowd.

He sips a diet Coke as if it is laced with speed, but I decide that he is just starved for someone to listen to him after driving for three days across country. It doesn't take but a couple of questions to get him off and running again.

The toughest thing I ever did, he says, was get off drugs. When I was eighteen, I slept in Dupont Park in D.C. and used my boots for a pillow. If I didn't sleep there, I'd find a squat, an old abandoned house to crash in. I panhandled for dope money. I've been straight for three years now. I even went back to high school when I was nineteen. That was scary and took even more courage than this trip. If somebody tried to sell me dope today, I'd punch his nose. No, more than that, I'd kill him. You know why? Because he'd be trying to kill me if he offered a fix. My music has had a lot to do with saving me. When I was fifteen I was a computer whiz. I was written about in *Newsweek.* I was one mean hacker. I could do anything a telephone operator could do. I once charged a guy I didn't like twelve thousand dollars on his phone bill. Getting busted helped straighten me out. I combined my computer ability with music and became a musician.

Sounds like things are going your way now, I say.

Yeah, he says, but I still wrestle with myself about some things. Take God, for example. I'm torn about whether He exists or not. If He exists, how can He let all the suffering go on in the world? You got babies born who are addicts. You got kids on the streets selling crack just so they can buy certain brands of tennis shoes. What's happening to our values in America today? I have an agreement with the members of my band. If we catch each other even drinking, we're to kick ass.

The massive mountains are green as we enter Utah and the tops are snowcapped. It is a bit sad to leave Wyoming, which was so good to me, but I become excited on seeing the lights of Salt Lake City. This is the first *city* I will have encountered on the Trail, and a new sense of adventure begins to brew. Fred suggests that we get a motel room together to save on money, but wanting my freedom for the night, I pass and wish him Godspeed on to San Francisco.

As I hike across town toward the American Youth Hostel to get a room for the night I'm spellbound by the beauty of Salt Lake City. The streets are clean and lined with trees, swaying in the breeze. There're certainly plenty of cars moving here and there, but I don't hear a single motorist honking in hurry or anger. Two girls skip rope and laugh on a sidewalk before a house as though they have nothing to fear in the darkness. On the steps of that same house a man and woman sit talking, their voices drifting through the night with tones of warmth and comfort. Then, as if looming from the sky itself, I spot a towering cathedral. When its bells begin to ring, I feel as though they sing to welcome me from the sometimes trying Trail. Even the great mountains to the east of the city seem to stand guard over this pristine setting, the moon offering its soft, soothing light.

I find the hostel, located in a cozy neighborhood with an American flag waving from a pole towering before its doorsteps. I've arrived just in time, for most of the rooms have already been filled with people from all around the world. As I crawl into my clean bed I hear a man and woman speaking French in the room next to mine. Their voices soon grow softer and I begin to hear moans of lovemaking.

I get a good night's rest and the next morning I leave the hostel for breakfast. The houses I pass along the street are so clean and beautiful that I almost wonder if they're real. Red and yellow roses bloom in all directions along fences, and the lawns are manicured. A dove coos from a cage hanging from a tree branch that stretches out over a patio. Less than twenty feet from that patio a man holds a hoe and digs around tomato plants, thick with lush red tomatoes. He has a scar on his chin and I wonder what happened to him.

You got some big tomatoes on those plants, I say to him.

Would you like one? says the man.

Thanks, but I'm in need of coffee right now.

Coffee's bad for you.

His tone is judgmental and his eyes harden, as if I have suddenly fallen from grace. I'm so surprised by his impassioned reaction in such a tranquil setting that it makes me wonder what else might lurk beneath the surface of this entire city.

I walk on down the sidewalk and soon spot The Roasting Company, a modern, two-story coffeehouse. I go inside, and sunlight coming from over the snowcapped Wind River Mountains is reflected in the natural pine walls. People of all ages sit around sipping coffee, nibbling pastries, reading, and writing. I get a coffee and take a seat.

Across the room is a woman in her early twenties sitting by herself. She's wearing shorts that reveal long, tanned legs, and a gold bracelet dangles from her right wrist. It jingles as she writes with great passion in what appears to be a journal. From time to time, she raises her head and looks my way with a faint but inviting smile. I'm trying to get up the nerve to go say hello to her, when she stands up to leave. I wish I had been a little faster.

Over here, honey, I hear a voice say from close by me. Looking up, I see a towering man in his fifties with a big red beard and a gut sticking over his belt.

The man, carrying two cups of coffee, sits at the table next to me. The woman, her black hair hanging almost to her waist, carries a suitcase and joins him. She places ten containers of Half & Half on the table along with ten packs of sugar.

Boy, does it feel good to sit down, says the red-bearded man, eyeing me.

Yes, I nod. This is a good place to rest.

Me and my wife here sure need that, he says, opening five packs of sugar to pour them into his cup. We been on the road for two weeks now. We're hitchhiking to D.C., where I got a son. We tried to hop a train in Las Vegas, but the railroad cops threw us off. So far this is a good town. I cleaned a man's windshield this morning and he gave me five dollars. These Mormons are real good people. I preached for seventeen years. That's how I met my wife here. She came forward to receive the Lord. She's a beautiful woman, but we both look a bit worn at the moment. I almost got killed three days ago in the desert. I was about to step on a rattlesnake when God opened my eyes. A snake is an evil creature.

I'm both amused and touched by this man. I may be totally wrong, but I get a feeling in my gut that he's trying to con me.

I worked in the New Orleans French Quarter for eight years and you learn to smell more than whiskey and perfume.

If you're short on money, I say, you can probably find a shelter here in Salt Lake City.

I'm sure of that, says the man, but we'll never stay in another one of those. Last time we did I awoke in the night to find a man over our bed. He had his hand on my wife. I can't put up with such as that. It's not easy to get a job, either. If I find one, what do I do with my wife in the meantime? I can't set her down somewhere like a box and then just pick her up later. I'll tell you the truth, mister, I'm getting afraid that all these military bases that Bush is closing down are going to be turned into camps for the homeless. I just hope they don't make us do forced labor.

No, I say, that wouldn't be much fun.

I get up to leave as the bearded man opens a sixth package of sugar for his coffee. His wife, on the other hand, is a fan of the Half & Half. Four or five drops splatter on the wooden table.

Good luck on your trip to D.C., I tell them. Hope you find your son.

The best to you, too, mister, the man says. We're all in the same boat whether we know it or not.

I head out the door with a sparrow of guilt on my shoulder. I don't have much cash, but maybe I should have given the man and his wife a few bucks. Who is to say that I won't be living off sugar and Half & Half by the time I reach the Pacific Ocean?

CHAPTER
TWENTY-NINE

 I'll have a gin and tonic, I tell a bartender that afternoon in a bar and grill named Sea Gulls.

You a member? he asks me.

I don't know, I confess. Of what, the human race?

The fat bartender wears a little black bow tie and a yellow pencil sticks behind his ear. He was using it to work a crossword puzzle when I entered Sea Gulls. Painted on a wall behind him is a flock of gulls picking locusts from the air, and a field of wheat. He finally grins.

You're not from Salt Lake City, are you?

No, I'm from the South. A little town in North Alabama near Chattanooga, Tennessee.

Thought I recognized that accent, he tells me. No, the drinking laws here are screwy. You got to be a member of each bar to get hard liquor, unless somebody who's already a member will vouch for you.

The bartender turns toward the end of the bar, where a man sits sipping a drink as he reads a newspaper. Crutches lean against the table next to him, his right leg in a cast. On the cast in big, bold letters is written SLOWPOKE.

Hey, Sammy, calls the bartender. Want to vouch for this man so he can have a gin and tonic?

The man looks up from the newspaper and gives me the

eye. Then he raises his hand as if to be counted for in some great decision.

Yeah, why not, he says. These damn Mormons can't keep everybody from having a drink or two when he wants it. Just watch yourself while you're in town, Alabama, some of the people here will try to tell you how to think and what to believe.

Thanks for vouching for me, I say. Could I borrow some money as well?

His eyes harden and then he begins to laugh. Finally, with his great vouching mission accomplished, his head disappears once again between the pages of the newspaper.

As I sit sipping my gin and tonic I study the painting of the gulls on the wall. It makes me remember a story I once heard about how the locusts were devouring the Mormons' crops. They prayed to God for help and the sea gulls came to eat the bugs. I've always been touched spiritually by such stories and, recalling this one now, it reminds me that one of the main reasons that Sir Richard Burton traveled to Salt Lake City was to meet the city's spiritual founder, Brigham Young. I'm still thinking about this when I return to the hostel, so I decide to see what Sir Richard wrote in his diary when he met this famous man:

> . . . His manner is at once affable and impressive, simple and courteous: his want of pretension contrasts favorably with certain pseudo-prophets that I have seen . . . He shows no signs of dogmatism, bigotry, or fanaticism, and never once entered—with me at least—upon the subject of religion. . . . His temper is even and placid; his manner is cold . . . but neither is he morose. . . . His powers of observation are intuitively strong. . . . If he dislikes a stranger at the first interview, he never sees him again. . . . His life is ascetic: his favorite food is baked potato with a little

buttermilk, and his drink water. . . . Of his education I can not speak: "men, not books—deeds, not
words" has ever been his motto. . . .

Closing the diary, I set it on my bed and ponder the con-
trast between what Sir Richard found when he met the Mormon leader, Brigham Young, and what the man at the bar
called Sea Gulls said about the Mormons. Deciding to write
about this in my journal, I take it out to the steps of the hostel
and sit down.

I'm starting to write when a woman comes up the sidewalk
to offer one of the prettiest smiles I've ever had the pleasure
to warm my eyes. I like that she now turns from the sidewalk
and moves toward the steps where I sit.

Hello, she says.

Hi, I say. You sound French. Are you?

No, she says. I am from Austria. Could I sit with you for a
while?

She's in her early twenties and her smile is not one of
flirtation as much as it is one of warmth and playfulness. I
can't stop staring into her clear blue eyes. Maybe I've been
even lonelier than I realized.

Please, have a seat. What's your name?

Andrea. She sits next to me.

How long have you been traveling? I ask her.

Three weeks. This is my first trip to America. I arrived in
Los Angeles three weeks ago to see a friend. Now I am traveling by myself. And *you*?

She wears shorts and her left knee has been skinned. Her
cheeks are sunburned. She wears her blond hair short; the
wind plays with a few strands that keep falling down over
her right eye. She eases them away as if innocent of how
such a simple gesture makes her all the more alluring. I doubt
if she has any true idea just how beautiful she is.

And *you*? she repeats. What are you doing here?

I'm retracing the Pony Express Trail, I tell her. I keep a journal and take photographs. Have you heard of this Trail?

Yes. Her eyes are impish. Where is your horse Trigger?

He's up in my room taking a nap.

And are all your letters safe? she asks me.

Those imaginary letters are certainly safer than my very real heart just now. I've just met this Austrian beauty and I already want to hold her. If it were simply lust, it would be much easier to look at her, but I already feel a kindred spirit.

I haven't had lunch yet, I say. Have you?

No. Shall we fix something in the hostel kitchen?

I saw a restaurant nearby that looked good, I say. Let's go there and I'll treat.

We go to lunch at Cedars of Lebanon, where the Middle Eastern food is good and cheap and where belly dancers perform on the weekends. I'm so excited to have met Andrea that I can hear the bells of the dancers jingling and jangling though they are nowhere in sight.

I play classical guitar, says Andrea, but I sold mine for five hundred dollars to make this trip to America. I also draw and paint, but I'm not sure yet if I have the discipline that it takes to succeed. A person must put his whole heart and soul into it. That's one reason I took this trip. I wanted to find out more about who I am inside and what I want out of life. It is also part of my father's dream that I am following.

I don't understand.

It is not so easy for me to understand, either—she lowers her head—after what happened in Los Angeles.

She takes a bite of food and chews as if trying to heighten my curiosity. Or maybe she is simply trying to decide how much she feels comfortable in revealing.

My father, she begins, was forced into Hitler's army when he was only seventeen. The war did things to him he cannot talk about. At least, he does not talk to me about these things. When the war ended, he wanted to come to the United States and start a new life. His first wife refused and he stayed for her. By the time they had three children, he was sad and trapped. His dream was gone, except now through me. His second wife is my mother. Now I am scared that I have killed his dream for the second time.

But you're here, I say.

Yes, I am here, but . . .

She trails off into discreet silence, but a haunting look moves over her young, sensuous face. Though I'm curious to know what is going on inside her, part of me says I'll be smart not to push for more information just now.

There is a piano concert tonight in the Mormon cathedral, says Andrea. The pianist is from Vienna, where I live. Would you like to go with me?

Yes, I tell her, thinking that I would like to go almost anywhere with her.

I'm glad. She smiles as if I were being welcomed into her home.

The sun begins to set as we leave the hostel to head for the piano concert. Sitting on the steps where I met Andrea, a German and a Japanese practice their English. The vocabulary is that of a four-year-old. They grope to tell each other about their journeys. How often I take my own language for granted. I am impressed that Andrea is fluent in both German and English.

I speak French, too, she says. But not so well.

Pink and purple hollyhocks bloom along our walk. Cherry trees, planted by the sidewalk near the grave of Brigham Young, hang heavy with the red fruit. I gather a handful from a low limb, and some of the sweet, sticky juice stains my fingers. I give half the cherries to Andrea.

See if you can catch one in the air with your mouth, says Andrea as she throws one overhead.

I try to catch it, but it falls to the ground. I throw one to her, but she misses it as well.

I don't think the circus will employ us, she says. Unless it is to clean up.

We walk down the hill from Brigham Young's grave to behold the towering cathedral. When we enter this pristine building, I follow Andrea to sit in a wooden pew near the front. The pianist soon appears and begins to play Mozart, an Austrian like Andrea. He plays with such power and beauty that I am touched, but I am truly moved when I see how it makes Andrea smile. She leans forward, as though a couple of inches can make a great difference.

As I listen to the music and eye her excited face the next thirty minutes I realize further how much I need things of beauty to help me deal with life's occasional ugliness. To a romantic like myself, the lips of a woman can go a long way in nurturing that beauty. At times, the mere sight of a sensuous mouth has helped me forget all pain. Now, as I study Andrea's lips and feel the passion they arouse within me, I know that this is one of those rare and welcome times.

The pianist stops playing, stands and bows, but a demanding thunder of applause inspires him to do an encore. Halfway through the new song Andrea's fingers, as delicate as the beautiful music, slip over my weathered country hand.

When we leave the concert, night has fallen over Salt Lake City. We walk back to the hostel and make it just in time, for the doors are locked at ten each night.

When the night manager turns out the lights at ten-fifteen, Andrea and I are seated in the gathering room with a woman from England. She has spent all day in the Mormon genealogy center trying to trace her family tree.

My grandmother was a Gypsy, she informs us. A real one who traveled about Europe in a horse-drawn wagon.

I know it sounds silly, says the night manager, but if you

stay up, you'll have to whisper. The owner lives upstairs and may come down to chew us out if he hears you.

Both my grandmothers died when I was a baby, I whisper.

When my grandmother died, Andrea says in a low voice, my sisters took all her antiques and things they could sell. I got the love letters my grandfather wrote her. That was all I wanted. They were tied in a bundle with a red ribbon.

When my Gypsy grandmother died, the English woman whispers, she was cremated in her wagon, which was set on fire.

I once spent three weeks thumbing from Alabama all through Mexico in search of a tribe of Gypsies. I finally found them living in a caravan, watching a TV set that was plugged into a wire running from a telephone pole. I wanted us to dance around a blazing fire rather than watch reruns. So much for that illusion. But here, now in the dark on the Trail, I feel again the great Gypsy spirit and see the flames of the wagon as the grandmother vanished into the Other World.

I must get some rest, says the woman, so I can do more research on my family tomorrow. Good night.

She leaves the room, and Andrea and I find ourselves alone in the dark. I'm wondering what to say to her when the night manager reappears.

I'm sorry, he says, but I'm uneasy about the owner coming down. Would you mind going to your rooms now?

There are two beds in my room, but no one was assigned to the free one. The owner was kind enough to give me a key to the room since was I concerned about my journal and camera being swiped. Andrea and I go there to continue a day that doesn't want to stop simply because the sun has chosen to go down.

And where is your horse? she asks, sitting beside me on the bed.

I do have something to show you, I tell her.

I reach into my pack and pull out the leather pouch. I open

it to pour the Trail's gifts onto the bed. The pieces of china from the wagon train destroyed by Indians back in Nebraska lie beside my tiny bottle of gold. My hawk-wing bone-whistle rests against the thumb-size piece of wood from the Cottonwood Pony Express Station. Andrea touches the clump of soft black hair that's lying among my treasures. She lifts it, her blue eyes curious.

It's from two dead buffalo, I say. I found their skeletons together back in Wyoming. They seemed to have huddled together for warmth from a snowstorm.

You are a strange person.

I feel a bit vulnerable, as if I have revealed too much of myself too soon.

I'm going to carve a pony, I explain. I kept the hair to use as the mane and tail.

I do not mean strange in a bad way, her voice softens. Sometimes my English is poor. I mean you are rare. You live in your heart and I like this.

I slowly place my fingers to her cheek and she kisses my hand. When my fingers find the warmth of her neck, she drops the buffalo hair onto the bed by the Trail's gifts. She smiles as I begin to rub her neck. A very faint moan comes from deep down inside her.

That feels good, she whispers.

I want you to feel good, I say, putting my lips to hers.

At first her lips barely part and I let the tip of my tongue touch hers. Then her mouth opens as she moans. I put my arms around her and she does the same to me. She has large, firm breasts, and I feel them tight against my chest as her breathing quickens and our kiss deepens.

Will you hold me? she whispers. I mean, only hold me? I am afraid.

I turn out the light and we lie on the bed free of the leather pouch and its treasures. We snuggle into each other and she rests her head on my chest, letting her fingers play in the hair. I kiss her neck and ear with a touch as light as breath itself.

I feel safe with you, she tells me.

I want you to feel safe. What are you afraid of?

Her fingers fall still on my chest. She takes a deep breath and releases a faint sigh.

I am afraid I may be pregnant. When I came to Los Angeles to visit my friend, we made love only once. But my period is three weeks late now. This is unusual for me.

Your body may simply be stressed, I say, because of traveling and worrying about this. Your period could start tomorrow.

I have considered these things. But my breasts are also tender to touch.

Why don't you take a pregnancy test?

No, I don't want to know the truth yet.

Do you love the guy in L.A.? I say. Do you want to have a baby?

I have known him for several years, she says. We met in Paris, but I do not love him. I'm not sure if I want to have a child or not. I think some part of me wanted to get pregnant, though, to force me into some direction with my life. If I go back to Austria and I am pregnant, it will destroy my mother. Her mind is not so open. My father's dream that I come to America and do good will be gone as well. I could have an abortion, but isn't that a form of murder? I'm not sure what to do. I had planned to leave for Seattle tomorrow, but now that I have met you . . . What should I do?

You can always bet on two sure things. First, few things are as they first appear. Second, when you open your heart to someone, you always run the risk of being hurt. Oh, but this is just a foolish defense some part of me is trying to put up to protect myself from love. I'm so drawn to this young woman that it already hurts to think that she might leave tomorrow.

We fall asleep in each other's arms, but a few hours later I find myself awake in the middle of the night. There is just enough moonlight coming through the tree beyond the window to trace the profile of Andrea's face. Her lips are barely parted. Yes, new life is sacred and precious, but I hope that she is not pregnant. It would complicate her life as well as our budding relationship.

She half awakens and takes my hand, moving it down onto her stomach. She holds it there against the warm, smooth skin.

CHAPTER THIRTY

Andrea has asked me whether she should stay in Salt Lake City or move on to Seattle today as she had planned. Though I dread the thought of her leaving, I can't bring myself to tell her what she should do about that any more than whether to have an abortion if she turns out to be pregnant. Sometimes I think all one human being can do for another when he is confronted by decisions is try to inspire courage anyway.

With a cool morning breeze drifting through the hostel window, we crawl out of bed and get dressed. Her body in early sunlight is as beautiful as her voice was in bed.

I think it is best that I leave today, says Andrea. But is your offer still good to phone your friend there about a place to stay for two or three days?

Now that Sean has left this world as surely as the Gypsy grandmother in a wagon of fire, Carolyn has an extra bedroom in her Seattle home. Andrea might be good company for her. It will certainly save Andrea some money, which is almost gone anyway. I phone Carolyn and she is warm and open to the idea.

I walk Andrea to the bus station and we gather some more cherries along the way. I am not very hungry, though, and neither is she. She promises me she will take them with her on her trip. It hurts to watch the door of the Greyhound open for her departure.

What are you feeling? she whispers.

Sad, I say, as we put our arms around each other.

Will you call me in a few days?

Yes, I want to make sure that you made it.

And I want to make sure you are okay in the desert, she tells me.

I take her orange backpack onto the bus and place it in the rack over her seat. When I step off the bus, I see her placing her face to the window. She holds up one of the cherries and puts it in her mouth, as if to offer one last kiss. Then, as the bus pulls from the station, she waves good-bye.

I head back to the hostel, but I'm too restless to stay there. I can't get Andrea off my mind. I begin to do what I may do best when I'm troubled. I walk. And walk.

That night, with hopes of feeling closer to Andrea, I return to the Middle Eastern restaurant where we had lunch. The food is excellent and the place is exotic and alive with belly dancers, their bells jingling and jangling about the customers where candles flicker on our tables. But for all the music, passion, and life, I only find myself missing Andrea more. It hurts to long for love, but it hurts even more to feel that you've gripped the thread leading to it and let it slip right through your fingers.

I return to the hostel and climb the stairs to my room. It's cool and I reach over the bed to lower the window. A single blond hair rests on the pillow where Andrea slept in my arms. I leave it there as I turn out the light and crawl into bed.

The next morning I awake thinking of Andrea, just as I did off and on throughout the night. Trying to cope with missing her, I walk over to The Roasting Company. After I've had a couple of cups of coffee, I'm reminded that caffeine can be a tiny curse, my restlessness now building up more steam. Then, as I start to leave The Roasting Company, I recall I have a promising piece of paper in my wallet. I take it out and unfold it. There it is—the phone number of Doug Kincell, who lives here in Salt Lake City.

I met Doug and his wife in a café back in Lander, Wyoming, the day I left with Sam to pan for gold. Doug grew up near where I was born and raised, and his southern accent caught my ear. We hit it off and Doug, a rescue pilot, invited me to spend a shift with him and go out on an emergency flight, should one arise.

Pulling a quarter from my pocket, I drop it into a pay phone at the street corner and dial his number. My hope fades as the rings go on and on. Even if Doug does finally answer, I suspect for him to say he has changed his mind about the offer for one reason or another. His insurance may not allow it, if nothing else. He answers the phone.

Sure, he says, his southern accent sweet music to my ears. Come over this evening when I begin my shift.

That evening I start to feel better about missing Andrea as I become excited about the possibility of flying through the Utah night on a rescue mission. I take a city bus out to the airport hangar where I am to meet Doug. For some reason, I envision him and another pilot sitting on the edge of a worn cot in a greasy shop while a plane engine runs, awaiting an emergency. Boy, am I wrong.

Doug appears and looks so official in his pilot uniform. I almost come to attention and salute. Jerry Ellis, alias Crane at Creek, reporting for rescue mission, sir.

Good to see you again, says Doug, very much the modest man I met with his wife in the Wyoming café over coffee.

When I was a kid, Doug had told me over coffee, I lived next to the old airplane graveyard in Tullahoma, Tennessee. I'd sneak under the fence and crawl into the cockpits of the World War II planes called Buffalo Busters. I pretended I could fly. I never got over it. I had to become a pilot.

He leads me out to his car and we get in. His headquarters is a few blocks away and we head there.

Have any unusual emergencies arisen lately? I ask him.

All the time, he says. Just a while back, I got a call to fly to a tiny town in Wyoming to pick up a real sick baby. My weather charts said there was a snowstorm there. I spoke to the doctor and he assured me the sky was clear. I took off in my jet and got to the town to find it was snowing. I couldn't see anything so there I was circling blind over a runway set in a pocket in the mountains. I finally made contact with the ground, but the man reading the controls was having a hard time. I asked him if this was his usual station? *No,* he said, *I usually just pump gas.*

You pulling my leg? I ask.

No, says Doug. I wasn't sure what to do. I didn't want to crash in a snowstorm, but I didn't want the baby to die, either. I took a chance and managed to land. We got the baby back to Salt Lake City and he lived.

You're a hero, I tell him.

No, I'm just a man who likes to fly planes for a living. I was once flying cargo in Africa when the engine caught fire. I turned off the fuel, but it kept blazing. I didn't know what I'd do. I finally found a stretch of beach along the Nile and set it down. I ran away from it just as it exploded into flames.

Doug and I arrive at the pilots' headquarters, a plush two-bedroom apartment suitable for dignitaries. A giant TV set also offers a VCR complete with a cassette library. The fancy computer on the desk by the wall gives up-to-the-minute weather charts. *Thunderstorms in Denver; 55 and cloudy in Seattle.* The painting of an Indian woman is hanging over the computer, and she seems to watch us as we walk about the room.

The computer also doubles as a video game, which the night's second pilot, Dick, suckers me into playing. He was a pilot in the U.S. Navy and has also flown cargo and corporate planes. He spent all day working on his motorcycle. He stands 6 feet tall and weights about 225. He has a wonderful laugh as we play video golf and I keep thinking of Baby Huey as I look at him.

Shit, he says as his video golf ball falls into the sand trap. I should have allowed for the wind.

And you call yourself a pilot? I tease him.

I didn't say I was a good one, he says.

I've never played a video game or real golf in my life, but I become as hooked on the game as Dick is. While we battle it out, Doug sits on the couch with a knife in his hands, sharpening it against a stone.

You checked the charts yet? Doug asks, still rubbing the knife blade against a sharpening stone.

I will in a minute, says Dick, swinging his electronic club across the video screen.

Doug runs his finger down the edge of the knife. He does not seem to approve of Dick being so lost on the golf course. The look in Doug's eyes reminds me that we are waiting for a tragedy to occur. No, that's not right. Rather, we are waiting to rescue someone. However you put it, the phone now rings; the golf game is over. Doug seems to take a deep breath as he answers.

Hello, he says as Dick and I listen, wondering what he is being told. Yeah, I'm on the way.

He hangs up the receiver.

An adult, he announces. Down near Bryce Canyon.

What happened to him? I want to know.

They never tell us that, Doug tells me. They think it might influence our decision to come. It wouldn't, though.

You guys looked at each other funny, I say, when you said Bryce Canyon. Something I should know?

The airfield lies at the foot of a mountain, Doug explains. It's the most dangerous place to land in Utah. It has a blind spot as we come in and take off. The side of the mountain, it . . . maybe you'd like to wait on another call?

No, I decide, trying to hide my concern. Let's go.

Dick now switches the computer from golf to weather. Doug phones the airport to chart our flight route. All of this is done with the grace and precision of Mr. Spock on the starship *Enterprise*.

Dick stays behind in case another emergency arises, and Doug and I hurry out the door to hop into his car. We speed to the hangar, where his small jet awaits us. The man fueling the jet with a giant hose has only two fingers on his left hand. When he detects my glance, he hides the hand behind him.

You going up with Doug? he asks. You're lucky. I've been wanting to for a long time.

He is twenty-one and studies criminal justice at a local college. I feel bad that he caught me eyeing his hand. He works the giant hose, however, as if it doesn't get in his way.

An ambulance arrives with two nurses trained for emergencies. Doug starts the engines and we all hop in the aircraft. I've never been up in a small plane or small jet, and I'm surprised when Doug has me sit in the cockpit with him.

Put this set of headphones on, says Doug, so you can hear what I hear.

He speaks with the flight tower and I can barely understand the communication. A pilot must have the ears of a composer, separating musical notes from the buzz of a bug. The control panel lights up before me. While we await clearance from the tower Doug points to a few of the instruments on the control panel and tells me what they do. One measures altitude, another speed, and another wind velocity.

There's not much to it, he says, eyeing more than thirty intricate dials and switches.

Yeah, sure, Doug. As the lighted instruments of the jet face me I might as well be in an all-night coffee shop with Albert Einstein drawing on a napkin to explain the Theory of Relativity while a fresh pot brews.

The tower clears us for takeoff and I become both thrilled

and anxious as we taxi onto the runway. I'm glad that I trust and admire Doug, for I have a horror of plane crashes.

We shoot down the runway and rise into the night as gracefully as a dove flying toward the top of some magnificent mountain. We climb to 17,000 feet and jet beneath the stars at 350 miles per hour. Bright yellow moonlight reflects off a river snaking between little towns. Their streetlights give faint glows all the way to the vast desert.

See how the towns are about fifty miles apart? Doug points out. When the Pony Express was replaced by the telegraph, that was the distance a battery could send a charge.

Some thirty minutes later, the side of the mountain appears in the dark of night. We'll crash straight into it if Doug doesn't come in at just the right angle and speed. I can't deny a quick prayer as we swoop down like a gull to a lake. I'm relieved when I hear the tires squeal against the pavement, Doug bringing us to safety. It's true, the earth is sweet.

An ambulance is waiting for us, and the two nurses, Doug, and I hop in. It takes only a few minutes to speed us to a small hospital, where we rush through the emergency entrance. The victim was not brought to the airport because he has not yet been stabilized for the flight.

A large man in his sixties is stretched out on a table in the emergency room. Wires and tubes run here and there from his body, as if he were caught in a web between life and death. The horrible smell of human excrement fills the room, for the victim has lost the dignity of bodily control. While the two nurses prepare him for departure the doctor joins Doug and me in the hallway. He fills us in on the patient, whose name is Alex.

He's from Canada, says the doctor. He and his wife have been on their dream vacation. Alex ate dinner, walked back to his hotel room, and collapsed with a massive coronary. Doesn't look very viable. He was out ten minutes before the paramedics got to him.

You mean he's brain-damaged? I whisper.

It doesn't look viable, the doctor repeats.

Alex is carried on a stretcher to the jet and I help others lift him inside. I then get back into the cockpit and Doug joins me. I'm handling the situation fairly well till the patient's wife boards the plane to sit behind me. She is tall and well dressed and has a beautiful face, which seems determined to show grace in the face of tragedy. Her dignity begins to fill me with an overwhelming sense of sorrow and pity.

I've heard that the hospital in Salt Lake City is among the best in the United States, I say, hoping to offer some kind of comfort.

Are you the other pilot? she asks, desperation in her voice.

For the first time, I feel like an ambulance chaser. The look in her face is breaking my heart.

No, I say. Doug, the pilot, is a friend of mine.

Alex loves the mountains, she says. We were having such a wonderful time. This afternoon we went to Inspiration Point. Nobody can take that from us. I can't believe this is happening. Maybe it was the altitude.

The jet roars down the runway and we lift straight up by the side of the mountain to that critical point where we disappear into a blind spot. No moon. No stars. Just total darkness and a prayer. Then seconds later we find ourselves in a world of fragmented but reassuring lights. Doug sets our course for Salt Lake City, which is one hundred fifty miles away. An ambulance awaits.

When Doug and I return to his plush apartment headquarters, it is three in the morning. Dick has gone to bed. He placed a pillow and a blanket on the couch for me. Doug goes on to bed, knowing full well that the phone could ring at any moment for the next emergency flight.

I lie in the darkness except for a tiny light near the computer. The painting of the Indian woman on the wall still seems to watch me, but I feel alone. I think of Andrea on a Greyhound somewhere in the night. I imagine Alex's wife in the hospital by his side.

I hear my heart beating in the dark. One day it will stop like the hearts of all men before me, and I begin to long to hit the Trail across the vast Utah desert. I want to live as much as possible while I still can.

CHAPTER
THIRTY-ONE

The next morning I get up early, relieved that no other emergency calls jarred the night. The pilots are still in bed and I write a thank-you note, placing it on the table by the computer. *P.S. Dick, stay out of the sand traps.*

I take a bus back into town and get out at the cathedral. The air is fresh and clean and gulls cry out as they perform feathered tricks in the sky. The cherries are now gone from the low limbs of the trees where Andrea and I gathered some the past two days. A crow jumps about the red fruit in the treetops.

I can't get Alex, last night's victim, off my mind. I keep seeing his gracious wife sitting by his side. When I get back to the hostel, I use the pay phone in the hallway to call the hospital and inquire about his condition. A woman answers.

Are you a member of the family? she asks.

No, but I was with the flight crew that brought him to Salt Lake.

Oh, her tone warms. He's in stable condition.

Will he be okay? I ask, wondering if he's hooked to a machine till he dies.

That's all I can tell you, sir.

Last night's sorrow and my missing Andrea so much make being around the lively hostel folks a comfort. I go to the kitchen to cook breakfast. It's packed with people from all over the world and I'm lucky to find a seat by a window while I await my turn at one of two stoves. Sitting next to me is a man in his early twenties. He smiles at me, making his robust and friendly face all the more handsome.

This is a busy kitchen, I tell him.

Sure is, he says, and I'm hungry, too. I've been waiting on a stove for twenty minutes now.

He's not that hungry, says a young woman with a Cockney accent at a chair across from us. He gave up his turn at the stove twice so those girls over there could cook before he did.

So you're a gentleman? I tease him.

No, nothing quite that noble, he grins. I was just practicing a little patience, something I usually have very little of.

What brings you to Salt Lake City? I ask him.

I'm headed back home to Richmond, Virginia, he explains. The past week I was washing dishes in a restaurant in Idaho to earn money to take kayaking lessons there.

I tell him that I hope to take a canoe down the Sacramento River along the route the Pony Express letters traveled by the *Antelope*, a steamer, from Sacramento to San Francisco. His eyes become wide and his face intense as he listens.

I can't recall who, I say, but you look like somebody I've met or known.

Because I look so all-American, he says, some of my class-mates in high school called me John Boy from *The Waltons* TV series.

What's your name? I ask him.

Albert Pollard. He offers his hand with the grace and confidence of a diplomat, making me think of John F. Kennedy.

Excuse me, interrupts the young woman with the Cockney accent, but *my* name is India. I heard what you were saying about looking for stories of adventure and all that. Could I join you? I came over from London a month ago and—

Pulling her chair closer to Albert and me, she looks about

the room, as if making sure the coast is clear. She lowers her voice to a whisper.

I landed in Los Angeles, she continues. I just got out of there yesterday. I'm still in a bit of shock. I was held for five days in a jail holding pen with four hundred other women. I was caught in a bank forging a check for three hundred dollars. I was doing it to support my boyfriend. I wouldn't have gotten caught, but I signed the check in the same handwriting I used to make the check out. I was high or I wouldn't have done it in the same hand. The public defender got me off with five years' probation, but I had to skip town before they realized I had written checks for fifteen thousand dollars the past two weeks. I know it sounds so crazy, but when you're in love—

How did you get the blank checks? I ask.

We had several people open phony accounts, she says. We paid them for the checks. In one case we bought checks whose owner had been dead for seven years. I just hope I get out of the United States without being caught. I couldn't take being locked up again. I miss my boyfriend, too. It isn't so easy just to stop this kind of life. You get addicted to the excitement. I'd really like to *rob* a bank or drive the getaway car. I don't know, but something about America makes me wild.

I don't like eyeing a mirror to see my wrinkles gaining momentum, but listening to India makes me realize I'm grateful to be forty-three years old and clear of youth's folly. Well, most of it, anyway.

Albert, the opposite of India, seems very grounded and sure of himself. When he returns to Richmond, he will campaign for a candidate in an upcoming election.

I'm getting tired of waiting on a stove, I say. Let's go to a café down the street for breakfast.

Yeah, says Albert, excitement in his tone. Sounds good to me.

As we leave the kitchen India drops a raw egg to the floor. The yellow splatters onto her bare ankles.

I hate to cook, she pouts.

Albert and I walk to a café and order breakfast. We're almost finished when his lips part, but close again.

Were you about to say something? I ask.

You don't have to answer right now, says Albert. But what you're doing is historic. I'd like to be part of it and walk with you across the Utah desert. Or if you don't want company all the way, I could just go along for two or three days. I want to see what it's like.

So much has happened since Tom, back in Nebraska, suggested the same thing. Missing Andrea as much as I do makes Albert's company most appealing. Still, a part of me has looked forward to being alone in the desert. Besides, Albert, like Tom, may only be caught up in the moment's dream.

Let's both sleep on it, I say. Make sure you really want to do it and we'll discuss it in the morning?

Suits me, he says. But I thought about it before I asked you. I'm sure I want to do it.

I get a good night's sleep and I'm excited about Albert spending a few days with me in the desert. He is still raring to go as well, and we pack our bags to leave the hostel.

We are about to walk out the door when we hear India on the hallway pay phone. She is crying and arguing with her mother back in London. When she hangs up, I ask her what's wrong.

I sent several letters in a package to my mother, she says. I asked her to put stamps on them to mail them to my friends there in England. One was a letter fourteen pages long to my best friend. It told *every*thing that has happened since I got to the United States. My mother said it was open and she read it. She had no right to do that.

No, I say, maybe not, but she was worried about you. Besides, it's almost like you wanted her to read it by sending it like that just to save a little on postage.

I see myself as kind, generous, and loving, says India. But sometimes I have a great capacity to be so stupid.

Good luck, I say as Albert and I leave the hostel.

You two be safe, she calls out to us as she takes a seat on the front steps. After Albert and I get into his jeep I turn to see India biting her nails and tapping her foot on the steps. Her expression is charged with such passion that, for all I know, she may be dreaming that she sits in a getaway car outside a bank being robbed.

Albert and I buy supplies and drive south of Salt Lake City to park his jeep at a lone farmhouse. We load our packs onto our backs and start walking. Two hundred miles of dirt road stretch before us along the original Pony Express Trail. The closest thing to civilization is Fish Springs, which is seventy miles straight ahead as the crow flies. But as two men walk?

This is the first time I have walked with anyone on a long journey, and it seems right that Albert is by my side on this adventure. The thought of making discoveries together warms me, and especially after some of the cold experiences I had on the wagon train, when I began to doubt my fellow man.

The Trail stretches before us as far as the eye can see and winds off into the hills. Jackrabbits hop about in the sage and disappear as quickly as the Rabbit Man when he descended into his hole-home. I just may get a Milky Way the next time I find a grocery store. A grocery store? How foreign such a thing seems now as we pass the skeleton of a deer near cacti blooming pink and yellow.

Anthills five or six inches high are everywhere. Thousands of ants go about their hurried business in and out of holes in the earth.

Look at them, I say. They don't even know we're here.

They know, Albert tells me. We just don't interest them enough to make them slow down.

Albert and I follow the winding Trail into the hills, where cedars defy the arid terrain. At the base of the hills we come to Lookout Pass to find the crumbling rock foundation of a Pony Express station. A tiny stream trickles from a spring between the hills and it is easy to see a Pony rider leap from his horse to kneel and scoop his hands into the cool water. He washes the dust from his eyes and face and takes a drink, a few drops running down his chin, before he leaps atop a new horse to gallop on. I also see Sir Richard Burton stepping from his stagecoach in 1860 to walk along the stream. He sits under the shade of a cedar and sketches in his journal. From time to time, his fingers twist his long black mustache.

I like that this tiny stream trickles between the hills so far away from the towns and cities. It has followed the same path for hundreds if not thousands of years, and here in the desert it stands a good chance of continuing to escape man's sometimes confused progress.

Besides thirst, I say, what is it about water that fascinates man so much? Is it the unknown, or because our ancestors crawled from the sea?

It's hard for me to imagine being away from water for very long, says Albert. I grew up within a stone's throw of Chesapeake Bay and began to sail solo when I was fifteen. I had my own crab traps. One summer I beat all the other kids selling raffle tickets because I could get to more houses in my boat. The water has always been a big part of my life. I got a theory, too, about growing up where I did. It was the same place where George Washington was born, and that has always filled me with the feeling that *I* can do something outstanding in history.

Albert does not say this with any hint of arrogance, but rather with a tone of challenge and responsibility. He gives me a good shot of hope about American youth. He is also carrying two gallons of water, which does not hurt our budding friendship either. Now if I could just get him to carry my pack as well . . .

We walk on past the stream, and the crumbling rock station disappears as we turn the bend. Now that we have crossed Lookout Pass the great wilderness opens before us like some endless world. Antelope loom from the earth so quickly at times that I can't prove they weren't jackrabbits only seconds ago, playing tricks they learned from the desert. A dust devil dances on the horizon, and a tumbleweed bounces. Here and there we come upon a ditch filled with dozens of the dried tumbleweed plants, as if they have huddled together for the night to seek peace from the pushy wind.

We walk all day and my feet hurt like hell. I don't care what my eyes say, we no longer walk on ground, but on red-hot coals. Albert impresses me and refuses to bemoan the fire.

Walking is only the constant redirection of gravity, he says, trudging forward. We must catch ourselves with each step before we fall.

Yeah? I say. My feet still hurt.

His Virginia grin does, however, take away some of the burn in the blisters between my toes.

At eight o'clock that night the sun is just going down and I feel like it's been a long day. We build a small fire from cedar and pine on a level spot on the side of a hill. We cook rice and scoop it into our mouths with tortillas. Food never tasted so good. Funny how something so simple can give so much pleasure.

As Albert and I eat, we sit on the ground with our shoes and socks off. We are two tribesmen happy with our kingdom of toes.

How's your rice? I ask.

Great, he says. How's your tortilla?

Couldn't be better, I say, wiggling my big toes.

When we finish eating, we sit for twenty or thirty minutes to savor the sunset and rest. Then we slip our socks and shoes back on and hit the Trail.

We are still walking at ten o'clock. The moon is full and comes and goes behind the hills, as if playing with us. When it does appear, it seems so close that we could almost hit it with a rock, or send a dove to sit cooing on the edge of a crater. Two owls begin to hoot and the faint orange glow of a very distant town seems like little more than a candle in a pumpkin.

We decide not to use my tent tonight. We simply grope about in the moonlit sage to find spots where we can lay our sleeping bags and hope not to lie on one of several snakes we saw today.

I lie looking up at the brilliant stars. It boggles my mind that each one is a sun. In the great distance a tiny red light flickers on a plane and I wonder if it is Doug or Dick out to save a life.

I become alarmed when I hear a rattlesnake within arm's reach. I lie frozen in my sleeping bag, wondering what to do as sweat breaks out on my forehead and my heart begins to pound. Finally I realize that it's the rattler on my hat, shaking in the wind.

Look, I whisper, up there. See it?

What? says Albert, rising to his elbow.

There, over there, I point. That ball of light.

I see it now, says Albert. It's a satellite.

The dust has hardly settled from the Pony riders and now we send letters through the stars on invisible horses galloping at the speed of light. I love life with all my heart, but sometimes things move too fast for me. Tonight I like having my body against the earth, solid and ancient.

Good night, John Boy.

CHAPTER
THIRTY-TWO

Sometimes there is a special place in the human heart that seems the most easily reached in the quiet of the night. Here, in the desert in my sleeping bag, I feel close to that place. The pines and cedars in moonlight, the sage swaying in the gentle breeze, all seem to have souls. All seem to be part of me and me part of them.

It's about two-thirty and I've been awake some ten minutes feeling this way as I sit up on the ground with the sleeping bag pulled up near my naked shoulders against the cool night air. I can't help but let these thoughts I'm having blend with those I sometimes have of my father. This is the time of night that he usually crawls from his bed and walks down the hallway with a small flashlight in his hand to show his way to the refrigerator. A diabetic, he pours himself a sip of orange juice and drinks it to keep his sugar level normal. Then he goes over to sit in his favorite chair by the wood-burning heater. He opens its door and watches its flames. Often our cat Rosco climbs into his lap and my father holds him with great tenderness, as if the animal understands him better than people can. Sometimes I'll get out of bed at this time of night just to go see my father and admire his face lighted by the flickers of the heater's flames. We don't usually say much, but sometimes our hands will touch as we stroke the cat together and what I feel says a great deal to me, and perhaps him, too.

Then he will close the heater's door, turn on his flashlight, and walk down the hallway to his room. I think that for as long as I live I will feel that this thread of connection we have with our cat by the fire is a rope that sometimes pulls me from despair, if I should get to thinking that I don't have a lot to be thankful for in life.

Anything wrong? comes Albert's sleepy voice as he raises to his elbow inside his sleeping bag, some eight feet away from mine.

No, everything's fine. I was just thinking about home.

Oh . . . His voice is little more than a whisper in the desert night as he lies back down and curls up inside his sleeping bag. He soon falls asleep again, his breathing becoming a faint song. Funny, but it seems that Albert and I, camping on the same speck of earth are, in a way, sharing the same home for the night. And he has, without even realizing it, entered into that special place in my heart where everything has a soul and where I sometimes reach out in the night to my father through the cat by the fire. It's okay that Albert has entered into this special place because, at least for the moment, I feel as though there's even room for more.

The next day Albert and I walk for hours and we have covered many miles when, in the great distance, we see what appears to be a tribe of twenty or thirty people walking across the desert. Their heads move up and down with each step they take moving down the dirt road toward us. They are too far away to see their faces or determine their ages, and their clothes and bodies seem to blend together into one big blob.

What do you think? I say. Their bus broke down and they're walking back to the highway?

Beats me, Albert admits.

We walk toward them and they gradually develop faces. All are kids except for four adults. They seem as surprised to see us as we are to see them. All the kids wear Boy Scout uniforms.

Yeah, says the adult leader, the boys are out to walk twenty-five miles of the Pony Express Trail to get badges.

Having fun? I ask.

Well, says one of the boys, it's fun when we stop to rest.

I dread going back to Salt Lake City, the leader tells me. After being out here it'll be hard to take the noise of cars. It's not natural to wake up at night with a siren going off, either. If it wasn't for earning money, I'd just come to the desert to live. Forget all that other stuff. You headed all the way across the desert?

Yes, I say, all the way to San Francisco.

We won't be back to our camp for a few hours yet, he says. But you'll see it in about four miles, at Simpson Springs. Help yourselves to food and water.

Albert and I walk on. We spot the American flag blowing over that camp long before we get there. The wind is so strong and rough that the boys' tents flap like masts on ships fighting a storm at sea. I expect for them at any moment to pull free and fly twirling across the desert past tumbleweed, antelope, and dust devils.

The sign over Simpson Springs says: DO NOT DRINK. I take off my socks and shoes, however, and stick my feet into cool, wet heaven. Is that steam I see coming from my toes?

Just below the spring are the crumbling rock walls of a one-room house. It was built in 1893—according to the brass plaque—from the Pony Express station that stood on this spot. It was built for a man's wife, but she never got to use it because she died in childbirth.

Albert and I make ourselves at home and cook lunch on the Scouts' gas grill. Judging by how the boys reacted when I asked if they were having fun on their walk, I can't help but suspect that they'd rather be here having lunch than putting badges on their uniforms and blisters on their feet.

*　*　*

On the third day we reach the tip of the Great Salt Lake Desert. The earth is so dry and white in some spots that dust blows into the air like sheets of flour or powdered salt.

When we reach the Fish Springs Wildlife Refuge, the clean, clear water appears in the desert like a mirage. Ducks and other waterfowl play in the stream and pond as if they, too, have been walking forever. *Splash, you fools,* they seem to say. *Splash to your heart's content.*

We find a picnic table under a giant cottonwood and build a fire from some of its fallen limbs to cook a meal. The tree's great friendly shade holds back the parching sun as a lone frog sings about this oasis in the desert.

That frog seems happy, I say, watching the smoke rise from the fire up into the limbs of the massive cottonwood.

So am I, says Albert, now that we're in the shade.

When we finish eating, Albert opens a can of Skoal; he takes a pinch of tobacco to stick into his mouth. It still strikes me as out of character with his genteel nature, but my Appalachian habit of spitting may not always endear me to some folks, either.

It's not easy to think about leaving this shade, I say, and walking through the sun again. Maybe we should set up camp here and rest till tomorrow before we push on?

We can't. Albert points to a sign on the other side of the tree: NO OVERNIGHT CAMPING.

Well, I say, we could stay here in the shade and rest till dark and walk by the light of the moon. It'll be cooler then.

That's a good idea, he says. But I've got to come to a decision about whether to keep going or head back toward my jeep. You know last night when I saw you sitting up and I asked if anything was wrong?

Yeah?

Your saying you were thinking of home must've gotten mixed up with my dreams. I awoke this morning wondering how my mother and father were doing. I've been traveling most of the summer and I'm starting to miss them. Might be good to spend a few days with them before I start work on that campaign I was telling you about.

If you head on back I'll sure miss your company, I tell him. But I understand. I'm starting to miss my folks as well.

Albert opens his map and we study it.

It's about seventy miles from here to Nevada, he says. Yeah, I better start back for my jeep today.

Good idea, I say, my tone less than excited.

Why don't we stay in touch? Albert suggests. Maybe you'd like to come up to Chesapeake Bay and we could go crabbing together.

And I hope you'll come down to see me, I say. I'd like to show you my cabin in the mountains.

We walk back up to the dirt road and remove our packs. Albert will go east and I will continue on west. Yesterday we walked for eight hours before a single car passed us. Who can say how long it will take him to get a ride back to his jeep?

I'll stay here with you, I say, till you get a ride or I do myself.

Though we wear hats, the sun beats down with such power that we both begin to sweat. It drips from our faces onto the dusty road. An hour passes and it's almost as though we're melting as the sweat drops build in the dust.

A car pulls up to the road from the wildlife refuge. It stops and a woman in her sixties sticks her head from the window.

My son, Bret, she says, works down at the refuge, where I do part-time myself. He told me what you're doing. I can put you up for the night. My home's west of here fifteen miles, in Callao.

That would be great, I say, placing my pack in the backseat of her car.

See you, Albert, I say, offering my hand. Thanks for taking

my cowboy boots for me. I'll have room now in my pack for that pony I'm going to carve.

Send me a picture of it, he says. I'll mail the boots to you as soon as I get home.

I crawl into the car with Leah Layman. As we head down the dirt road I turn back to see Albert still standing in the sun with only his tobacco juice for company. I feel just a bit guilty leaving him there, but he looks pretty determined, shading his eyes from the scorching sun. Brave, for a young man. I hope he never loses faith that history has great things in store for him, just as it did for another hometown boy, George Washington.

Have you lived here long? I ask Leah as we continue down the rough, dusty road.

I've lived here my whole life and love it. Sometimes outsiders stop at the refuge center and say it's dead out here. This really bothers me that they can't see or hear. The desert is as alive as you and me.

I cannot imagine a human soul not caring for Leah within minutes of meeting her. She has a beautiful face and her body appears agile and tough, like Tanya's mother, who helped brand cattle on the Pathfinder Ranch in Wyoming. The warm gleam in her eyes tells me, too, how happy she is to meet a stranger and make him feel welcome.

My hot-water pipe broke yesterday, Leah tells me. But my daughter, ReaJean, lives behind me and you can shower there if you like.

Yes, I could do without a pound or two of dust.

And when you're ready, I'll be happy to cook you something to eat.

You're a kind person.

No, I just try to treat people like I'd like for them to treat me.

We arrive in the tiny town of Callao, which has only eight

or ten houses scattered here and there along empty dirt streets. There isn't a store or gas station in sight.

You can't tell it now, says Leah, but back in the twenties we had has many as thirty or forty cars a day coming through here. This was part of the first Transcontinental Highway. Now if you see five or six cars in a day you've got your eyes full. My daughter drives a hundred miles every day just to get her two kids to school and back.

Her daughter, ReaJean, lives in a trailer, and I take a shower there. A child's plastic dinosaur lies on the wet shower floor, as if it had crawled in from the desert to get a drink. Looks like it swallowed so much, it just decided to keel over and sleep for a while.

I come from the shower refreshed. Leah and I go out the back door of the trailer to her log house, which she tells me was built in 1918. The towering cottonwoods were planted by her father when she was a little girl. How curious that she can mark her life by something that now reaches the sky.

Some ten years ago, says Leah, I went to Salt Lake to live for a while, but I began to miss the desert and came back here. My kids got scared when I told them that I had come home to die. I didn't say I wanted to die anytime soon and had to get that straight with them.

We go inside and the log house smells of woodsmoke because Leah built a fire in the old potbellied stove this morning. On the floor by the stove is a stone the Indians used for grinding corn, nuts, and seeds. On the wall hangs a shotgun that Leah took duck hunting over the years. Below the gun sits a potted plant, and sticking from the dirt is a nude woman ten inches tall carved from pine.

My husband carved that, she says. He lives just down the way there in the house on the other side of my son Bret's home. For several years he scratched out a living for me and the kids by trapping coyotes, foxes, and badgers to sell their furs.

On the wall is the picture of a cowboy on a bucking horse. Two others watch him as he hangs on for dear life. On the bottom of the picture is written LIVEN UP THE DAY.

That belonged to my grandfather, says Leah. He was a real cowboy. The museum up in Fillmore, Utah, has a lariat he made from cowhide. When I was a child, I remember helping him make ropes from horsehairs. I've always liked working with my hands. When I retire, I want to spend my time making things from wood.

I've just arrived, but I already feel at home here. The house is cool, a breeze blowing the curtains.

The doors are always unlocked, she says. Just do whatever you want. I have a few errands to run.

Could I get a needle, thread, and button? I ask.

She brings a little box from her bedroom and I find what I need. I sit outside and sew a button on my jeans. The needle also does a sharp job of deflating a couple of new blisters.

That evening the sun paints the sky with pinks, blues, and yellows in ways I've never seen before as it sinks over the hills where old gold mines await new hopes and dreams. It is those same hills that grew the pine logs that built Leah's house and the fruit cellar.

That cellar sits some twenty feet to the right of her home and I step down into it to see the shelves lined with jars of fruits and vegetables; quaint handwritten labels mark each jar. The floor is hard-packed dirt and it fills the room with the smell of exotic earthiness.

Wandering over to the wooden shed just beyond the cellar, I discover rusty traps dangling from chains on bent nails. I hear the cry of the animals they caught, but I can also see the food they put on the table for Leah's family.

Bret, Leah's son, arrives in his car with his sister, ReaJean. He sticks his head from the window.

I see you made it to Callao, he calls. We're going for some beer. You drink?

I could go for a cold one. How far to the beer store?

Round trip, says Bret, is one hundred sixty miles. You want to go with us?

Not that far.

I give him money for a six-pack and they take off down a dirt road toward Nevada. One hundred sixty miles? Damn, what a beer ad.

As twilight settles over Callao I sit on the foot-high porch and play fetch with Leah's dogs, Amos and Jack. Amos is the older one and he taught Jack the game. Jack is so pushy to get the stick at times that I only pretend to throw it into the approaching darkness. He runs to get it while Amos waits with humble mouth open by my side. Sometimes I simply place it between his teeth. Jack returns and seems to wonder how Amos found the stick so quickly and made it back as if he never left. Watch closely, young Jack, the desert has many tricks.

The human voice creates the greatest music I have ever heard and it reveals more about a person than many of us would like to know. A single thought can sometimes alter the vocal cords with such beauty or tension that a few simple words can tell a whole story. The human tongue is not part of the mouth, but an extension of the heart and mind. These are my thoughts as I sit on the porch with a stick in my hand and hear Leah's voice in the twilight.

Brittany? she calls. *Brittany,* where are you?

Leah is calling her granddaughter, who is three years old. I cannot see either one of them, but Leah's words ride upon the wind again in search of *Brittany.* The voice is filled with fear and layered with a tenderness of love. Can a child really just disappear into the desert, as if a dust devil carried her away at sunset?

Leah steps out of her log house, her white-blond hair blowing ghostly in the wind and dark.

Have you seen Brittany? she asks.

No, I say, and rise to help her search for the child.

Leah does not stop walking to hear my reply. She moves on past the dogs and disappears around the house into the dark. I hear her voice once again rise and fade in the wind as she calls out like a prayer for her granddaughter to reappear. How foolish I was to think that all was safe here. But then, like an answered prayer, Leah appears from behind the fruit cellar with Brittany in her arms.

She's here, says Leah. She was just playing a game and wouldn't answer.

I have met many such adults who play this game. I am happy tonight that I am free of them. In truth, I feel free of everything. It is only nine o'clock and Bret and ReaJean have not returned with the cold beer. But I go on to bed to savor the songs of the crickets in the wind as cottonwood leaves quiver over the old log house, woodsmoke in the air. Leah, in the next room, hums as she holds Brittany in a rocking chair. How safe and sound the world seems as I fall asleep.

CHAPTER
THIRTY-THREE

 The next morning the smell of coffee lures me from my bed and I go to the kitchen to pour myself a cup. Leah is already there, moving around the kitchen, getting breakfast.

I'm a Mormon, says Leah, and my religion doesn't really allow me to drink coffee. But I don't see how a cup now and then can hurt anything. Did you rest well?

Sure did.

I have a couple of bicycles. You want to go for a ride?

We ride to her little modest church and go inside. Her face glows with pride as she shows me around. Why, the church even has a telephone. She uses it to call David Bagley, who lives just down the Trail less than a mile. He owns the old Willow Springs stagecoach and Pony Express station.

Yes, says Leah, hanging up the receiver. He said he and his wife would be happy to see us.

We crawl back onto our bikes and pedal down the dusty road. I haven't ridden a bike in years and despite all the walking I've been doing there are muscles in my legs that start to ache already. Leah, on the other hand, bikes like an old pro.

This is great, she says. I was telling ReaJean this morning before you got up how good it would feel to have somebody to ride with.

This woman melts my heart with her simplicity, openness,

and warmth. I like it when we stop pedaling and coast side by side, because the look in her eyes makes me feel like a kid again, when everything was timeless and filled with wonder.

After a few minutes of riding, we arrive at David Bagley's farmhouse. He's waiting for us outside his door, a weathered old man. He has a grin like a possum with a touch of bulldog thrown in for good measure. He wears rubber boots that come up almost to his hips. His faded coveralls speak of a man who is not afraid of hard work and sweat.

You know what that is? He points to a tree as big around as a truck camper.

The giant tree towers over a log cabin, which was the Pony Express station. It sits only fifty or sixty feet from David's home and is bordered by an old picket fence with a wooden gate, hanging by a single rusty hinge. Just beyond that is a muddy pond.

It's a cottonwood tree, isn't it?

It's not just a cottonwood tree, says David. It's the second-largest Frémont cottonwood tree in all of America. You just check your record book and you'll see. Know what those poles are leaning against it? Those are genuine telegraph poles I gathered on my ranch here. I'm not so smart sometimes myself. I threw away a dozen of the wooden insulators before I realized what they were. They're right out there in mud in the middle of that pond now. See that wire going into the cabin? That's the original wire that replaced the Pony Express. When they stopped riding, this became the telegraph office. It's been in my family for over a hundred years, and Mother and Daddy lived in it before they built the house me and my wife now call home.

We go inside the dusty old log cabin. It is filled with ancient pots and pans and spurs and bridles and all kinds of Old West junk, but I cannot keep my eye off the telegraph wire that dangles free overhead.

You like that, don't you, says David. Yeah, a lot of people

do. We helped get our daughter through college by framing pieces of it and selling it. There's not a lot left now. But let's see if we can't find you a piece.

He reaches into a drawer and removes a pair of pliers. He cuts a piece of wire two inches long and hands it to me. His possum grin reappears and I become a kid on Christmas morning who just unwrapped what he always wanted.

Yeah, son, says David, this old shack is where Mark Twain and Sir Richard Burton stayed as well as the Pony riders. Back in 1935 it became an important part of my own history. I was to ride in the Pony Express Association Race when my horse got kicked in the knee. I got discouraged. My sister offered to let me ride her horse, but I didn't want to take a girl's animal into the race. I did, though, and I set a record. I galloped ten miles in thirty-five minutes and one second. I can't even get on a horse today and this old shed is just filled with junk.

I like old stuff, I tell him.

I'm glad my wife does, too, says David. Otherwise I wouldn't be here today.

Could I get a limb from the tree? I ask.

A limb?

I want to carve a pony, I say, as I continue on down the Trail. It would mean a lot to me if it came from this spot here.

I know just the limb, he nods.

He gets a saw and we go down to his barn, where a giant tree limb has been dragged. He eyes it as if it yet lives.

That thing almost killed me, David confides. I was working under the tree and just stepped inside to get something when the wind tore it free. It crashed on the spot where I had been working. Maybe it'll give your pony some kick.

It's just the right size. Want me to saw it?

No, I can manage.

He saws a foot-long limb as big around as my forearm

from the record-setting cottonwood. I carry it back to his house, where Leah and I get back on our bikes.

Don't cut off a finger carving that pony, David cautions me.

I'll remember.

Leah and I pedal our bikes down the dusty road past ten or twelve old tombstones. When we pull into the yard in front of her house, we find Bret getting into his banged-up, rusty old car.

You look in a hurry, I say. Making another beer run?

Your friend has been at the refuge all day and night, Bret tells me. He can't get a ride out of the desert and I thought I'd give him a lift back to his jeep.

Tell him I said hello?

Sure thing, Bret agrees as he heads off down the dirt road.

Leah goes into her house and mixes flour and milk to make bread. I wander into the shed with the rusty traps to get a hammer and hatchet to split four legs from my pony wood. It feels good to work with my hands. I imagine that a creature is wanting to spring from the cottonwood; Amos and Jack, on the other hand, think I want to play fetch. It would be easy to get caught in a serene place like this.

I go inside and Leah is kneading bread dough. Her hands are strong and caring. Her face soothes me as I watch her work.

I hope you like fresh bread, she smiles.

I do, but I think I'll move on today. I've been on the road now for two months and I have a piece to go yet.

She stops kneading the dough as it becomes as thick as cheese. Her eyes are those of a friend.

You're sure welcome to stay, she invites. You're not in any-body's way.

Maybe you'll come visit me in Alabama one day?

They do have those tour buses, she says, her wonderful voice lightening.

It is now that I begin to realize what I felt in bed last night that the desert was starting to tell me. This journey is catching up with me. My heart and soul are filling with all those I have met and it is a bit sad to think that the trek will soon be over. Still, I feel pulled toward the Pacific Ocean, as though the undertow of the great waves themselves are at work on me.

Leah gives me a lift twenty-five miles down the Trail to Ibapah, near the Nevada border. With my pack by my side, I watch her old car vanish into the desert, followed by a trail of dust. I am not sure why, but I like knowing that the bread dough awaits her at home. I can see her hands kneading it as the wind comes through the window to blow her hair.

CHAPTER
THIRTY-FOUR

The trail of dust left by Leah's car drifts off the road back into the hills, disappearing among the rocks and sage. I lift my pack from the ground and turn to face a small grocery store with two gasoline pumps outside. A sign in the window promises a U.S. post office inside as well as bread and beer. A car arrives and two Indians get out. One is an old woman, and her wrinkled face has the charm and beauty of the desert.

Hello, I say.

She eyes me with a look of caution. But when she sees my smile, she offers one, too. I open the door for her and she enters the store. I leave my pack outside, but follow her.

I gather an onion, tomato, cheese, tortilla, and small bag of rice in my arms. The old woman approaches the single clerk with her loaf of bread and milk. He is a white man in his late forties.

How are you today, Morning Flower? he greets her.

I'm doing okay, Don, she says. I made a new basket this week.

He places her food into a bag and she leaves. I set my items on the counter and introduce myself to Don, the owner.

Are there a lot of Indians here in Ibapah? I ask.

Mostly all Indians, says Don. The Goshute Reservation is just a few miles from here. Me and my wife took over the store five years ago. I ran casinos in Reno and Atlantic City for twenty years. But it got to be too much of a rat race. All the crime finally got to me. It wasn't easy when we first moved here. It took a long time to build trust with the Indians. Now they know we don't cheat them and we never put anybody before them just because they're white. The Goshutes were the heathens thrown together from other tribes. Nobody wanted them. Most of them today are shy and gentle.

I go to the picnic table outside. I slice cheese and onion for a tortilla. Ibapah was the Deep Creek Pony Express station and, as I chew, I dig into my pack to get Sir Richard Burton's diary to see what he saw when he came through here in 1860:

> The Mormons were not wanting in kindness; they supplied us with excellent potatoes, and told us to make their house our home. We preferred, however, living and cooking afield. The station was dirty to the last degree: the flies suggested the Egyptian plague; they could be brushed from the walls in thousands; but, though sage makes good brooms, no one cares to sweep clean. This, I repeat, is not Mormon, but Western: the people . . . apparently disdain any occupation save that of herding cattle, and will do so till the land is settled.

Two flies buzz about my tortilla. As I try to knock them down with my hand I wonder if they are cousins to the very ones Sir Richard speaks of in his diary. Indians come and go from the lone grocery store and all are kind to answer when I say hello. Some of the fat Indian girls, looking a lot like my Cherokee great-aunt, just respond by giggling. When a red truck arrives with two Indian men about my age, I go to them and ask what's going on.

Just out for a ride, says the passenger, a rifle between his legs.

Having trouble? I look at the gun.

No, he says. But you never know what the Feds will do.

The driver returns from the store with a bag in his hand. He gets in the truck and starts the motor. The passenger reaches his arm out the window. Our hands grip each other as if it were as natural as breathing.

Back in Wyoming, I say, a Sioux made me a Brother to the Serpent. Do you know what it means?

I'm a Goshute, he says. I don't know.

The truck moves forward and he nods good-bye. Thinking more about Meadowlark making me a Brother to the Serpent takes me back to Casper, Wyoming, where I learned of Sean's death and spoke to his mother, Carolyn, in Seattle. I begin to ache to know if Andrea made it there safe and sound and go to the pay phone on the side of the grocery store to call her. I prepare to hear Carolyn answer the phone, but the *hello* comes from the sweet, sensual voice of Andrea, inspiring a vision of her clear blue eyes. I feel like new life is breathed back into me.

Are you okay? I wonder.

Yes, she says, I am fine. But I was beginning to think you would never call. I was worried about you in the desert.

This rare magical desert. It strips me bare and in only a matter of seconds I am wanting and needing to hold Andrea close and tenderly.

How was the trip on the bus?

It was long and boring, she tells me. But nothing since then has stopped flying. I am sleeping in Sean's room, where he hung himself. I took the test and the little tube showed the circle. I am pregnant.

My heart sinks. For a split second I want to believe that the test is mistaken, that things could be simple. But I am only grabbing at straws.

How do you feel about this?

At first, says Andrea, I was excited. Then I was scared. I phoned my roommate in Vienna and she told me she just learned that she was pregnant, too. So I slept on it and became happy again. I wrote her and told her that we would have the babies together. But she phoned this morning after getting my letter. It arrived a day late. The day before she went for an abortion. Now I am confused again. I phoned my friend in Los Angeles to tell him, but he lives only in his head. He said I could have the baby and give it to him. What kind of human being says such a thing? I could not carry my own baby for nine months and give it away. Maybe I should have an abortion, but isn't that murder? I am confused.

Perhaps you should see someone who counsels in such things. There's no charge.

Yes, she says, this might be a good idea. Right now I only know I want to see you again before I leave for Vienna. Is there some way we can do this?

A part of me now wants to run away because I chance being hurt if I get more involved with Andrea and have to watch her vanish over the Atlantic Ocean back to Austria. But I'm willing to take that risk. Life's too short to throw love out the window.

What do you have in mind?

You said the Trail takes you around Lake Tahoe?

Yes, I say, feeling some of the hope and thrill I felt when I was a teenager and in love for the first time.

I looked at a map. There is an American Youth Hostel at Lake Tahoe. We could meet when you pass through.

Yes, I say, surrendering to my heart. We can meet there.

I hang up the receiver and return to my pack. I slip it onto my back and start walking into the desert. I got a feeling that something like I have never known awaits me.

*   *   *

The sun is beginning to set when I find an expensive-looking cowboy hat resting on the desert floor, as if it were some kind of bait. Who owned it and how did it get here?

I lift the hat and brush the dust from it. I place the new hat on my head and it fits as if it had been waiting for me. But I already own one and so I place the orphaned hat on a sagebrush to dance back and forth in the wind. I hope one of the Indians will find it and consider it a gift from the desert.

As I walk on, the sun sinks farther into the horizon and the wind picks up. From a nearby gully, two big antelope leap forward and charge across the desert, a trail of dust following. They are almost out of sight when I discover the tracks and droppings of wild mustangs. It is as though I have arrived at some rare spot in the desert. Even the bleached bones of a sheep that now appear excite me. They do not make me think of death, but rather make me all the more thankful to be alive and to have met so many kind people who have helped me survive to this point.

As night falls I pitch my tent and build a fire to cook rice and make coffee. When my stomach is full, I behold the tiny glowing orange light of a distant town. Miles beyond it a lightning storm flashes yellow over the Great Salt Lake Desert. Where I now stand was once covered by a sea and I think again of the Pacific Ocean calling me. There is a spot there in San Francisco where I want to end my journey by a cliff; waves crash against it to create a kind of music. Many years ago, when I lived in San Francisco, I saw a whale rise and fall and rise and fall as he swam northward just beyond this point. I have never forgotten the mammal's grace and strength, something I admire.

Tonight, however, I am sitting by my fire in the Utah desert and it is exactly where I want to be just now. I take the cottonwood limb from my pack and open my knife. I begin to carve a pony with his powerful head lowered, as if in an eternal gallop.

My fire begins to fade as I carve into the night. The moon and stars are now brilliant and a coyote howls from the hills. I can see the cowboy hat still dancing in the wind on the sagebrush.

As the cottonwood limb slowly takes shape the knife handle rubs blisters between my thumb and index finger. I welcome a pain that creates life in my very hands. I take the buffalo hair from my leather pouch and hold it to the neck and hips of my crude wooden horse. It blows in the wind and inspires me to see the finished creature. I will call him Buffalo Pony.

I finally grow tired and put away the wood, knife, and buffalo hair. I take the hawk-wing bone-whistle and blow into it. The faint, delicate music is little more than a man's breath in the wind. Still, it allows me to touch my cabin on the hill. With the whistle in my hand, I begin to chant. I'm connected to the deepest part of my voice now. It is as clear and strong as my heart is open and it resonates through the night and out over the hills. It is a song of celebration of life.

I crawl into my faithful sleeping bag and fall asleep with Andrea in my arms.

CHAPTER
THIRTY-FIVE

The Great Salt Lake Desert fades into the hills behind me the next day as I walk on toward Nevada. I take a certain pride in having my clothes and old faded hat filled with Utah dust because I survived the trek across such a rugged and desolate land. But when I reach Ely, Nevada, I'm itching to take a merciful shower and have a real bed with clean sheets.

I get a room in the Copper Queen Casino and Hotel. How odd to be in a room with four walls after being in the desert for so long, where the only walls are distant hills and those self-imposed. The TV is connected to CNN, and world news jolts me into recalling how small and insignificant I truly am. Still, with all the chaos across the globe, it also reminds me how free and uncomplicated my Trail life is.

I set Buffalo Pony on the nightstand by my bed. His head begins to have a mouth and ears. His strong back is starting to ripple with muscles.

The door from my room opens to the casino and, as I stand shaving before the bathroom mirror, I hear loud bells every time someone hits a jackpot. Those damn bells ring so often that they begin to work on my curiosity and greed. Why, I could use a pocketful of that money myself. I finish shaving, get dressed, and head out the door into the casino. What a carnival! Lights blink and bells ring as if in competition with each other to see which can get the most attention. A man in a bright red shirt with yellow flowers and a gold chain around his neck pulls the long silver arm of a slot machine. It blinks as quarters roll to jingle-jangle into a pile.

I sit and face a computer screen to play Jokers Wild. It swallows my nickels like a starved man eating peanuts. From time to time I win a buck and press the button that releases the pile of won nickels. I want those around me to hear the winner's music. My God, I am getting as caught up in this obsession as the man with the gold chain around his neck. I do, however, come back to my senses after donating ten dollars to help support human folly.

I take my dirty and smoky Trail clothes down to the Smoke Shop Laundromat on the Shoshoni Reservation. As I stick them in the washer it dawns on me that I left my favorite blue shirt hanging on a limb at the campfire where I began to carve Buffalo Pony. It does not take more than a coffee shop shrink to guess that some part of me wanted to stay there.

Throughout the night the casino rings its Jokers Wild bells as I try to sleep. I am relieved the next morning to pack my clean clothes and head on down the Trail with Buffalo Pony. I have grown to depend on the smell of sage, dust, and campfire smoke, and also the silence. A casino is no place to find peace.

Miles west of Ely, the hills are dotted with abandoned copper mines. I climb a hill to look down into one. It is covered with wire, and a wooden sign, dangling by a single nail, warns that the air down there is bad. Snakes abound and shafts may cave in at any second. But as I peer down into the dark mine a cool breeze shoots from the cave, as if the earth itself were blowing breath over a snowcapped mountain.

Two black lizards rest side by side on a sunbaked boulder by the mine and I guess I'm part reptile, for I feel closer to them right now than I did to the strangers I saw gambling in the casino. I've always believed that Nature and her creatures care for me, though I've sometimes wondered if Man does.

Maybe I'm just some foolish romantic, but even if I am I don't care. The farther I go down the Trail, the more I accept myself. And as I look closer at my two friends the lizards, resting side by side on the sunbaked boulder by the mine, I decide that this is an ideal spot to sit for a while and carve on Buffalo Pony. Why, he might even start to breathe some of that cool air blowing from deep down in the mine. After all, hasn't the earth for millions of years shared its magic with trees, one of which has donated a limb I now begin to carve with my knife?

The knife's silver blade reflects the sunlight as I press the sharp edge into the wood to create two eyes for Buffalo Pony. The lizards seem to watch me and approve, I hope, of my humble attempt at vision.

That afternoon, I walk toward a sign by the roadside that reads: GARNET HILL, 5 MILES. An arrow points down a second road and I'm tempted to follow it, for I learned from the hotel clerk back in Ely that the hill is filled with garnets, free to those who choose to find them. Yes, now that I think more about it, *I will* detour from the Trail those few miles with hopes of finding two of the precious stones to set into the sockets of Buffalo Pony's eyes.

By the time I reach Garnet Hill, covered with rocks and pines, I've built up a hardy appetite. And while I'm eager to find some gems, I'm more excited about eating first.

It doesn't bother me in the least that the clean clothes on my back begin to smell of smoke again, my campfire popping and crackling as I cook a pot of rice. I'm about to have my first bite when a camper-truck arrives. A man and a woman get out.

I didn't think anybody was around for miles. I greet them.

We just pulled in from Reno, says the man, who introduces himself and his wife as Gene and Norma Elliot. We're on vacation and Norma wanted to try her luck at finding some of these garnets they claim are here.

Care for some rice? I invite them.

No, Norma thanks me, we just ate at a café back in Ely.

Norma hurries into the pines with her head lowered and her eyes searching the ground. Gene, on the other hand, sits across from me at the picnic table where I enjoy my rice dish. Norma isn't even out of sight when five minutes later she turns and calls out.

I found two already.

Damn if I don't feel a bit like I did when I was with Sam and got gold fever. I gobble the rest of the rice and head into the pines along with Gene. Fifteen minutes later I still haven't found a single garnet. Norma reappears from the grove of cedar and pines with fifteen in her hand. I do not get it. I can usually find arrowheads and other Indian artifacts on the earth with the glance of an eye. Have I been looking too hard? Does a man constantly have to adjust his vision, depending on what he seeks?

How does your wife do it? I call out to Gene.

Beats me, he admits. I haven't found one yet, either.

Ah, you boys stop your pouting, Norma grins. I'm not above sharing.

She walks to me and holds out her palm, covered with garnets half the size of peas.

Take a couple, she offers.

You mean it? I ask her.

Sure, she tells me and I pick two of the pretty stones and drop them into my pocket.

We have plans to meet some friends this evening, says Gene, so we better head on back toward Ely. You want a ride back to the highway?

Thanks, I don't mind if I do.

How are you fixed for water? Norma asks me. You're headed into some remote countryside.

My canteen's about half full.

Here, she insists, let's fill it up from our jug. We'll get more water when we get back to Ely.

She takes the cap from their water jug and fills my canteen. It runs over, some of the water dripping to the dusty ground.

When I get thirsty on down the road, I say, I'll have a drink and think of you two.

En route to their truck, I find—at last—a beautiful dark red garnet eyeing me from the dust. It seems to wink at me as I pick it up.

Arriving back at the main road, I part with Gene and Norma. I watch their truck disappear toward Ely and I head on to the west, my pack growing heavier with each step.

That evening, as I walk on, I hear the cries of sheep in the twilight; an owl begins to hoot. The cries grow stronger and louder till, finally, the darkened hillside comes alive with hundreds of white sheep. They seem to float in slow motion across the desert like the foam that gathers after great waves have surrendered to the earth. A lone horse with a rider moves alongside them. I wave and he does the same. We are little more than shadows in each other's lives and soon even that passes. He and the sheep vanish over the hill and into the night.

As I travel through the Nevada darkness I wonder if an Indian found my blue shirt hanging on the tree limb over my cold campfire. What about the cowboy hat I placed on the sagebrush? These things are so small, but when you are alone walking in desert at night you sometimes ponder the thread that ties fragile life together. It may, after all, be the loose ends that help determine who we are and who we become as we move on down the Trail.

Nevada Highway 50 bills itself as "The Loneliest Road in America." It sure feels long to me as I finally stagger into the town of Eureka, bordered by Diamond Mountain. I must look as if I've been tied to a rope and dragged by horse halfway across the state. My clothes are so dusty that I can beat them with my hands to create a personal little dust storm. The sun has further faded my old hat and I'm just a bit too embarrassed to enter one of the newer-looking cafés to eat breakfast.

The Alpine Lodge, however, looks perfect for the likes of me, and this is where I'll eat. It is a turn-of-the-century block building three stories high with some of the windows broken and boarded up; it is an ornery old man who has seen better days. A single pine tree, four feet tall, grows from the sidewalk near the door I now enter.

Booths, spread with red and white checkered tablecloths, line the green walls. A mirror-covered light as big as my pack and shaped like Saturn hangs from the center of the ceiling. Six stools line the counter, and a yellow and red neon sign says BAR and CASINO at the other end of the room. It smells of bacon and eggs and fresh coffee, but what really makes it seem so down home is the dog stretched out on the couch with his head on a pillow. He looks like the Walt Disney version of Old Yeller. Yes, sir, I can be as real as the sweat in my hatband in this here café.

The only folks in the Alpine are an elderly couple seated at the counter. I join them and ask if the food is any good.

Best buckwheat pancakes I ever ate, claims the man.

They are delicious, adds his wife. I was beginning to wonder if we'd ever find a place to eat. This desert goes on forever.

We're from Iowa, says the man. On the way to Sacramento to see our daughter. She just had her first baby. A girl.

The couple is beaming with pride. A moment later, a man in his sixties appears from the kitchen. He wears a floppy leather hat and his mustache is so big that it hides his whole mouth. Red suspenders hold up his pants and he seems as down home as Old Yeller over there on the wrinkled couch.

These folks say the buckwheat pancakes will go down if you drink enough coffee, I tell him.

If you don't like them, says the man, you don't have to pay for them. I mixed the batter myself.

I tell him what I'm up to and he introduces himself as Frank Escobar. He speaks in a deliberate manner, as if to savor each word, born with feeling and thought. Frank has owned and operated the Alpine Lodge since 1972. For twenty years he lived in Los Angeles, where he was an aeronautical engineer. Six other years he was a sheriff's deputy in Austin, Nevada. He lights up when I tell him where I was born and raised.

We got something in common, says Frank. I'm a *Nevada* hillbilly.

It is curious to watch Frank speak because with each word his lips appear from behind his curtain of mustache. It takes very little imagination to see Mark Twain standing before me.

That your dog? I ask.

Yes, says Frank. Sassy cames into my life over a year ago. Some city people from back East were driving across Nevada when they saw him in the desert back near Ely. Somebody had poured motor oil all over him and they thought he was a coyote. When they stopped to take his photograph, he got in their car and wouldn't get out till they stopped here to eat. I cleaned him up in my bathtub and he's been with me ever since. Are you my friend, Sassy?

Sassy raises his head from the pillow on the couch. The sagging skin over his sleepy eyes springs into action. Yes, Frank, he seems to say, you are my master and I am your friend . . . as long as you feed me.

What is the little stage used for? I point to the area just above Sassy.

Nothing now, says Frank, except collecting clutter. It was built by Saxophone Blanche when she retired from the road. She was a singer who traveled all across America. She sang her last song in here when she turned seventy. She was murdered and her body was found right over there on the floor. A while back my bar was robbed by a guy with a gun. He locked the bartender in the back room and took off with several rolls of silver dollars. He was drunk, though, and I was able to track him down. Those coins kept falling from his pockets and he left a trail of silver on the streets. If you're going to have those pancakes, I better get to the batter.

Frank disappears into the kitchen and I go to the couch. Sassy wags his tail as I rub his head. When I return to my seat at the counter, I'm surprised to see a man with shoulder-length black hair step out of the kitchen.

Did you want coffee? he asks.

I nod and he pours me a cup.

Frank told me what you're doing, he says. That's something. I always wanted to paddle down the Mississippi River, but I'm too old for such as that now. I'm forty-one. My name is Ashbury. Well, that's what most people call me, anyway, because I went through the whole Haight-Ashbury trip in San Francisco. I started to work here six days ago. I met Frank at the employment office in Reno. I had lost all my money gambling. Now all I want to do is get back on my feet and buy some land in Oregon. I want to get as far away from pavement and concrete as possible. I've spent all my tip money so far, though, on those one-arm bandits back there. Some woman from Wyoming stopped yesterday for a cup of coffee and put *three* quarters in one machine. Then *bingo*—fifteen hundred dollars came rolling out. That was *my* money. I sure like your hiking shoes. As soon as Frank pays me I'm going to buy a pair of boots with steel toes.

Two men around twenty years old hurry into the room. They wear tie-dyed T-shirts that say GRATEFUL DEAD 1991. Their hair is long and necklaces and bracelets abound.

Can Frank give us a lift down to the garage? says the one who calls himself Beaver.

I guess, Ashbury shrugs, but maybe you should phone first and make sure your van is ready.

Beaver uses the phone and Ashbury disappears into the kitchen. I feel as though I have stepped back in time again. It is 1860 and 1968 in one breath.

Your van break down? I ask.

That's right, Brother Man, says the Dead Head. Six of us in the family went to a concert in Denver. Beaver and his girl got married during the show. Beautiful happening, Brother Man. Then we headed back to the Bay Area when our water pump went out. You met Frank yet? He's got God in his soul. He gave us all a free room last night. Till we came in here nobody in town would give us crumbs off the floor.

Shit. Beaver hangs up the phone. The van won't be ready till tomorrow. They got the wrong water pump.

What are we going to do? says the other Dead Head. We don't have money for the pump and a room tonight, too.

Ashbury comes from the kitchen with a stack of hot pancakes. Sassy raises his head from the pillow and the two Dead Heads eye my breakfast as well. I got a feeling that I've landed in a most peculiar shade in the Nevada desert.

CHAPTER
THIRTY-SIX

I begin to eat my buckwheat pancakes as the couple from Iowa heads out the door. The Dead Heads run upstairs to tell their friends about the bum water pump and Ashbury snatches the Iowa tip from the counter. He changes it for four quarters at the cash register and hurries back to the one-armed bandit. Frank reappears from the kitchen and shakes his head when he spots Ashbury being sucked dry in the little cracker box casino.

Some people never learn, says Frank, compassion in his tone.

Could I see a room? I ask, finishing my pancakes.

I follow Frank up the stairs and Sassy follows me. What a trio we make as we walk down a hallway lighted only by the sun shining through a cracked window. Someone has drawn a red rocket as big as Sassy on the wall. It appears flying a mile a minute into outer space.

There're dog hairs everywhere, says Frank, but the beds are clean.

He unlocks a door and pushes it open. Someone has written in pencil on the wall THIS IS A LOUSY HOTEL, and two naked wires dangle from the ceiling as if they do not know what to do with themselves.

It's perfect, I say. Is there an extra charge to draw on the walls?

Frank's lips appear in a slight grin from behind his curtain of mustache. We go back downstairs and I pay sixteen dollars for the room. When I tip Ashbury for breakfast, he returns again to the slot machine.

The mapmakers won't print it, says Frank, but back up there on the other side of Diamond Mountain is where the old Trail came through. Two squaws were picking piñon nuts one day when they discovered two Pony riders caught in a homosexual act. Ever since then the locals have called that ridge Cocksucker Peak.

Frank speaks in the same slow and gentle tone with which he talks to Sassy when he rubs his head, as though he is simply passing on folklore without prejudice or judgment. I don't know if the story is true, but it seems that for such folklore to live this long may say something about America and its preoccupation with sex.

Who did the pastels? I ponder, walking into the small BAR and CASINO.

On the wall over two slot machines are two powerful pictures of Albert Einstein and Mohandas Gandhi. Between them, over a piano, hang two Mexican sombreros. On another wall is the pastel of a striking woman I do not recognize.

I drew them, Frank tells me. The woman was my wife. She died a few years ago. We have a son in L.A., but we haven't talked in a long time. He lives with some woman and they have a son. He's a lazy bum and won't work. They take money from the government. The last time I saw him I had on my cowboy boots. When I kicked him in the ass, he must've rolled some ten feet. The picture of Gandhi has a happier memory. Some years back when I was working on planes in Los Angeles, the University of Southern California had the president of India over to speak on economics in that country. The auditorium was packed with students and teachers and the general public. When the speaker got to the mike, I raised that picture of Gandhi over the sea of heads. The Indian president wanted to know where I got it. He liked it so much that he said he would help me any way he could. I told him he could help me now by speaking on my hero, instead of economics. He was put on the spot, but took a vote from the audience. The professors who brought him to speak were pissed, but democracy won. He spoke on Gandhi.

A man wearing faded jeans and boots enters the bar. Long white hair falls from his hat where tiny American flags stick from the band. Tomorrow is the Fourth of July.

Want a cup of coffee, Cowboy? Frank inquires.

No, Frank, says Cowboy. Think I'll get on to a good cold beer.

Cowboy sits at the bar and Frank hands him a bottle of Miller. A customer enters the café and Frank goes to check on him. It isn't even ten o'clock in the morning yet and I wonder what is with this man called "Cowboy" as he downs such an early brew. I introduce myself.

I was raised to be a Mennonite, says Cowboy, back up in South Dakota and Idaho. I've spent most of my life logging and cowboying. I'd like to play in a country and western band, but so far I haven't done too much about it. I was so shy when I was a child that my grandmother made me sing solo before the whole church. I guess I need her help now to get me going again. I lost my fourth wife two years ago and it hasn't been too easy since. We went to bed happy, but when I woke up in the morning to kiss her she was cold. I had her cremated and went up in a plane over Diamond Mountain. I scattered her ashes. Those hills ain't been the same to me since.

If I came looking for America along one of the most famous Trails in this country's history, I sure am getting it left and right. I can't decide if it is more fitting to cry or laugh sometimes. I buy Cowboy a beer to swim in and head out the door to stroll about Eureka, which got its name from the expression a man used when he spotted silver oozing from rocks he had placed around his roaring campfire here among these very hills.

That afternoon I am honored and pleased when Frank invites me to join him and Sassy for a ride back among the hills. His old car is as beat up and dusty as his hotel, café, and casino, but I could care less as we rattle up a dirt road into a canyon.

I take Sassy up here every day, says Frank. He likes to run free. Sometimes he gets carried away, though, and takes off after a jackrabbit.

I don't feel sorry for Frank, but I am moved by him. His wife died and he kicked his son the last time he saw him. He seems to think the world of his dog that someone poured motor oil on, and sometimes he gives free rooms to people like the Dead Heads whose van broke down. Then, too, he gave Ashbury a job when he was down and out. Now that I think more about it, Frank does not run a hotel. It is a kind of halfway house for folks lost or stranded in the desert.

All these hills you're looking at, says Frank, hold some of the world's richest veins of gold. Only those in Africa and Russia outdo them. It's a shame, though, that the miners have used cyanide to separate the gold from the ore. It gets into our water supply. I don't go along with such as that myself. But then I don't agree with a lot of things others think are just fine. You take the rodeo for example. I can't see men having to prove themselves against animals. I know a man whose son got thrown from a bronc and broke his back. He'll never walk or use his arms again.

Frank stops the car and opens the door. Sassy hops out and runs as free as the desert wind through the sage. I like the look on Frank's face as he watches his best friend.

We return to the Alpine Lodge and I go to my room. I

stretch out on the bed. JESUS has been penciled near the two naked wires dangling from the ceiling.

I must have been more weary than I thought, for I awake at about eight o'clock that night and go downstairs to the CASINO and BAR.

Cowboy is seated at the bar with a guitar in his hands. He looks as though he just struck it rich—in a vein of empty beer bottles that line the counter before him. Next to him sits Beaver and his new Grateful Dead concert wife, Lisa, who is nineteen.

Any special requests? shouts Cowboy, as if he could pick a tune right out of the air.

The bartender, nicknamed Chicago, has come to Eureka from that city to work in the Alpine Lodge for the summer. He's here to see how business is going. His father just might buy the whole rootin'-tootin' show from Frank.

How about an Elvis song? suggests Chicago.

Just name it, Cowboys offers, tiny American flags sticking from his hat like a marching parade.

"Hound Dog," Chicago calls out.

Could I have another beer? asks Ashbury, setting an empty Budweiser can on the bar and grinning as though he were back in Haight-Ashbury in 1968.

You can have all you want. I'll just mark them down here on your bill.

Frances, Frank's friend in her sixties, plays the slot machine under the pictures of Einstein and Gandhi. She pulls the silver arm and some fifty quarters fly out from the machine. This music sends Ashbury into a mad frenzy of joy and frustration.

Oh, he says, just look at that. Oh, I wish I had a quarter.

I pay Chicago for a beer. He gives me change and I give Ashbury two quarters. He lights up as if he just found a long-lost friend.

You won't regret it, he says. If I hit it, we'll split the money.

Cowboy begins to sing "Hound Dog" and, frankly, he is so drunk that he sounds like a dog. I'm surprised that Sassy, stretched out on his couch throne, does not start howling. Beaver, however, also is three sheets to the wind, and slaps Cowboy on the back as if he were the next Hank Williams.

Beautiful, Brother Man, says Beaver. Just beautiful.

Frances, having gathered her pile of quarters, returns to the bar to sit by me. Ashbury approaches her slot machine, and Einstein and Gandhi seem to watch him.

He won't win anything now, says Frances. I worked here for Frank for years. I know those machines. They hit only once in a blue moon. They're dogs. They'll bite you if you don't watch out. You looking for work? I got a house two blocks away that needs painting before I can sell it. That's why I'm in town from Wisconsin. I can't take living here anymore. Not since my lover died. Too many memories make a place a graveyard.

Maybe this Grateful Dead bunch is looking for work, I say. Their van broke down and they're low on money.

They ain't looking for work, says Frances. They're looking for handouts.

Ashbury staggers away from the one-armed bandit and disappears out the door into the night. Cowboy—at last—drops from the charts; he lays the guitar on the counter. He orders himself and Beaver another drink.

You're from another generation and another world, says Cowboy. But it don't matter to me. I love a man for who he is inside.

I feel the same way, Brother Man, says Beaver.

Beaver now takes Cowboy's hand and kisses it. Cowboy does the same with Beaver's.

Beautiful, says the bride, Lisa. Just beautiful.

Makes me want to throw up, Frances whispers out the corner of her mouth.

Some people see skin, says Cowboy, before they see the real person inside that skin.

That's right, Brother Man, agrees Beaver. You're one smart human being.

Four more Dead Heads hurry into the cracker box BAR and CASINO. I cannot prove that they have been smoking grass, but they smile as if they just ate cosmic canaries. Two are young women wearing enough gold and silver bracelets to make any Gypsy envious. They stand before the slot machines as if they could guess their weights, heights, and fortunes. They have robust suntans and neither wears a bra. One of the young ladies has on coveralls and her hands roam around inside her clothes. I try not to stare, but each time her fingers ease up from her waist to her neck inside those loose clothes, she pushes them forward to reveal naked breasts as big as cantaloupes.

I don't care if a man is black, red, blue, or striped like a zebra, says Cowboy. We all got to love each other.

I love you, says Beaver.

I love you, says Cowboy.

They now kiss each other's hands again, but this is not enough. Once men are inspired, no flood or fire can stop them. Beaver and Cowboy now put their arms around each other and kiss their cheeks. The tiny American flags sticking from Cowboy's hat wave back and forth as if in victory over all prejudice and hatred. Frances, however, is making a face as if, at any second, she may pour her beer over the impassioned philosophers.

Frank enters and stops in his tracks to behold the show. The look on his face, however, is as accepting as the look on his old buddies Einstein and Gandhi.

Frank, says Beaver, coming from his barstool, I have something for you.

Beaver takes a necklace from his neck and places it over

Frank's head. A stone the size of marble is fastened to the center of the necklace.

Thank you for all your kindness, says Beaver. The stone is from Stonehenge. We have a hundred people in our family and our leader made a special trip to England for us. He paid a thousand dollars for a piece of Stonehenge as big as a softball.

Everyone stares at Frank and it is so quiet that you could hear a silver dollar hit the street a block away. Frank eyes the stone dangling below his neck and then looks at Beaver.

Thank you, says Frank with a warm tone, his face perplexed.

Sassy appears. He follows his master through the bar and out the door, Frank's fingers fondling the necklace's rare stone.

I wish the president were like Frank, says Lisa. That old fart that's in there now can't do a thing. I hate him.

Wait a second, I wonder. What happened to all that talk about love?

You're right. Her tone softens. I don't hate him, but he's out of touch with what's really going on in America. Maybe he can't help it because he's so protected by his bodyguards. I'd like to take him camping in Golden Gate Park. When I was fifteen that was where I was living. When you live on the streets, you get to know the real world.

Frances shakes her head and gets up to go to the bathroom. Beaver comes over and puts his arms around Lisa as Cowboy takes the guitar from the counter. He begins to pick and sing "This Land Is Your Land" by Woodie Guthrie.

Wondering if Woodie is turning over in his grave, I drift out the door. The Nevada night air is cool and fresh and I find Frank seated on a concrete wall two feet high. Sassy is curled up at his feet.

Some night, I tell Frank.

Yes, says Frank, his Mason's belt buckle silver in the moonlight. Some night. Are you aware of the sabotage?

Sabotage?

That bartender, says Frank. He didn't like it when I hired Ashbury. He gave him all that beer on credit tonight just to get him drunk so I'll have to let him go. When I hired him, I told him he'd have to stay sober.

Ashbury steps from behind a building across the street and staggers toward us. He mumbles something and goes into the bar. I see more compassion than anger in Frank's face.

You think and feel a lot, Frank. You can see it in the pastel you did of your wife.

I wrote her a poem one time, says Frank. *The New Yorker* bought it for seventy-five dollars some years ago. I don't know if it was published or not.

Could I hear it?

Men are hosing down the street two blocks away to clean Eureka for the Fourth of July tomorrow. The water now streams along the sidewalk past Frank, Sassy, and me. Frank's lips slowly appear from behind his curtain of mustache.

Warmth, life, and love abound, says Frank. Flowers bloom, and song is in the air. For she is mine. She waits for me. I long for her, to feel her cheek on mine, to tell her what I have in mind, of plans I have for us to share. And she is mine, until reality taps my shoulder, to tell me it's a dream, that the day is cold, and I'm alone.

CHAPTER THIRTY-SEVEN

I awake in the night with voices drifting through my opened window from the Nevada sky, brilliant with stars. At first I am a bit spooked. Then, coming more awake, I realize that the voices belong to the Dead Heads, sitting on the roof.

They're up there, I hear Beaver saying. Up there watching and laughing at what we do down here.

I guess, says the girl whose hands played inside her clothes down in the BAR and CASINO. But we can't be sure. It could just be all ice and fire with darkness in between.

A part of me wants to stick my head out the window and tell them to *shut up. I want to rest.* But I lie back down and fall asleep with their whispers floating about my room.

The next morning I am jolted awake by the sound of someone pounding the door next to my room.

Ashbury? Frances is yelling. *Ashbury,* you lazy bum. Frank's looking for you. You're thirty minutes late and he needs help in the kitchen. Don't expect me to keep doing it. *You hear me?*

Ashbury mumbles as if his head is under a pillow and I hear Frances's footsteps fade down the hallway, two or three of the loose boards squeaking. I get dressed and go downstairs.

It is the Fourth of July and I find Frank and Frances seated at the bar. They have bowls of soup before them. Frances uses a spoon, but Frank—his giant mustache covering his mouth—uses a straw to suck the soup from the bowl. As he leans toward the soup his Stonehenge necklace swings over the center of his chest.

See anything of Ashbury? Frank asks.

No, I say. But I heard him grunt when I closed my door.

He should've left when those young hippies did this morning, says Frances. You should've seen that van. It was packed full.

Cowboy enters with his tiny American flags sticking from his hat. His white hair falls down his back. He takes a seat at the bar.

What happened? he asks.

You and that hippie hugged and kissed. Frances seems to delight in her information.

Oh, Cowboy sighs. I wasn't sure if I dreamed it or what. Mind if I help myself to a coffee?

I'll get it for you, says Frances, pouring a cup. I still don't know what I'll do about painting my house. I got to get back on that Greyhound by the fifteenth headed for Wisconsin before my ticket expires.

I'd do it for you, Cowboy offers, but I'm not very good at painting.

I'm not looking for the job to win any awards. Frances hands him the cup of coffee. I just want to get it done so I can sell my house.

The truth is, Cowboy confesses, I'm afraid to get up on a ladder.

Sassy wanders into the room to curl up by Frank. He continues to suck his soup through his straw, the liquid disappearing into his giant mustache.

I go to my room upstairs for one last time and pack my bag. I'm about to leave when I see THIS IS A LOUSY HOTEL penciled on the wall. I set my pack on the floor and unzip one of its pockets. I pull out a pencil and write on the wall to change the complaint to read: THIS IS A LOUSY HOTEL, BUT YOU LEAVE IT FEELING THAT LIFE IS WONDERFUL AND RICH.

When I get downstairs, Frank is almost finished with his soup. The straw slurps in the bottom of the bowl. Frances is playing the slot machine and Cowboy is pouring himself more coffee. I rub Sassy on the head.

Well, I invite, let's head on toward California.

Happy Fourth, says Frank. Come back sometime.

You can count on it, I promise, and head out the door.

That night, around my campfire, I cannot get Frank and Sassy off my mind. I sit on the ground with my knife open, trying to give Buffalo Pony some personality. Silver does not ooze from the rocks encircling my fire as it did for the man who cried *Eureka,* but I gained something from my stay in that town that will be with me for the rest of my life. I feel that I am carving some of that warmth into the cottonwood as I sit beneath the Nevada stars. Is that a heart I hear beating inside Buffalo Pony, or just the wind in my ears?

It's about sixty miles from Eureka to Austin, Nevada, and when I arrive there I find the tiny town built on the side of a hill. It seems to be a dividing line between the rough, rugged wilderness and the trendy influence of the West Coast, for hairstyles and clothes are changing. My waiter in a Mexican café looks like somebody on MTV. This is fine and dandy, but it doesn't compare to a dust devil's ancient flare.

When I leave Austin the next morning, I behold the vast desert before me again. But only a mile away a most peculiar oasis, half a city block square, sits before me.

As I walk toward the green oasis I see that it is a cemetery from the 1800s. The rusty iron gate squeaks as I enter to behold the weathered tombstones. I am surprised at how many buried here came from Europe. A marble angel almost as big as myself stands over one grave in the shade of a cedar. Here, only a few feet below my boots, are the bones of the pioneers and cowboys who built the Old West. What a reminder that I, too, will one day bite the dust. I'm not worried about that right now, though, since I've almost made it down the Trail to California. As I wander about the graves, I read some of the inscriptions on the tombstones:

> GONE TO MEET HIS MAKER
> ABNER LOWRY
> BORN IN IRELAND 1845
> DIED HERE 1885

> GONE, BUT NOT FORGOTTEN
> OUR BELOVED MOTHER
> ELIZABETH BROWN
> 1834–1894

Sometimes I'm too sentimental for my own good, for reading about someone's mother being dead always gets to me. I walk from the cemetery into the scorching sun and discover a herd of cattle scattered before me behind barbed wire. I walk on only a few more feet, however, when I discover a bull staring at me. He has escaped the wire and is as free to roam as a stray bullet. His horns are at least three feet long and their tips are as sharp as ice picks. His eyes are as big around as the barrel of a shotgun. I take another step and he begins to pound the earth with his hoof. Dust rises and drifts toward me in the breeze.

I stop in my tracks with hopes that it will calm the bull. Sweat drips down my face and adrenaline jars my system to rush fear to every muscle. I'm ready to run like hell but I'm not sure *where* to if he charges.

The few pines and cedars are too small to climb, so forget them. I can make a run for it and dive over the fence back

into the cemetery. Yes, how appropriate. Or I can chance my
luck and keep walking . . . very slowly. The bull pounds
the earth again with more dust rising. He seems to enjoy
watching me squirm. I take a step forward. Then another and
another. There's no turning back now. I take another step.
He pounds the earth again, lowering his head, showing me
the tips of the horns.

I keep walking straight ahead into the desert as I watch
him from the corner of my eye. When I'm a hundred yards
away from the bull, I'm so relieved that he didn't charge that
the vast, waterless desert with its scorching sun is a welcome
sight.

I've often thought that it would be horrible to run out of
water in the desert, and this is just the very thing that happens two days later. My mouth is dry and my lips begin to
parch, my clothes wet with sweat. There's not a shade in
sight and my old faded hat can cover only so much of me. My
buddy, the pack, isn't much of a friend in a situation like this;
its weight on my back makes me more thirsty with each step I
take.

I finally drop the pack to the side of the road and begin to
hitchhike. There're very few cars out here and each one appears from around a curve in the hills some ten miles back
like a shiny trinket in the sun. It seems to take forever for
each car to get to me so I can see if I'll get a lift or be passed
by like an unwanted cactus.

At last, mercy comes when a car pulls over with two teenage boys inside. They're headed all the way to Carson City.
This will not only put me near the California state line, but
also close to Lake Tahoe, where I am to meet Andrea. I can't
wait. And what a great bonus: They're carrying a jug of icy
water, which I almost choke on as I drink and drink.

What you're doing is cool, says Chad, the driver. We're in
the Explorers Club. We got Dale Evans, Linda Evans, and

Robert Conrad as members. We're trying to get Clint Eastwood.

We won the 1989 Clean-up Award, says Ken, his companion. We cleared an old Indian trail to the top of a hill where the Indians used to build bonfires to signal each other. You could see the flames all the way to Las Vegas at night.

On the hood is strapped a Cabbage Patch doll. His stuffed face grins from ear to ear as we fly down the road.

What's with the doll? I ask.

Him? says Chad. Oh, we dollnapped him. His job is to watch the road when we forget to.

The radio is blasting and a song soon comes on by the Grateful Dead. I tell Chad and his friend about the Dead Heads I met back in Eureka.

We saw a bunch of those guys at a nuclear power plant demonstration, says Chad. We pounded them with raw eggs. We didn't have anything against them. It's just that we're from a small town and sometimes we get bored.

When we arrive in Carson City, I get out and walk to the old Pony Express site. A sign hangs over a beautiful little house and reads VICTORIA WEDDING CHAPEL. It's a quickie marriage place and the only one in Carson City. I've always been intrigued with folks who swear to love each other and stay together till they die. Being a veteran of such a wild promise myself, I wonder if the chapel houses some unusual stories about couples who got married as quickly as a Pony rider once leapt from horse to horse on the very spot.

With the pack on my back, I march into the chapel as if looking to tie the knot. But my timing is off. The place is packed with the friends of two couples about to get hitched.

Come back in an hour, says Irene, owner and operator of the chapel. I got my hands full now.

Like a rejected lover, I leave the chapel. I go into a grocery store—oh, it's so wonderfully cool in here—and buy a cantaloupe. When I exit, I sit under the kind shade of a tall cottonwood and slice fruit with my red-handled pocket knife, dulled from carving Buffalo Pony. The yellow-orange fruit is just ripe, like thick, sweet water. Across the street, two men play horseshoes. From time to time the air *clanks* as metal strikes metal.

The first legal hanging in Nevada Territory took place in Carson City in 1860 and the rope claimed a Pony rider, Carr William. He had killed a man during a quarrel.

It was also in 1860 here in Carson City that the Penrod Hotel was turned into a fort because of the Pah Ute War that broke out. Ever since 1849, when white men raced westward to stick their greedy hands into the gold found at Sutter's Mill on the American River, the Native Americans had been outraged. Many of the white men showed no respect for their culture or their land. They trapped their animals and cut their piñon trees, which furnished nuts for their survival. The Indians finally swore to regain their homelands, dignity, and honor. They began to attack the whites, and that included the stagecoach and Pony Express stations stretching from Lake Tahoe to Salt Lake City. The Pony riders were put out of commission for a whole month. When things settled down, the Pony Express had lost 150 horses. Seven stations had been crippled and 16 men were killed.

I finish eating the cantaloupe. My hands are sticky from the juice and I wash them with water from my canteen. The men across the street are still swinging horseshoes when I dig into my pack for the diary of Sir Richard. I turn to his section on Carson City:

> . . . A gambler or professional player, who in the Eastern States is exceptionally peaceful, because he fears the publicity of a quarrel, here must distinguish himself as a fighting man. A curious story was told to illustrate how the ends of justice might, at a pinch, in the case of a popular character, be defeated. A man was convicted of

killing his adversary after saying to the bystanders, "Stoop down while I shoot the son of a dog (female)." Counsel for the people showed *malice prepense;* counsel for defense pleaded that his client was *rectus in curia,* and manifestly couldn't mean a man, but a dog. The judge ratified the verdict of acquittal.

I could do without all the fancy lawyer talk, but is sounds like if a guy called a man a son of a bitch before he shot him he could live to brag about it. Too bad that Carr William had manners when he killed his man, or he might have dodged the rope. An hour passes since I stuck my head into the chapel so I stuff Sir Richard's diary back into my pack and head that way again.

I go inside the Victoria Wedding Chapel and find the place empty except for Irene. She now looks relaxed and relieved to have sent more newlyweds galloping off on honeymoons.

Sorry I wasn't so friendly before, she says. Sometimes it gets pretty wild in here.

She gives me a tour of the chapel, which has three rooms. Each one gets bigger and more flowery than the other and costs a bit more, but they all end with *I do.*

How long have you done this? I ask her.

I've had the business for fourteen years now, says Irene, an attractive woman. Before this my husband and I had a flower shop in the Bay Area. You wondering about those little bunches of seeds tied in veils? I let people throw them instead of rice because I read that birds eat the rice and some of it isn't good for them.

Have you had any unusual customers?

Oh, my, yes. Once we even had Hell's Angels get married. He was forty-four and she was twenty-three. Must've been almost a hundred motorcycles. We spend forty-five minutes lining up the bikes the way they wanted them. Then we had to reverse the order of the bikes. They were drinking and I just knew they would go wild any second. I get a lot of drop-ins, but other customers were afraid to stop when they saw all those bikes. I finally explained it to the leader and he was nice about it. They got married and all of them blasted off like a bunch of wild Indians. I used to be open twenty-fours a day, but now I keep more sane hours. I have several ministers and I can phone the one that is most appropriate; he'll get here in fifteen minutes. He usually gets tipped fifteen dollars, but sometimes he'll get as much as a hundred. People have used everything under the sun for rings. Cigar bands. Hair. Bolts. Sometimes the younger ones don't put rings on their fingers. They exchange earrings. One man in his twenties was so nervous he couldn't put it through the hole in her ear. I helped him. The saddest ones are those who are pregnant and get married because they feel forced into it. The happiest couple I ever saw was this black and white couple. Something about them made everybody here feel so good. Even the minister felt it. After all these years I still cry sometimes when people get married. Some of them I have to hug. I just can't help myself. Some of the customers are repeats. I had this one man who was married twelve times. I can see three or four but *twelve*?

A man and a woman in their twenties enter. She is fat, and his shoulders are slouched as if the world had been strapped to his back. But their eyes are filled with joy, excitement, and great hope.

We'd like to get married, she says, smiling at the man who lowers his head and eyes to his shoes.

That's wonderful, says Irene. Let me give you a tour of the chapel.

As she leads them from room to room I slip into my pack and start for the door. Irene's sweet voice drifts into the hallway, where I hear her telling them what a handsome couple they make and how happy they'll be together. I hope that she's right, but I can't forget what she just told me a few minutes ago about the man who was married twelve times. I wonder if she told each of his new brides the same story.

CHAPTER
THIRTY-EIGHT

Arriving at the American Youth Hostel a day before Andrea gets there, I leave my pack in my room and go down to the great lake. Beneath tall pines, I sit on a bed of needles. Sassy might like it here to curl up nearby as I carve the legs for Buffalo Pony; they'll be fastened to him with wooden pegs when I get to a drill.

That afternoon I paint the body as red as the wings of a cardinal. After making yellow circles for the sun on the back and sides, I color the powerful legs black, as if they charge through the desert night. White flashes in the carved eyes, as if they flame with sacred vision. Tiny moons roll down the legs to be pulled by earth's great gravity into thundering hooves. I hold the buffalo hair to the mane and tail areas, which will be planted when I drill the holes. The wind blows from Lake Tahoe, and Buffalo Pony is coming as alive as the ripples on the water and the memories of all those I have met so far on the long Trail. I do not forget that the limb he is born of almost killed David Bagley when it crashed to the ground.

The next day I leave the hostel to go to the grocery store. When I return, I find Andrea on the porch. We melt into each other's arms.

I thought the bus would never get here, she says.

It feels so good to see Andrea's face that it does not matter what we do. I want only to have her near. Her clear blue eyes and rosy cheeks add to her sensuality, but her full lips and voice, and what they reveal, are the delicate forces that strip me bare. I cannot and do not want to hide from her who I am inside. As much as it lingers, long gone are the days when I drove my first love of seventeen to the drive-in movies to see Clint Eastwood in *Fistful of Dollars*. I thought a man was to show no tenderness or complexity. He was to be only clever steel. He bit a bullet when a red-hot knife blade dug into his arm to remove the arrowhead. He might grunt, but that was the extent of his emotion. Yes, I'm almost certain now that some of the brighter girls laughed at all us macho boys trying to become men. Forgive me for reaching so far back into the past again, but this trek continues to make me ponder so many of the myths that American males seem to find necessary to keep them marching on, but into what and under whose command but that of our own demise?

The next day I come from the hostel shower and go to our room. I find Andrea standing before the window, where sunlight warms her face. She holds a towel to dry herself, but now places it over her chest in modesty.

The water, she whispers in her German-French accent, it felt so good on my skin.

I didn't think we would ever see each other again, I say. You came and went in my dreams when I crossed the desert.

Yes, she whispers.

She pushes the towel to her side for me to see her breasts in the sunlight. They are big and firm and the nipples are unusually large and as pink as her moist mouth. She takes my hand and kisses it.

You are not afraid of your body, she tells me, and that helps me feel comfortable with mine.

She still holds my hand and I gently raise the index finger

to touch her cheek. She puts the finger in her mouth and makes it warm and wet.

I did not realize, she says, how much I needed to make love till last night when you held me. I feel so good this morning. I'm not worried about anything.

She moves my hand to her cheek again and kisses it. I put my other hand into her wet hair, and the bed is soft and warm as we crawl into it. I have never wanted to make love to anyone as much as I do Andrea now, her blue eyes watching me. I take her hand and lick her fingers.

The night in Salt Lake City, I begin, when we heard the pianist from Vienna, you placed your hand over mine for the first time.

Mmmmm . . . she smiles.

I wanted to hold you then, I continue, so bad I couldn't stand it. I wished I could have played the piano for you and made you happy the way the pianist was doing. I envied his hands.

The tip of her tongue traces my lips.

Your fingers know things his will never know, she whispers.

Her mouth opens as I pull her close and we kiss, her naked breasts pressing against my chest. Our arms now wrap around each other as our thighs slide together, her skin next to mine feeling like something I've been needing for so long that it hurts to admit. Part of me wants to hurry inside her now, but I try to hold back and enjoy the sound of her excited breathing. I want every moment to last in my memory, for I fear a time that might come when I won't be able to touch her.

Late that afternoon, Andrea and I go to the lake to pitch my tent among the thick pines. Steller's jays cry out as they hop from limb to limb, their royal crests magnificent over their blue bodies. We toss them pieces of bread and they snatch them from the ground like starved orphans running from the law.

We walk down to the water. It is as clear as a great spring and Andrea lets her fingers wade about in the ripples.

Let's come back tonight, she says, and take off our clothes to swim in the moonlight.

That evening we build a fire near the tent and cook a pot of rice. I savor the shadows on her face.

Could I use your knife? she asks me.

What do you want it for? I nod, fishing into my pocket for the knife.

Just something. She takes the knife.

She opens the blade I used to carve Buffalo Pony. Taking a seat at the wooden picnic table, she lowers the tip of the blade into the wood. She slowly carves ANDREA JERRY.

I will not carve the AND or LOVES parts, she says. Everyone does that. Besides, I cannot define who we are here tonight. I only know that we are here and this makes me happy by the fire. If I were an animal, what would I be?

A deer perhaps. An otter sometimes.

You are a bear by day, she says. A big dog in the evening and an owl at night.

Darkness falls as we sit on the ground by the fire and eat our rice. It is getting cool and the flames warm us. Except for Albert back in the desert, this is the first campfire I have shared with anyone on this journey; its end approaches and fills me with that peculiar mixture of sadness and excitement. I am grateful that Andrea is with me to keep me from thinking too much about that just now.

The glowing coals, she says, are a world of their own. I see a canyon in them. It is deep and winding. It is orange and red and blue. I can't imagine being without my eyes. I could not paint or draw. I could not see your face or the face of my baby when he is born.

That reminds me, I say, reaching into my pocket. I have

something for you. They're two garnets. A woman and her husband gave them to me in Nevada, where we looked for them together in the desert. I thought of them as eyes for Buffalo Pony because the woman had such good vision. But I decided that they belong to you. Maybe they will help you see.

She holds the dark red gems in her palm before the red and orange canyon of fire. The flames' shadows flicker on her face, a most rare gem itself.

They will help me remember, she says, sadness in her voice.

Mosquitoes begin to bite us. That, along with the cool night air, make us skip the moonlight swim. We crawl into the tent and eye the flames only a few yards from our feet. We have been together for two days now and tomorrow we part. We lie in the darkness as if denying this.

I must tell you something, she whispers, I think I am so drawn to you because I need you so much right now. I am not really so attracted to your looks and you are too old for me.

I am jolted. I would be no less surprised if Lake Tahoe fell ten feet in the night. When I was with the wagon train—my God, another time, another world—the mules and horses sometimes spooked when they saw a large rock or tree stump as if they were monsters. The animals would turn sideways, trying to run away from a simple world they knew that had suddenly become distorted. The mules and horses could not trust anything or anyone—even their masters—when this happened. We with the leather reins in our hands had to hold tight till the animals saw that stumps were as firmly planted in the earth as large rocks were bound to soil as well. They were safe. Here, now by Andrea in the dark, I must hold the reins to myself. It is true that I am much older than she, but I like my age and who I am. My looks may not be what some would like, but some have not found them cruel. Several horrible seconds pass till I finally realize what is happening inside Andrea.

I will miss you, I say. I want to be your friend.

Yes, she whispers, and takes my hand. I ask forgiveness. Please let me back in. I am afraid of leaving you and I only wanted to hurt you for a moment because of that.

We put our arms around each other.

Will you rub my stomach? she whispers, easing my fingers to her warm flesh.

Did you phone your parents in Austria?

No, I will not tell them till I see them in person. But it does not matter. I want this baby and I will do what *I* think is right. I know them. Money will be the first concern. Their lives center around it. I am mostly concerned about my father. He so much wanted me to live out his dream to come to America after the war. I have failed him, but I cannot change that now. It is as it is. My mother will cry when I tell her that the father of my baby is black. When he and I walked together in Los Angeles, both blacks and whites stared. Some white man in a car shouted nigger. I hope no one will call my little baby an ugly name.

I'm sure he'll be a beautiful child, I tell her.

The last few days before Beethoven died, he did not play the piano, but banged the keys. This is how I feel about leaving you. I wish this baby were yours.

She stops my hand from gently rubbing her stomach. She presses it against her skin as if I might make more contact with what she feels inside.

Yes, I surrender. I wish he were, too.

With the wind blowing through the moonlit and swaying pines, we fall asleep as the fire fades into the night. Sometime later, I awake and study Andrea's face as I did the first night we were together at the hostel back in Salt Lake City. I hear her breathing. It is a sound that I may need at some point to help breathe love back into me.

* * *

The next morning we return to the youth hostel and she stuffs her clothes into her orange backpack. I reach into my pack and pull out Buffalo Pony. I hold the buffalo hair and legs to him to show how he will look when he's all put together.

When we met, she says, you had only the hair and a dream to create him. Now he is real. He looks alive.

It breaks my heart to walk her to the bus station to return to L.A. to fly back home to Vienna. I can't believe that she will vanish before my very eyes in only a matter of minutes.

Will you come to Vienna and see me one day? she asks, tears rolling down her eyes.

I hope so. Maybe one day you'll come to see me in Alabama.

Yes, she whispers, with my baby.

The Greyhound arrives and opens its door. Andrea and I embrace. Tears roll down her cheeks onto mine. Or are they my tears as well? She boards the bus and vanishes behind dark-tinted glasses. The bus roars away and disappears down the long road into the pines.

CHAPTER
THIRTY-NINE

As soon as Andrea's bus is out of sight, I return to our room and place Buffalo Pony in my pack along with my clothes. I discover that Andrea left behind a red sock under the bed. I slip Buffalo Pony into it and put it back in the bag. I can't stand being in this room without her now. The wrinkled sheets haunt me.

I exit the hostel with my pack. I'm headed south around Lake Tahoe when I spot a bookstore. I feel drawn inside and discover a book titled *American Indian Myths and Legends*. I turn to the index and find "The Snake Brothers" listed on page 404. Intrigued by my encounter with Meadowlark and his making me a Brother to the Serpent, I turn to that page and read the tale.

Countless moons ago, long before the white men came to their hunting grounds, four Sioux brothers shot a buffalo with arrows and killed it. Then a voice spoke.

Take plenty of meat, said the voice. But put my head and hooves and all other parts back together.

Only the youngest Sioux brother believed the voice. His older brothers said that they only imagined the voice. They took the meat and went back to their camp. The youngest brother, however, stayed and put the buffalo's parts back together as he chanted the Buffalo Prayer. When he finished, the great animal was whole and alive again. The youngest Sioux watched him run over the hill.

The older brothers returned to gather the skin of the killed buffalo. They accused the youngest brother of hiding it. They refused to believe him when he told them what had happened.

That night all the brothers awoke around the campfire when they heard loud rattles. All but the youngest were being turned into giant rattlesnakes.

We are being punished, said the oldest brother, because we did not listen to the inner voice.

It is what the Great Spirit has willed, said the youngest brother.

Yes, said the brothers, but though we are snakes we are still your brothers. We will help you when we can.

The youngest brother carried them to the hills, where they crawled into holes to live. Sixteen days later, the youngest brother prepared to go to war. He went to the hills and asked his snake brothers for help. They could only hiss now and one pushed forth a medicine bundle from the hole. It was snake medicine and protected the young Sioux in battle. He returned home in victory with many horses.

I close the book and leave the bookstore with my pack. I will let others judge if it was only a coincidence that Meadowlark appeared when he did to reach out to Crane at Creek with the Buffalo Prayer and the snake medicine to help me get back in touch with my innermost voice for strength to chant and continue the long journey when I was down.

We smelled each other in the wind, Meadowlark had said. We have met for a reason.

I do not doubt that the Great Spirit had a hand in that wind any more than I doubt the magic of life and love. It is that belief that I now draw upon as I walk the Trail around Lake Tahoe and hurt so from parting with Andrea.

This depression will pass, I tell myself, but I must walk and walk till I have paid the toll. I want new blisters and sweat and throbs in the legs and back.

Finally, as the sun begins to set over Lake Tahoe, I start to digest the past two days, and a sweetness, however faint, begins to replace the salt. I have chosen a life of Trails and I must bear the occasional sorrow with as much grace as possible, not so much out of nobility as out of the practical. I have many miles yet to go and I can only appreciate them if I see getting to know Andrea as a blessing and gift from Fate, if not the Great Spirit Itself. Still, for all my rationalizing, I wonder if I made a mistake in letting Andrea vanish back to Europe. Should I phone her before she leaves and ask her to stay?

Twilight is settling over the water when I enter the town of Lake Tahoe. It buzzes with tourists who have come to gamble and to escape the ho-hum of their lives. Outside the famous casino called Harrah's sits the bigger-than-life sculpture of a Pony rider on his horse. They gallop with such speed that the very steel of which they are made seems as soft as silk, rippling in the wind. I stand before it to stare as a few of the tourists gawk at me and my pack.

I step into the casino, but what a mistake. The flashing lights and ringing bells shove me out the door and back into the approaching night. How beautiful the moon is over the massive and towering pines as I walk on down the very Trail where the Pony rider Robert Haslam ("Pony Bob") galloped. He once rode 36 hours and covered 380 miles. A fiery old man, he worked his last few years at the Congress Hotel in Chicago. He had business cards with drawings of him when he was twenty and tough as nails. He spun his yarns of adventure to the hotel guests, who eagerly paid him to take them for a ride down memory lane.

The lights of Lake Tahoe fade into the night as I walk on with only the moon and Buffalo Pony at my side. How good it feels to be in California—my last state. I do not use my tent tonight. I simply crawl into my sleeping bag, resting on a bed of pine needles. Andrea said that I was an owl at night. But a real one now hoots from the dark forest. It's okay, I accept that I am a man.

I awake in the night startled by a dream. I was riding Buffalo Pony. He was as big as the giant sculpture back in Lake Tahoe. He leapt from mountaintop to mountaintop. We could fly with grace and ease as I held to the buffalo mane. Then, back on earth, he walked with a limp. One great leg was made of wood. I loved him all the more.

The Trail leads over the Sierras and across the American River to Placerville. In the days of the Old West it was called Hang Town because a lot of folks dangled here from ropes. The site of the old hanging tree is now a bar in the quaint little downtown. A tree limb sticks from the second floor out over the street and a dummy swings from it with a rope around its neck. Pride in history knows no limits. As I stand studying the scarecrow-type dummy I wonder what his crime was. Did he abandon a cornfield or perform unnatural acts with a wayward mannequin? Perhaps he simply swiped a stuffed horse from a toy store and an example was to be set.

Placerville, save for the dummy, appears to be a charming little town. It is clean, with flowers and houses perfect-looking enough for any magazine. Wondering where my best buy is on a motel room for the night, I approach two female joggers sitting on a bench with sweat dripping down their red faces. Their eyes harden just a bit as I get closer. Maybe I look more like a bum at this point than a humble adventurer.

Sorry to interrupt you, I say. Do you know this town?

Yes, says the older woman. You're in Placerville, California.

She seems as serious as the sweat dripping down her face. But does she truly think I don't know where I am? Maybe I should take a good, long look in the mirror to see if something is going on in my face I'm not aware of. I feel just fine. In fact, I'm amused. How can I not be? I'm almost to Sacramento.

No, I say. I mean do you know the town well enough to direct me to the best buy on a motel for the night?

I'm sorry, she says, finally laughing at herself along with her jogging partner. I thought you meant . . . I'm Joan McClintock and this is Tina Scaline. Welcome to Placerville.

I introduce myself and explain what I'm doing. Then they escort me up the street toward the Days Inn. I am used to people getting excited and joining in the spirit of my journey because they want so much to do the same, but these two—sucking water up straws from plastic bottles—become thrilled as if they decide right on the spot to abandon their daily lives and hit the Trail with me. Tina has been up since four this morning, when she cleaned out the milk bin at the grocery store where she has worked for years. Joan, who teaches physical education at the local college, and Tina are training partners for marathons.

Joan is no ordinary woman, says Tina. She ran a race last year that covered a hundred miles.

Joan, an unusually beautiful woman, has a body as athletic as that of any Olympic star. I admire this quality in women as much as in men. I have always been amazed at the human body and all that it can do when treated with respect. But a woman who can run a hundred miles? This is no trendy jogger, licking the boots of the physical fitness craze.

A hundred miles? That's fantastic.

I didn't make it all the way. I did seventy miles.

The look in her eyes and the tone of her voice impress me more than those other thirty miles because I see and hear the surface of what appears to be some great undertow trying to pull Joan in over her head. In a few minutes we arrive at the point where my street to the motel parts from their path.

I regret we got here so soon. I look at Joan. You two are fascinating.

I have an idea, Joan suggests. Tomorrow, why don't we

take you to Sutter's Mill, where gold was discovered. Isn't that what got the Pony Express started?

Sounds great, I nod. Does your husband have a drill?

A drill? says Joan, as if I don't know where I am again.

I've carved a pony. I need to put holes in him to fasten his legs with wooden pegs.

Yes, says Joan, he has a workshop. I'm sure he must have a drill.

We make arrangements on the time to meet tomorrow afternoon and I check into the Days Inn. I certainly haven't gotten Andrea off my mind, but I'm so excited that I'm almost to Sacramento to begin the canoe trip that my missing her is easier to handle. Then, too, Joan was so warm and friendly that I feel a touch of home here in Placerville. It will be a real treat to get that drill and put the legs, mane, and tail on Buffalo Pony. Yes, everything is coming together.

CHAPTER
FORTY

The next afternoon I stand outside the Days Inn to await Joan's husband, Ed. A car pulls up and a man sticks his head from the window.

You must be Jerry, the man calls. Joan said you'd have on a hat with a feather in it.

Are you Ed? I ask, a bit surprised because he looks so much older than Joan.

That's me.

I get into the car with Ed and find that he carries a cane. As he drives from the motel, he eyes the feather in my hat.

I see you met a Steller's jay.

Yes, I say, I found it back on Lake Tahoe where a friend and I camped one night. She had to return to Europe. How'd you and Joan meet?

She was teaching where I was principal. The reason I noticed your Steller's jay feather is that I'm an avid bird-watcher. Last year I identified one hundred fifty different birds on my two-acre farm.

When we arrive at the farm, he shows me his walnut trees. He amazes me when he begins to do bird whistles beneath the branches. That he must lean on a cane to support himself makes his songs of breath all the more dear. I cannot always control what my mind flashes before me and now, as his bird whistles fill the air, I see Joan running like a mountain lion while he drags his cane in the dirt to leave a trail like a lone, lost snake.

Ed gets his drill and I am glad that this man with birds in his heart will become part of Buffalo Pony. He is showing me the different sizes of drill bits I can choose from when Joan steps from the house.

You have an interesting husband, I tell her.

I think so, too, she agrees, tenderly touching Ed's shoulder as she comes closer. Shall we head on out to the old mill?

Ed and Joan drive me to Sutter's Mill, only a few minutes away, where the Gold Rush in 1849 started on the American River. Wooden beams of the old mill have been saved and—as I watch the river roar down from the mountains with kids riding the rapids—I think how these banks once rattled and clanked with crazed men digging and panning for gold. Many had abandoned their ships and torn down the hemp sails to build tents here while others struggled across the desert to seek their great fame and fortune. In time, those letters from back home must have helped save those whose dreams became only wet sand.

That evening Ed does not feel so well. He will not say what is bothering him.

Is your leg hurting you? I ask, hoping that he might tell me what had happened to it. But he simply frowns.

You and Joan go on and have dinner, he says. I'll be just fine.

When Joan and I get to Old Red—a neon-lighted but tranquil kind of honky-tonk—we have to wait a few minutes on a table. It still surprises me from time to time that I'm, finally, in *California*. When I was the age of the Pony riders, I believed that this golden state offered the end of the rainbow. Weren't all the girls here tanned and beautiful? Didn't the waves crash to shore just to honor the passion and glory of all those who trained on Muscle Beach? Weren't all minds open and wise and welcoming to newcomers—even those of us who grew up in the mountains of Alabama?

I lived in California several times from the age of eighteen to thirty-eight, I tell Joan. Years passed between each stay. Each time allowed me to realize just how important home was to me. That realization finally lead me to walk the Trail of Tears. Ever since, I have had no desire to live anywhere but home, near my family. So here tonight in old Hang Town awaiting a table for chicken, I owe a great deal to California.

This sure is good chicken, I remark, licking my lips. We've finally been seated at a cozy table off to one side of the restaurant.

I'm glad you like it. We'll get Ed a plate of ribs to take home. You *walked* here from Missouri?

I've mostly walked, but I took a few rides. When I went on the Trail of Tears, I did all nine hundred miles by foot. I was inspired by a touch of desperation. I had to prove something to myself. I'm knocked out that you *ran* seventy miles. That puts you in the top 1 percent of the physically fit.

I still feel like I failed, though. I guess I have something to prove to myself, too. What you were saying earlier about being so close to your family really hits home.

The human face and eyes take on certain features when someone is about to drop his masks. I see that nakedness now in Joan. It makes me need to make a decision. Shall I just keep eating this chicken, or go with her down into the canyon of her soul?

What do you mean? I rest the chicken on the plate.

In 1989, she says, the San Francisco earthquake almost destroyed my father's home. We've always been close and I took off from work for two years to oversee the rebuilding. It made me feel good to get it back in order. Ed was understanding about my being gone a lot of the time. He had his birds, but . . . when I finished the job and got back home, I got a letter in a few weeks from my father. It crushed me. He is ninety years old and my sisters convinced him that I had wasted a lot of the money. I couldn't believe it. . . .

A part of me now wishes that I had stayed with the chicken, for Joan is on the verge of crying. This may be the first time she has told anyone about this and it appears that we are now just below the surface.

Then, she continues, when I entered the Western States Endurance Run last year—we had to run over mountains and across streams—the sun was hell. I had a pacer with me, but she was not allowed to touch me. Not even a little finger. I collapsed after seventy miles. I just couldn't do it anymore. My pacer tried to talk me up again, but all I wanted to do was just lie there on the ground. I just wanted to rest.

A tear slips from her eye.

That night, she says, I couldn't believe that I failed. My whole life seemed to depend on that run. Nobody in my family phoned. *Nobody.* I wanted my father to tell me he loved me.

People often tell me their secrets, but I never get used to it. I reach over and touch her hand. Sometimes that's all we need, isn't it—just to know that someone, even a stranger, will listen with care?

That night back in the Days Inn, I plug the electric drill into the wall. I drill holes in the cottonwood carving and begin to attach the legs with wooden pegs. As Buffalo Pony becomes whole I see the tears running down Joan's cheeks, but I also see the fight and determination in her eyes. I hear as well the beautiful bird songs of Ed. We did, indeed, discover gold today where others thought it had washed away.

The next morning I am packed and ready to head down the Trail toward Sacramento when Joan stops to get the drill. She is hot and sweaty and in her jogging clothes. I see the mountain lion alive in her eyes today, but perhaps more importantly than that I hear peace in her voice.

I'll see you on the news, says Joan, when you start down the river. Drop us a postcard from San Francisco?

When I get to Sacramento, I am in ecstasy. I walk down to the Sacramento River, where the Pony Express letters were carried by the *Antelope,* a steamer, to San Francisco. Another bigger-than-life pony and rider sculpture has been erected here, like the one in St. Jo where I began the Trail. I brush my fingers against the iron hoof of this giant galloping horse, and I'm so happy that I feel bigger than life myself. Why, I just might reach up any second to pull a leaf from the top of this tree towering over the swift water. Damn, now that I take a closer look, this river really is moving pretty fast. And what about those swirling pools here and there? I haven't canoed since I was seventeen, and that was just for kicks for less than a mile with my two buddies who are now in the Great Beyond. I'm not so positive that I can handle a canoe. Still, charged with the warrior and led by the fool, I rent a canoe for tomorrow and buy supplies.

Early the next morning a crew from Fox Television shows up along with folks from another TV station and a photographer from the *Sacramento Bee.* I haven't even taken the canoe for a test run. Is the stomach of a grown man supposed to feel this uneasy? As I am interviewed on the docks I have visions of crawling into the canoe and shoving off into the center of the swirling river to turn in circles while those on the bank laugh and sing *Row, row, row your boat* . . .

With cameras rolling for all of America to see, I step into the rocky canoe. Well, at least I can make a splash in my life. *Merrily, merrily, merrily, merrily, life is but a dream.* . . .

CHAPTER
FORTY-ONE

Many onlookers have gathered at the dock along with the media people to watch me try to head downriver. A woman holds a little girl in her arms and is motioning to her that she should wave good-bye to me. I'm excited by all the attention, but frankly, this very moment, I wish I were simply alone with the canoe and the water so we could get acquainted. I'm hardly seated and already the canoe seems determined to give me a rough time, rocking under me like the back of some great prehistoric creature awakening from a nap. I finally get the ropes untied from the dock and drop them into the canoe at my feet. Lifting the paddle, I place one end to the dock and push away from the onlookers. With my first four or five strokes, the boat is such a stranger that we wobble like a conversation between two people who don't like each other but try to carry on nonetheless. I'm still seated and it feels awkward. Hoping to find a more agreeable position, I lower to my knees and the canoe shakes with such force that I fear it will turn over.

But I regain my balance and this position makes me more secure. I'm out in the middle of the river and the current pushes me downstream as I alternate left and right strokes. I'm so busy that I forget the media. I paddle under a giant bridge and eight or ten pigeons flutter overhead, a single feather floating down to the water.

The massive columns supporting the bridge mark my passage and I'm amazed at how fast I'm moving. My anxiety is replaced by thrill. I glance back and the docks and the folks watching me are now part of the past. I am on my way and the very gulls themselves seem to say so as they cry out, drifting over my head. The canoe, paddle, and my body begin to find their kinship in a kind of dance I have never known before. I like making my chest, shoulders, and arms work. At last my legs can take a break. I bought a pair of gloves, but I prefer to feel the wood in my bare hands. It puts me closer to the water and already I begin to respect its power.

A man sitting in front of a cardboard shack on the bank waves as I pass. He wears an old U.S. Army cap and watches me longingly. Then, only moments later, he disappears as I drift around the bend.

The sun beats down to glare on the river and my face begins to burn. I am paddling nonstop and my shirt becomes soaked with sweat. Thank goodness I had enough sense to get my dark shades from my pack before I pushed away from the docks. From time to time the canoe crashes against a wave with such force that it sends merciful mist blowing into my face. My shoulders and arms ache, but I like the kind of pain that allows me to feel the strength and ruggedness of my body. Just as my hands and my knife carved Buffalo Pony from a tree limb, sun, wind, and water can carve a person's outlook. The boy within me joins forces with the man and now I understand how Huck Finn might have felt when he drifted down the mighty Mississippi on his raft to celebrate freedom, adventure, and the beauty and the mystery of the river itself. All these things now come together within me to create the kind of wonder I experienced in childhood, and isn't it wonder that always gives birth to magic in the human spirit? If so, maybe that's why Meadowlark had said that a man who has lost the boy has lost the man. Be that as it may,

I know I have never before this moment on the river felt a greater sense of my manhood and childhood in the same breath.

I round the bend to discover two boys climbing a tree. A rope hangs fifty feet from the massive limb of a cottonwood out over the river as they follow rungs nailed into the trunk. When they reach the rope, they take turns swinging above the river. They are twenty feet above the water and let go to turn flips in the sky before splashing and disappearing, only to emerge with enough joy in their faces to paint a dry desert with glorious rain.

That looks like fun, I call out to them.

It is, says the first boy. You should try it.

But I am moving so fast downstream that I can barely hear him. The second boy, showing off—and I don't blame him— hurries back up the tree to do it again. As he lets go of the rope he shouts *Geronimo*. Their dog barks from the bank each time they splash, as if he wants to do it, too. It is just a bit sad to take the next bend, for the circus performers now become lost behind earth and trees. The faint barking of the dog grows weaker and weaker, replaced by the cries of gulls.

I have been paddling for almost five hours when I spot a sandy beach under trees for shade. I aim the streamlined eighteen-foot canoe that way. We slide onto the sand like a gull floating from the sky onto the water.

It feels odd to place my feet on earth again. I open a bag and get out an avocado and a tortilla. The food, cool shade, and rest are wonderful. Then I am startled when I hear twigs snapping. I spin around to see an enormous man with only shorts and shoes on. He smiles and I spot two gold-capped teeth. He stands pondering the canoe and me.

How are you? I finally ask.

Good, he says. I good. Boat yours?

I don't recognize his accent. He comes closer, eyeing the

canoe like it were something he has always dreamed of own-
ing.

You want something to eat? I offer him the food bag.

Not hungry, he says.

He moves closer to the canoe and towers over it. He bends
to pick it up and I wonder if he plans to take it home with
him.

Good, he says. Not heavy. I like. I like very much. Good.
Very good for water.

He lowers the canoe and his gold-capped teeth reflect the
sun. He seems happy now that he has touched the canoe and
determined its weight.

One day I own canoe, he says. Two years now in America.
Russia bad. I never go back. America *good*. I like all America.
Job, food, apartment. *Three* rooms. You wait. I back.

He disappears into the trees and returns with a plastic milk
jug. It is filled with water and ice.

Cold, he tells me. You drink. Go, drink.

I have ten gallons of water in the canoe, but there is no
way I can refuse this hospitality. It is a toast to our meeting. I
raise the jug to my lips.

Good? Cold?

Yes, I say. It is very good and cold. Thank you.

Good, America good.

I think back on some of the bigotry and narrow minds I
encountered on the Trail, and it still saddens me. But most of
the people I met were kind and caring. Yes, I agree with my
new Russian river friend. *America is good.*

That evening—I have paddled for ten hours now and covered almost twenty miles—the wind picks up and it begins to
get so cool that I must slip into my leather jacket. Eight Viet-
namese line the bank with fishing poles as I drift by them.

Catching anything? I shout above the wind.

A boy of about nine or ten reaches into the water. He lifts a line with a bass that is eighteen inches long. The entire family smiles at once to make a perfect family photograph with their Catch of the Year Award. The boy lowers the squirming fish back into the river as I sail on.

As twilight falls the wind becomes so strong that I can hardly move the canoe forward. I keep getting blown into the steep rockbanks. I become a bit spooked, for the nearest beach area for landing was over three miles back. The last thing I want now after such a wonderful day is to be flipped over into dark, cold waves, capping as I continue to fight the water.

As I work my way foot by foot down the rocky banks, water splashes into the canoe. The twilight is thickening into darkness, and my anxiety is becoming plain old fear. The wind is howling in the trees and I begin to chant against the night for strength. My voice seems to ride upon the capping waves.

Hope appears when I spot a light in a house atop a hill overlooking the river. It has a private dock and I head that way.

What a great sense of peace to feel the canoe stop against the wooden landing. I tie it to the dock and go up a flight of stairs toward a beautiful Victorian home. I have no idea how those inside will receive me. I cross my fingers and hope for the best as I knock on the door.

Sorry to bother you, I say. But I'm in a canoe and—

Yes, says the blond woman in her forties, I saw you on the news tonight.

Her teenage son and daughter now step from the back room of the plantation. All three are California-perfect. Straight white teeth. Glowing complexions. They are charged with intrigue and excitement about my drop-in visit and before I know it we're all down at the dock. They want to examine my canoe and pack and hear about my journey. I feel like a sailor spinning yarns as night falls around us. The mother offers for me to take a shower, but since her husband isn't here with us to second the motion, I decide my going into the house might be an intrusion on his territory. Besides, an old salty sailor like myself doesn't mind a little dirt and sweat. Why, I remember once on the high seas when . . .

A pear orchard sits only some fifty yards from the grand Victorian house. The limbs are bent with ripe fruit and I slide into my sleeping bag on thick grass on the bank by this Garden of Eden. I am exhausted, but I am as happy as I have ever been in my whole life. I like looking out from my sleeping bag to see that the light in the house is on and that a family is there together.

The wind is so powerful that the limbs over my head sway, threatening to break and blow across the river. I hear the water splashing against the bank. When the moon appears, it shines on the pears and the river alike. I am on solid ground, but my body continues to feel rocked by the water. Yes, my lover, the river, she has such a sweet way of putting me to sleep.

I awake in the night and the wind has stopped. The moon is now over the river and it is so silver and looks so solid on the water that I almost believe I could walk across it to the other side.

CHAPTER
FORTY-TWO

I awake at dawn. The trees are even thicker with pears than I thought and the river is so calm that a single whisper might make it ripple. Then the calm and silence are broken when the surface erupts. Two otters, near the bank, raise their heads out of the water in perfect unison and then dive back toward the bottom. For all I know, they are saying hello, welcoming me back to the river.

I want coffee, but decide not to build a fire to make it. The sunrise is charged with such splendor that I don't want to miss a moment of its magic.

I go down to the dock and am relieved to see that my canoe didn't get blown away in last night's gusts. I crawl into it and take Buffalo Pony from my pack. Tying him to the bow, I push from the dock to send ripples all the way across the river. It is so easy to drift downstream this morning that I feel like Buffalo Pony and I are flying, gliding toward San Francisco.

Less than hour later, I spot a café at a small marina. Three men inside gawk as the canoe slides along the landing. I go in and have coffee and breakfast. What a treasure to look out the window and see Buffalo Pony galloping at the bow, his mane and tail blowing in the morning breeze.

If you ask me, says an artichoke farmer seated at a table next to mine, you got a loose screw to be out there alone with just a canoe on that river. I wouldn't mind trading places with you, though. Driving a tractor isn't the greatest adventure in the world. But I don't have to worry about drowning.

Buzzed from three cups of strong coffee and my stomach full of potatoes, eggs, and toast, Buffalo Pony and I sail on. My navigational charts intrigue me with all the different waterways running here and there and connecting as wondrously as veins in the human body. When I get to the old Chinese town of Locke, I bear left down the Georgianna Slough. In some spots it is only some fifty or sixty feet across and the banks are thick with blackberry bushes. Birds peck at the rich black berries. A blue heron sits atop a dead limb and watches me glide past as if he had never seen a pony in a canoe before.

The slough is more narrow than the river and as a result is more private and intimate. I cannot see as far downstream either and the unknown keeps me pulled forward.

Hours later, I spot a man and a woman fishing from a boat. I slow down.

Having any luck? I say.

Been great, says the man. Even my wife caught one.

Don't listen to him, she laughs. I caught most of them.

He reaches into the water and lifts a string with fifteen or twenty fish a foot long. Three or four flip their tails in the sunlight and water drips from them into the slough.

Want to sell me a couple for my lunch? I ask.

No, says the man. But we'll give you two.

I find a place to land and build a fire on the bank. While the fish bake in aluminum foil, I dig into my pack for letters the fifth-graders gave me way back in Gothenburg, Nebraska. I have been savoring them around my campfires at night and reading only one or two at a time. I have only five or six left. I unfold wrinkled pages to this:

Dear America,

What I would like to change about America is that there should be a law that no more cigarettes are made. Another thing is America should try to clean up the lakes and rivers. I hate to see papers and tires on the beach. One other thing is no more war. I think there should be peace all over the world.

Dear America,

I don't want to change a thing about you. If I could change something it would be the cars. They make a lot of noise.

Dear America,

I wish that America would stop using drugs and make more security guards work. They look lazy. I wish you could stay all day in our class. Will you write me two postcards from each town on the Pony Express Trail? At least one, please? Don't you get kind of hot wearing that leather coat? I think what you are doing is funny. When I get older, I will do it too. Don't you get cold at night.

A touch of nostalgia runs through me as I reread the letters, recalling the beautiful and vulnerable faces of the kids who wrote them. Placing the letters back into my pack, I wish the kids were here with me now to share the fish. After lunch, I crawl into the canoe and push out into the slough. Buffalo Pony leads the way, his mane and tail blowing in the wind.

That evening, as twilight falls, I find myself like last night caught in gusts. It is all I can do to handle the canoe. I finally find a public camping area, but I must carry the pack, supplies, and canoe itself up a flight of squeaking dock stairs and over a hill to make sure no one steals them in the night. I'm disappointed in Buffalo Pony, refusing to offer a hand in the moving ordeal.

Two boys and a girl—ages eight to eleven—gather around me when I set up camp. I slice my block of cheese and share the tortillas. We sit together at a picnic table and talk and laugh as if we were old friends who had planned to meet here and swap stories about our summer.

When you write Rabbit Man, says the eight-year-old boy, will you tell him I said hello?

Me, too, the other boy tells me. Tell him I'd like to have a hiding place in my backyard, but I'm afraid to dig there. We have water pipes somewhere.

I wish we could go with you in the canoe, says the girl. But we go back home this evening. I dread it when school starts up again.

Okay, you kids, calls out a man standing by a van down the way in another campsite. Let's load up and head home.

Sorry we have to leave, the girl tells me. We enjoyed meeting you.

The cheese and tortillas weren't bad either, says one of the boys.

It makes me a bit sad to watch the kids load their van with their father and drive away. But I soon become sleepy and crawl into my sleeping bag, stretched out on the ground alongside my canoe.

I paddled from dawn to dark today and I awake in the night with my forearms feeling crushed. Two of my fingers in my left hand are numb, and I'm concerned that I may have damaged the nerves. I hope I'm able to paddle tomorrow.

The next morning I am disappointed to find that my fingers are still numb. I carry the canoe, pack, and supplies down to the water. A gentle breeze blows and I push from the wooden dock. My left arm hurts like hell, but I can still use it and that is what counts.

I am, according to my charts, about three miles from the San Joaquin River. When I hit it, I plan to bear west toward

Richmond Point in the Bay Area, where I can return the canoe to Sacramento's sister store. All along the river, people have been warning me that the San Joaquin is too powerful and dangerous to travel by canoe. I don't believe them.

But an hour later, I paddle into this monstrously beautiful river. If I have been traveling on the back of a fiery dolphin, this river is an enraged shark. The wind is so strong that I can barely move. It takes all my strength to inch forward. The tide is coming in and currents converge, creating swirls like giant mouths opening to swallow me. I became frightened at night when the wind bounced my canoe from the rocky banks, but that was only a walk in the park next to this. I am a note in a bottle, bobbing up and down at sea. I like to at least imagine that I am fairly brave, but just now it takes all the courage I've got to keep from being sucked into a state of panic.

The river is so huge that a U.S. Navy Patrol boat roars by *way over there,* on the other side of the river. On the far roadside, a man in a truck stops and gawks as if he is seeing things.

It takes an hour to travel only a mile, and the wind and water are getting worse. I decide to bow out with what I hope is a touch of grace and turn back toward a marina I spotted as I entered the San Joaquin.

On the return, however, I get caught in the currents and am pulled sideways back toward the distant Pacific. The cold waves are capping and water crashes over Buffalo Pony and into the canoe onto me. I feel like a man fighting for his life. If I have been needing to be humbled, I now get it with both fists in the face. *If only I can make it back to the marina,* I keep telling myself. *Yes, I can do it. I must just stay calm. Take it an inch at a time. Don't panic.*

I crash into a wall of tule, bullrushes as big around as my numbed fingers and sticking from the water like hundreds of tentacles ready to grab me and pull me down to the bottom of swirling brine. But once I pass through them I am back in control of the canoe and I paddle behind a jetty with trees that block the wind. What a great and comforting sight the marina makes. It looks as peaceful as the face of a child who sleeps with parents he loves.

My hands are trembling a little as I tie the canoe to the dock. But when I step onto the landing, away from the water, I begin to calm down again. Spotting a café with a sign saying Pirates' Lair, I go inside and order a cup of coffee. The locals are curious and friendly. I've been on the Trail for almost three months now and the journey begins to end with a great sense of celebration within my heart.

John Martin, an artist who makes a living by painting signs, is drinking coffee at the table next to me. He is in his late forties and wears a goatee. Each finger sports a ring. They look like ten silver moons in a row. He has a van and offers to give the canoe and me a ride down the road to Richmond Point.

I just need to stop by the house first, says John, and tell my wife.

His home turns out to be a houseboat at the end of a wooden dock. I go with him to meet his wife, and his son, who just turned two yesterday. John delivered him on the houseboat.

His godfather bought this antique Spanish sword as a gift, says John. We cut the birthday cake with it. It'll be a tradition now for the rest of my son's life.

With the canoe sticking from the end of the van, John and I head down to Richmond Point. It seems odd to leave the canoe on land at the store. I wonder who will rent it now and what they will encounter.

Like so many fine people I have met, John insists on buying lunch. He even makes me take back part of the money I gave him for the hauling job.

It's only money, he says. Besides, you got me out on the road. I just wish I were going farther.

It's less than twenty miles to San Francisco from here. I want to savor the last two days of the journey, however, so I splurge in Berkeley and get a fifth-floor hotel room overlooking the bay. That night the lights of San Francisco are magical in the fog as I stand staring out the window, feeling so much a mixture of joy, sadness, thrill, and thankfulness that I almost wonder if I'm truly this close to the long journey's end.

CHAPTER
FORTY-THREE

I take a shower and leave the hotel to walk out into the Berkeley night. Getting a slice of pizza at a street corner on Telegraph Avenue, I wander down the sidewalk past coffeehouses to mingle with college students. A crowd of them has gathered around two cops who check ID's. They boo and hiss as the cops shine their flashlights to read their papers. Relieved to walk on past them, I find myself facing a man with a beard and a bottle in a paper bag; he hurries toward me.

Hey, man, he says. Spare a dollar? How about fifty cents? You know, other people like to eat pizza besides you. A *quarter*?

A car horn honks and a man crossing the street slaps the fender of the car as he walks on. This world seems so jarring and abrasive after the world I have been living in for three months. I go back to my hotel room to savor the lights in the bay from a distance. A foghorn sounds, the only sound to penetrate my solitude way up here on the fifth floor. When it sounds again in the fog, I find myself remembering how beautiful the fog is that sometimes floats over the creek near my home. *Home*—what a simple word with such complex meaning after my being on the Trail for three months. I haven't talked to anyone at home in almost a week now, and I feel I should phone Sandra to see how Ken is doing. I dial her number.

Oh, says Sandra, her voice breaking. You haven't heard. Ken let go two days ago. I had him cremated. The service is tomorrow.

I had hoped to see Ken before he died. Though I knew his end was near, this news still knocks the breath out of me.

Why don't you come to San Francisco, I say. It'll help you with the grief and it would mean a lot to me to see you. We can still try to celebrate the end of my journey like we talked about a few weeks ago.

Yes, says Sandra. I told Carolyn about it. She wants to meet us there, too.

The mention of Carolyn instantly brings to mind the suicide of her son, Sean. And I can't think of him without envisioning Andrea, who stayed in Seattle for a while and slept in his bed. I feel somewhat haunted by the thought of Carolyn joining Sandra and me in San Francisco, but I agree to the plan. We'll meet in two days.

The next day I enter San Francisco. I love the cable cars and their bells, sending music down the streets. I walk down to Montgomery Street and the California National Bank, site of the old Alta Telegraph Office, where the historic Pony rider arrived with the first letters from St. Jo on April 14, 1860. That rider was William Hamilton.

When Hamilton boarded the *Antelope* in Sacramento, it steamed down the river to set a speed record and arrived in San Francisco at twelve thirty-eight in the morning. As Hamilton hurried from the steamer, bells clanged and rockets exploded blue and red against the night. East and West had, at last, been connected by man and horse. The grand marshal waved his hand and the California Band began to play "See, the Conquering Hero Comes." The sidewalks were packed with merrymakers who shouted, clapped, danced, whistled, and stomped their feet as Hamilton and his horse carried the *mochila* down the street to end the wild parade here where I now stand at the Alta Telegraph Office. The only slipup in the great celebration was that the Monumental Fire Engine Company failed to get the powder to fire a triumphant salute.

I must confess that I'm a bit overwhelmed by my own reception on this historic spot. A car offers a victorious back-fire-salute and two pigeons land on the sidewalk. They're thrilled to see me; I can tell. But I'm so happy to near the end of the Trail that I begin to whistle a tune as I walk on into Chinatown, past the open-air vegetable and fish markets.

I now have only to go to that rare spot by the ocean where I once saw a whale just beyond the cliff; then the journey will be completed.

Fifteen years ago I undertook another journey. I was waiting tables in a New Orleans restaurant when I served a woman named Dianne. She'd just finished law school in California, where she was born and raised, and was treating herself to a car trip across America before starting to work for a big law firm. Somewhere between my serving her a glass of wine and a French meal, we discovered that we were kindred spirits. I ditched my less-than-hilarious job as a waiter and traveled with her for three wondrous weeks. She became one of my dearest friends and I have made arrangements to stay in her guest room in her new home in San Francisco. It's been several years since we've seen each other, and I'm thrilled that we'll soon share company. We are to meet at her house at five o'clock, when she gets in from work. But I get there two hours early and sit on her porch steps to write in my journal. When I finish that, I reach into the pack for Sir Richard Burton's dairy. This is what he found when he arrived in the city:

> . . . I was weary of the way; for eight months I had lived on board steamers and railroad cars, coaches and mules; my eyes were full of sight-seeing, my pockets empty. . . . It was far more grateful to *flaner* [wander] about the stirring streets, to admire charm-

> ing faces . . . than to front wind, rain, muddy roads
> . . . and the solitude of out-stations.

Amen, Sir Richard! For the last time on this trek, I place his dairy, wrinkled and coffee-stained, into my pack. When I get back home, I will place it in a special spot on a shelf over my desk.

Growing hungry, I hide my pack in a walled corner of Dianne's porch and walk to a little Italian café only three blocks away for a good meal and a glass of wine to toast the Trail.

I'm eager to see Dianne, who will get home in only an hour from now, and I head back to her house. I've remembered much more that I want to write in my journal while it's on my mind and clear to my heart.

When I arrive at her house, I begin to look around on the porch for my pack. I don't see it and I become horrified at the thought that it's been stolen. But it couldn't have been, surely. I must've placed it somewhere else and . . . no, I put it *right here* on this spot. It *is* gone. Damn it, *it is gone.* Forget the camera and equipment, but I feel lost without my journal, Buffalo Pony, and the letters from the kids. How could I have been so stupid as to leave all those things out for someone to take them? Where the hell was my mind? And who is the son of a bitch who swiped them? If I get my hands on him . . . I hurry to the street, determined to do *something* with this rage.

I bang on the door of the house next to Dianne with hopes that someone is home and saw the thief. I pound again and the garage door opens. An elderly man with white hair holds a wooden model sailboat from the 1800s in his hands. Two other model ships sit on a shelf in the workshop behind him. I mumble an explanation of my situation.

You may be in luck, he says. I saw Dianne's car out front

about twenty minutes ago. Maybe she put your things inside her house.

I grab at this meager straw and return to her steps. She arrives only minutes later and I feel like a man saved from a storm at sea. Yes, she put my pack inside. All of my valuables safe, I throw my arms around my dear friend, overcome with happiness.

You're here, she says. You made it.

Yes, I say, as if to make sure it's true. I made it.

She leads me to her guest room and there in a cage in the corner is her pet rabbit, Scampers. He looks up at me with his playful nose and eyes as if to say hello. I place my pack against the wall next to him. Sometime in the middle of the night, I half awake and turn on the lamp by my bed to make certain that my pack is truly with me. It is and the rabbit seems to assure me that it is as safe as his gentle nature. I turn off the lamp and go back to sleep.

The next morning I awake refreshed. Well, okay—kind of refreshed. My arm still hurts from canoeing and my lower back and shoulders ache. Still, it's amazing what a couple of cups of strong coffee can do. I place my leather pouch and Buffalo Pony into a bag and start walking toward the Pacific Ocean, only two miles away.

As I walk down a street toward the cliff a jet zooms overhead and telephone poles and wires line the sky. At the traffic light, turning red, a man in a car speaks into his mobile phone. Have we come a great distance since the Pony Express closed October 26, 1861, and the telegraph with its "talking wires" took over, followed by the railroad to connect East and West? Do Americans now truly communicate better with each other? Perhaps those answers lie in the stories of those I met along the way and in the letters of the children from Nebraska—heartland of America. For all our faults, I want to believe the best.

The Pony Express was a financial failure. William Russell was even arrested for swiping almost a million bucks from the Indian Trust Fund in hopes of pulling the Pony Express out of debt. The Central Overland Mail, under Ben Holladay, on the other hand, began to prosper. Of the three Pony Express founders, only Alexander Majors recovered, at least for a while, from the fall. He remained in the freighting business and later went to work for the Union Pacific Railroad. The Pony riders themselves, who thundered into American history, vanished almost as quietly into obscurity as dust into desert wind.

The bright side of the Pony Express and its glorious daredevil riders and horses is that for 18 months they risked their lives and made 308 trips each way. They covered enough miles—616,000—to circle the earth 24 times. Of the 34,753 pieces of mail they carried, they lost only a single *mochila*. Perhaps far more important than these numbers, however, is that the Pony riders became our heroes. And we are, indeed, a people hungry—if not starved—for myths and legends larger than life. I know, for I have struggled with that hunger since childhood. It led me to train with weights, which built my confidence to risk thumbing all over the world. I walked 900 miles along the Trail of Tears. That same hunger drove me to follow the Pony Express Trail, where I had rare adventures, new experiences. I learned more about who I am and what it is to be a man. Perhaps I even learned a little about being human.

With all this in mind, heart, and soul, I now arrive at the base of a cliff at the Pacific Ocean. I place Buffalo Pony on a rock as waves crash against that cliff near where I once saw a great whale rise and fall as it swam northward many years and Trails ago. This is where I once came when a friend of mine had been shot and crippled for life. I groped for understanding, but now I know that much in life is never understood. It is only felt. And feeling, at least for this man, is a blessing as much as adventure and life itself. From my leather pouch I pull the hawk-wing bone-whistle and blow a faint tune out over the ocean, where it blends with the wind and the waves, crashing against the cliff to drift out over the Great Mother, the ocean. When I put the whistle aside, I feel such strength and joy that I want to release it in a loud, earth-shaking chant. But when my lips part, I catch myself and watch and listen more closely to the humbling ocean, washing against the shore like an eternal poet writing about time and my small history in the sand at the end of the Trail.

EPILOGUE

One month later.

I'm back home now and it's the beginning of September. The nights are getting just a bit cool as air drifts down into the valley where I live between Lookout and Sand mountains. My parents are well and relieved that I made it back in one piece. My two fingers are still numb at times, but they're getting better.

Sandra and Carolyn joined me in San Francisco for two days before I left. Sandra's husband, a few days before he died, asked that his ashes be taken from Arizona to Colorado and scattered in the mountains where he once lived. My nephew placed those ashes in a box in the trunk of a man's car who was going to Denver. My nephew went along, but once they got to Denver, they failed to communicate and got separated. The ashes are still in the trunk without the car owner's knowledge and rattling against the spare tire somewhere in Colorado. My sister claims that her deceased husband had such a good sense of humor that he would find this amusing, but I'm not so sure about this.

Buffalo Pony now hangs on my cabin wall beneath a bow and arrows I made, and when the window is open the mane and tail dance in the breeze. On his back rides the leather pouch with the bone-whistle and all the little Trail gifts people offered me along the way. I placed the poem Tom gave me in Nebraska in there, too.

Yesterday I went to Wal-Mart and picked up all the film I had developed from the Trail. I have five hundred pictures. Each one looks back at me like an invitation to step through the door of another world where I can journey whenever I choose.

A picture of David and me on his wagon inspired me to phone him. Charlie, the wagonmaster, had his dream come true to see his wagon wheels leave tracks on the Oregon coast. But before he and Ted, the trail boss, got there they got into a fistfight. No one was clear why.

David's wife finished the Oregon Trail quilt—with a wagon on it—two weeks after David got home. But a week later she passed on to what I hope is a more gentle world.

I got a letter a few days ago from Andrea. The doctor says that she's in great health. The day she wrote she had heard her baby's heartbeat for the first time.

This afternoon I walked down to the mailbox. I found a letter postmarked *Kansas*. I opened it and became startled when I saw that it was from Larry, the fellow who took groceries to the Rabbit Man each week. I feared the worst and began to read:

> Dear Jerry,
> I hope you made it home safely. Ernest had a run of bad luck. He was in his trailer where he keeps his ice-cream and animal feed, when a bolt of lightning stuck the trailer. It burned to the ground. But don't worry. He survived and is back in his hole as happy as ever.

I can see the playful eyes of Rabbit Man. I have no desire to live in a hole, but I hope I am as carefree as Ernest when I get to be an old man and still love life as much.

I'm letting my body, mind, and spirit rest for a while. But

already I find myself starting to sniff the wind to see which Trail I might follow next. If you see me coming, I hope you'll kindly stop and say hello. We just might have something in common. You never know.

AFTERWORD

November 24, 2001—two days after Thanksgiving. It's been ten years since I made my trek along the Pony Express Trail, and eight years since the first edition of this book appeared. If the "young, skinny, wiry fellows, not over 18," who once rode at breakneck speed along the Trail to connect America's East and West could see just how fast our e-letters zoom around the globe compared to the handwritten letters they carried, they might yell as if they were riding atop the meanest bronco that ever kicked. Some of them would surely race straight for the hills, just to escape it all.

A year after I met the Rabbit Man he surprised me by hopping out of his enchanting Kansas hole to become a featured story on CNN. You just can't keep a good rabbit down. Andrea lives in Austria and we write from time to time; she sends photos of her handsome son. The carving of Buffalo Pony hangs on my cottage wall with other Native American folk art, his colors fading and his buffalo mane and tail thinning. Still, his legs are forever caught in a gallop down the Trail as if the best of the Western spirit will never die. Of course, people do die, and that's what happened to my father the year after I returned home from the Trail. He fell dead in our garden while planting seeds. He lives on in my mother, my two sisters, and me.

I have received a number of thoughtful letters about this book. The one that touched me most was from a psychologist in Washington DC, who told of how men she led in a weekly discussion group opened up after reading this volume, talking about things they had kept hidden since their youths. There are so many different kinds of horses to ride.

In 1994 the Pony Express Trail in Utah came back to me in ways I could not have dreamed when I first walked along the dusty road that leads into Callao. My friend, Debi from Tacoma, had reached a crossroads and wanted to spend forty days and nights alone in the wilderness to attempt to solve her pressing riddles. Bret, the ranger at the Fish Springs Wildlife Refuge, escorted her to a remote part of the desert and left her without phone or weapon. The second night there she almost died when a freak blizzard hit. Her book about her ordeal earned her a guest spot on *Oprah*. The forty days and nights alone along the Pony Express Trail truly changed her life.

We have since married and traveled to Asia and Europe, where we live six months of every year. I continue to write and lecture about my adventures. We are currently building a three-story chalet in the Alabama mountains where I grew up. The spot overlooks Wills Valley, where Sequoyah invented the Cherokee alphabet in the 1820s. The building of the chalet is the first major step in the creation of the Tanager Writer's Colony, which we plan to open in 2003.

Don't be a stranger. I welcome e-letters: tanager@tds.net.

BIBLIOGRAPHY

Burton, Sir Richard Francis. *The City of the Saints*. New York: Harper & Brothers, 1862; repub. Niwot, Colo.: University Press of Colorado, 1990.

Cody, William. *An Autobiography of Buffalo Bill*. New York: Cosmopolitan Book Corporation, 1920.

Henderson, Paul, and Merrill J. Mattes. *The Pony Express, from St. Joseph to Fort Laramie*. St. Louis: The Patrice Press, 1989.

Reinfeld, Fred. *Pony Express*. Lincoln, Neb.: University of Nebraska Press, 1973.

Settle, Mary Lund, and Raymond W. Settle. *Saddles and Spurs: The Pony Express Saga*. Lincoln, Neb.: University of Nebraska Press, 1955.

BIBLIOGRAPHY